TRANS~~LATION~~,
RESISTANCE,
ACTIVISM

TRANSLATION, RESISTANCE, ACTIVISM

Edited by

MARIA TYMOCZKO

University of Massachusetts Press
Amherst and Boston

LC 2010009004
ISBN 978-1-55849-833-4 (paper); 832-7 (library cloth)
Designed by Jack Harrison
Set in Adobe Minion Pro by Westchester Book, Inc.
Printed and bound by Thomson-Shore, Inc.

Library of Congress Cataloging-in-Publication Data

Translation, resistance, activism / edited by Maria Tymoczko.
    p. cm.
Includes bibliographical references and index.
ISBN 978–1-55849-833–4 (pbk. : alk. paper)—
ISBN 978–1-55849-832–7 (library cloth : alk. paper)
1. Translating and interpreting.   2. Intercultural communication.
3. Globalization—Social aspects.   4. Political culture.
I. Tymoczko, Maria.
P306.2.T7394 2010
418'.02—dc22
                    2010009004

British Library Cataloguing in Publication data are available.

Contents

Foreword

Without the work of Lawrence Venuti this book would never have been written. Venuti's writing on translation as a mode of resistance and his calls for action addressed to translators were central in motivating discourses about translation, ethics, ideology, and agency in translation studies. The result has been a productive conversation about these important topics, as a result of which Venuti's ideas have been interrogated, critiqued, and also enacted. This book rests on the foundation that Venuti built, but it attempts to go further: to go beyond resistance and delineate the current state of thinking about translation and activism. Although Venuti's ideas have been seminal, they have also been criticized as being not fully transitive, not sufficiently applicable to a wide enough range of cultural and political circumstances. In certain ways they are both too loosely stated and too rigidly prescriptive. The essays in this volume open up discourses about translation to a larger range of translational options for activist interventions.

The limitations of resistance as primarily a reactive rather than a proactive form of activism will be considered in the introduction. One way of stating the problem is to compare activism in translation to the three stages of writing often discussed by postcolonial theory. Initially there is a tendency in postcolonial cultures to introject the colonizers' values and standards. A second stage is marked by the tendency to reject those values and define the colonized culture's identity in terms of polar oppositions to the culture of the colonizers. A third stage is marked by transcendence of this sort of polarized thinking in favor of the attempt to define an autonomous cultural stance distinct from that of the colonizers, irrespective of the colonizing power's approbation or condemnation. In a sense resistance as a form of ideological and programmatic translation can be compared to the second stage of postcolonial thinking. The polarized nature of resistance, where attention is focused on opposing the force of a defined and more powerful opponent, is an unnecessarily limited view of translational activism.

In *The Left Hand of Darkness* Ursula Le Guin has a character reflect, "They say here 'all roads lead to Mishnory'. To be sure, if you turn your back on Mishnory and walk away from it, you are still on the Mishnory road. . . . You must go somewhere else; you must have another goal; then you walk a different road" (1969:153). In a sense activists cannot simply oppose or resist social and political constraints: they must also be able to initiate action, change direction, construct new goals, articulate new values, seek new paths. They must, so to speak, be able to leave the Mishnory road. This volume explores activism and translation in the widest possible sense, looking at a broad range of opponents, affiliations, goals, objectives, and strategies from many cultures and many historical circumstances since the end of the eighteenth century. The essays demonstrate that thinking about translation and activism has moved well beyond a focus on binaries in this domain as it has in most other areas of inquiry in translation studies, and thus it has moved beyond the focus on resistance.

The book was initially begun as a joint project between Edwin Gentzler and myself. Edwin read most of the essays as they came in from contributors and his comments were important in the shape that the essays took during the process of revision. The book is significantly stronger for his contributions to the editing process. To my regret he withdrew from the project for personal reasons. I continue to be indebted to him for the success of this project, and I am most grateful for his support of the project since he withdrew.

Translation has been a central element in the research and teaching missions of Comparative Literature at the University of Massachusetts Amherst since the program was founded in the 1960s. Indeed translation is a common interest that binds together members of all the language and literature departments of the University, as well as faculty members in those departments at Amherst College, Hampshire College, Mt. Holyoke College, and Smith College, which together with the University constitute

Five Colleges, Inc., the oldest and most successful post-secondary consortium in the United States. In the last half century, this joint faculty has been notable for its abiding concern with translation and for the presence of many eminent translators among us. This interest has sustained the long-running Faculty Seminar in Translation Studies and the Five College translation journal *Metamorphoses*. Since the expansion of the Translation Center at the University of Massachusetts, under the able leadership of Edwin Gentzler, that shared interest in translation has had a special focal point. This has been an excellent ambience for thinking and publishing about translation, resistance, and activism.

This volume grows out of an international lecture series in translation studies at the University of Massachusetts and follows an earlier publication, *Translation and Power*, edited by myself and Edwin Gentzler. A selection of preliminary versions of the present essays appeared as a special section of the *Massachusetts Review* (2006, volume 47.3) under the title *Translation as Resistance*, and I am indebted to the *Massachusetts Review* for permission to print the essays by Brian James Baer, Mona Baker, Nitsa Ben-Ari, and John Milton in an updated form. My colleague David Lenson, editor of the *Massachusetts Review*, has provided enthusiastic support of this exploration of activist translation throughout, including the expansion of the collection to the present volume. I am also grateful to William Moebius, Director of Comparative Literature, and to Bruce Wilcox, Director of the University of Massachusetts Press, for their counsel and encouragement in bringing the project to completion. The synergy linking Comparative Literature, the Translation Center, the *Massachusetts Review*, and the University of Massachusetts Press has been one of the great pleasures of working on this book.

My gratitude as well for special assistance from Julie Hayes, Carol Maier, Elizabeth Fitzpatrick, Cristiano Mazzei, Lenita Maria Rimoli Esteves, Alexei Tymoczko, Katherine D. Scheuer, and Carol Betsch, each of whom made important contributions to the scholarly finish of the book. Special thanks to Paul Kostecki, Joel Martin, and Julie Hayes, whose commitment to research made the publication of this volume possible. Above all I thank the contributors of the essays themselves, who were all gracious and assiduous in their responses to editorial suggestions and patient in working together to bring this joint project to light.

MARIA TYMOCZKO

TRANSLATION,
RESISTANCE,
ACTIVISM

MARIA TYMOCZKO

Translation, Resistance, Activism: An Overview

For Gideon Toury

T HE essays in this volume examine key translations and translation movements that have been instrumental in changing societies in
many parts of the world during the course of the last two centuries. These
texts and movements have participated in ideological and political dialogue and struggle in their own times and places. In "Translation and the
Emancipation of Hispanic America," Georges L. Bastin, Álvaro Echeverri,
and Ángela Campo outline the centrality of translation in the revolutionary movement that led to the liberation of the colonies of Spain in Hispanic America. Two studies describe the effects of more recent cases of
colonialism, detailing the relationship of colonialist translation to the sub-
ordination of populations and focusing on translational resistance in the
responses of the colonized groups. In "Covert and Overt Ideologies in the
Translation of the Bible into Huao Terero," Antonia Carcelen-Estrada analyzes the function of Bible translation in the "pacification" of the Huaorani
in the Amazon, looking at translation of identities and resistance to translation as well. Pua'ala'okalani D. Aiu discusses the colonization of the
Hawaiian Islands in "Ne'e Papa I Ke Ō Mau: Language as an Indicator of
Hawaiian Resistance and Power," defining the parts that both translation
and refusal to translate have played in the Hawaiian renaissance since the
mid-twentieth century.

Other studies focus on the use of translation to challenge more general
ideological oppression, including cultural straitjackets, illustrating ways
that activist translation has been instrumental in cultural liberation and

1

important cultural shifts. In "Secret Literary Societies in Late Victorian England," Denise Merkle details how translators in England circumvented censorship with secret publishing and distribution networks, thus opposing the sexual prohibitions of the dominant culture in the second half of the nineteenth century. In a paired study, "Reclaiming the Erotic: Hebrew Translations from 1930 to 1980," Nitsa Ben-Ari demonstrates that a variety of translation types—from pornography to medical manuals—ensured that the erotic would have a place and a vocabulary in modern Hebrew and emerging Israeli culture, countering the dominant puritanical ethos in cultural nationalism as the state of Israel was taking shape. During roughly the same period, translation of Western literary classics into Russian was used to create counterdiscourses to some of the most culturally repressive policies of the Soviet Union, as Brian James Baer indicates in "Literary Translation and the Construction of a Soviet Intelligentsia." Moving to the current moment, Paul F. Bandia examines cultural subversion in contemporary writing in the "postcolonies" of Africa and effective modes of translation for representing that subversion in his essay "Literary Heteroglossia and Translation: Translating Resistance in Contemporary African Francophone Writing." All these studies indicate the powerful roles that resistant and activist translations play in social change.

Two additional essays highlight the pivotal nature of translation as a political force opposing dictatorships. In "The Resistant Political Translations of Monteiro Lobato," John Milton argues that the translations of José Bento Monteiro Lobato promoted the modernization of Brazil and undermined the policies of the Getúlio Vargas dictatorship between the 1920s and the 1940s. The later dictatorship that dominated Brazil between the 1960s and 1980s is the subject of "Growing Agency: The Labors of Political Translation," in which Else R. P. Vieira recounts her own personal experience as head translator of a history revealing foundational events in the formation of the government; her work helped topple the power structure.

Theoretical perspectives on the nature of translation, resistance, and activism bracket the collection. Mona Baker extends sociological approaches to narrative theory in "Translation and Activism: Emerging Patterns of Narrative Community" and then uses this theoretical framework to assess activism undertaken by contemporary associations of translators who translate documents silenced by dominant news sources and who interpret for nonprofit organizations that oppose multinational, globalizing, and military interests, so as to further a more balanced circulation of ideas in the world at large. In the conclusion Maria Tymoczko matches the broad spatial and temporal range of the main essays with a longitudinal analysis of the Irish translation record to show that activist translation strategies—including those associated with revolution and cultural nationalism—are minutely situated in space, time, history, and political contexts; because these strategies are subject to stringent felicity conditions and rapid change, she concludes that prescriptive recommendations for activist translators and activist translation strategies are misplaced.

We will return to a more detailed assessment of the individual chapters of this volume and their significance as a whole in the concluding essay. Before attempting such a summary, however, it is useful to consider some more general questions about the nature of translation and the ways that it participates in social formation. Let us begin by asking some basic questions.

How have we arrived at a position where translations are read and discussed as records of cultural contestations and struggles rather than as simple linguistic transpositions or creative literary endeavors? How have scholars come to explore translations as a means of fighting censorship, cultural repression, political dominance, and physical coercion? Of fostering cultural nationalism and even revolution? In these essays translators are recognized as crucial agents for social change and translations are documented as central cultural expressions rather than as derivative, peripheral, or marginalized productions. Translation is seen as an ethical, political, and ideological activity, not simply as a mechanical linguistic transposition or a literary art. Even when literary translation is the subject of these essays, the ideological implications of translational innovations are sounded.

As scholars in the field know well, these approaches have emerged from the development of translation studies as an academic discipline since World War II.[1] Early in the history of descriptive translation studies, investigations of translations and translation movements led Gideon Toury to declare that *"translations are facts of one system only*: the target system" (1985:19, cf. 1980:28; original emphasis). Although studies of translations in the last three decades have shown that there are exceptions to Toury's dictum, in general the determining role of the receiving culture has been sustained and demonstrated to have even stronger political and ideological implications than Toury foresaw at the time.[2] It is not an exaggeration to say that studies of resistant and activist translation have their roots in Toury's articulation of the importance of the receptor cultural system for translation strategies, norms, and functions, as well as the programmatic purposes of the translated texts themselves.

For centuries Western Europe has imaged translation as a type of transfer, whether that transfer took the form of passing on the methods of rhetoric or oratory from the Greeks to the Romans or whether it involved moving lexis and semantic meaning to a target culture. The metaphorical conceptualization of translation as primarily a process of cross-linguistic transference—a communicative process in which content is transmitted from one language to another—is reified in the English word *translation*, which comes from Latin roots meaning 'to carry across', as well as words in other dominant Western European languages, including Spanish *traducción*, French *traduction*, and German *Übersetzung*, which are based on similar conceptualizations.[3] Western writing about and theorizing of translation have also commonly been rooted in similar assumptions about the primacy of semantic meaning and communication in translation, often resulting in normative and prescriptive statements about the process and products of translating.

World War II challenged these views, introducing complexities appropriate to imperative concerns during the war that affected the theory and practice of translation equally. Because of the global reach of the conflict, a central factor in the new thinking about translation was the necessity of negotiating a greater number of linguistic and cultural boundaries than ever before. Beyond the obvious fact of having to accommodate more types of cultural and linguistic difference and greater degrees of difference as well, two major preoccupations shaped thinking about translation during the war: first, the necessity of "cracking" the complex linguistic and cultural codes of enemies and allies alike, and, second, the construction of cultural products that would mold public opinion in the many cultures of the world. These preoccupations were overriding because translation was instrumental to the war effort on both sides, with most translators involved in gathering intelligence, strategic negotiations, and production of propaganda.

Reflecting these activities, after the war the early schools of translation studies concentrated on the instrumentality of translation, stressing functionalist aspects, and on linguistic and machine translation that had clear ideological agendas in its focus on the asymmetries and anisomorphisms of languages and cultures.[4] Within two decades translation studies was consolidating into an academic discipline, steadily widening the purview of the field and developing many new approaches. Beginning with questions about language, codes, and strategies for achieving specific goals, inquiry expanded to include philosophical questions, sociological considerations, sociolinguistic issues, systems analyses of translated texts, questions about the nature and purposes of translated literature, and insights pertaining to politics and power.

These expansions in translation studies traced a trajectory away from technical questions about *how* to translate per se toward larger ethical and political perspectives on the activity of translating, on the functions of translation products in relation to power, and on the agency of translators. Implicit in many of these discourses are ideological questions, including the constructivist aspect of translation, the nature of representation in translation, and the transculturation of cultural forms and values. Perhaps most important, translation studies demonstrated that translation is more than *intercultural* transfer; interest has shifted in many investigations to the *intracultural* functions of the products and processes of translation. These approaches have converged on the ethics and politics of translation, where the interest in ideology is akin to the focus on ideology in contemporary literary, historical, and ethnographic studies. Postpositivist views of knowledge in translation studies, as in other fields, have moved inquiry away from simple questions of how to translate "correctly" toward larger questions pertaining to the perception of difference and to self-reflexivity about perspective in relation to the nature of translation in diverse cultural contexts.

A significant step in rethinking the nature of translation was the development in the 1970s and 1980s of descriptive translation studies, as we have seen, with Toury as one of the principal architects of the approach. Descriptive translation studies moved away from prescriptive approaches in favor of describing actual translation products and practices in relation to their cultural and political contexts. A major branch of descriptive studies used systems theory to analyze the part translations play within larger literary and cultural systems.[5] Itamar Even-Zohar (1978, 1990) and others have demonstrated that literary systems include translated literature as a central component, forming a subsystem in itself. Much of what any people considers "their" literature, for example, is in fact translated literature. In Eurocentric cultures people think of the Bible and Greek and Roman literature as part of "their" literary system, even though very few people read

Hebrew, Greek, or Latin at present. Similarly Buddhists around the world claim the sutras for their own, as Islamic cultures do the Qur'an, whatever the vernacular language of the culture.[6] Within social systems as a whole, translations ground cultures, establish affiliation, construct identities, and enable appropriation. Descriptive studies have also established that the role of translation across systems is far from uniform: it is correlated with dominance and power, as well as local norms. Thus, in cultures such as the United States, translations play a smaller part in and constitute a smaller percentage of the total field of publication than is the case in Italian or Norwegian culture, for example.[7] Awareness of the function of translation in constructing the asymmetries of cultural systems and inequities in cultural power becomes ever more urgent as media translation inserts quantities of material from dominant societies into the social space of peoples around the globe.

Toury's seminal realization that translations are largely "facts" of the target system has therefore been gradually expanded to include many more parameters than those explored by early systems scholars. Early descriptive scholars focused on the ways that translation was enlisted in literary struggles and the partisan roles that it played in literary shifts within receptor cultural systems. What these scholars perceived less clearly was that translation could be and often was also enlisted in broader cultural struggles and that strategic and tactical interventions embodied in translations and practiced by translators constitute a form of participation in fundamental ideological contestations within and between societies. As these factors became clearer, descriptive investigations of translations expanded relatively quickly beyond literary questions, exploring the impact of the receptor system on translation within more extensive frameworks, as we have seen.

Interventions of translators can be traced through the shifts they introduce in the texts they produce, including shifts in content, textual form, and political valences. What is not translated in a particular context is often as revealing as what is translated. Thus silences and gaps in specific translated texts—like the non-translation (or zero translation) of entire texts—are fundamental in revealing the politics of translation in a particular cultural context. What became apparent from descriptive studies—in some cases shockingly so—is how many shifts in translated texts are attested in the historical record: many more shifts and more radical ones than can be explained simply by linguistic anisomorphisms and cultural asymmetries.[8]

Descriptive studies have correlated translation shifts with larger historical and geopolitical patterns in receiving cultures, revealing political constraints on translators' choices and implicit cultural and political initiatives undertaken by translators. The studies have clearly established that translation is much more than a matter of transfer and communication. In turn, as presumptions about linguistic fidelity and the communicative values of translation have given way to deeper investigations of how translations work within cultural systems and how they are shaped by historical and geopolitical frameworks, the role of translators as active figures in history, art, politics, ideology, and belief systems has become ever more manifest. Through such analyses descriptive studies have documented the many ways that translation has been used to change societies and social structures, at the same time revealing the ways that translation is limited by constraints within specific contexts.

In the 1990s, partly in connection with the influence of cultural studies, partly in response to the achievements of various translators (including feminist translators, translators in Quebec using translation to further cultural nationalism, and the "cannibalizing" translators of Brazil), partly in recognition of the cultural interventions of translators throughout history documented by descriptive studies, and partly as an outgrowth of the interest in ideology and power in translation, there were calls for translators to become activist agents of social change, most famously embodied in Lawrence Venuti's "call to action."[9] The writings of Antoine Berman (1992 [1984], 2000 [1985]), Philip Lewis (1985), and Lawrence Venuti (1992, 1995, 1998a, 1998b, 2008) are particularly associated with calls for translators to become involved in cultural and ideological struggles. Venuti appealed to translators to become "visible," eschewing what he saw as the presumptive invisibility of translators in dominant Western literary and commercial practices. The result has been a lively and energizing debate about strategies that are appropriate to and effective in activist translation practices. The essays in this volume are contributions to this ongoing exploration of power, ideology, agency, and activism in translation.

There are two principal terms in common use related to activist translation practices. The term *resistance* in translation studies has been borrowed from the designation for clandestine activist movements opposed to oppressive forces, notably those that opposed fascist governments and armies in Europe during World War II. There is a problem with the terms *resistance* and *resistant* when applied to translation, however. During World

War II and similar agonistic conflicts, the opponents of resistance movements were obvious and can still be presupposed in discussions of the events. In the case of translation by contrast, there is no obvious opponent or ideological target to which resistance in general can be presumed to refer. Case studies generated by Venuti and others at times discuss resistance as if the antagonist or opponent were obvious, but descriptive studies of translations using this terminology ascribe resistance in translation to diverse and highly variable opponents including colonialism, imperialism, neoimperialism, capitalism, Western domination, specific regimes such as that of the United States, various oppressive social conditions, the patriarchy, bourgeois norms, Christianity and other religions, dominant discourses (in a variety of cultures), dominant literary conventions, dominant linguistic norms, and many others. Sometimes the object of resistance is unstated and vague in the extreme. No agreement exists among translators or translation scholars as to what can or should be resisted in translation situations in general or even in a given context. As the term has been used with reference to translation, resistance often appears to be an open-ended enterprise without predefined or well-defined targets that translators or critics can delineate or agree upon.

Translators must make choices, and emphasis on the translator's choices and decision making was one of the first steps in exploring the agency of translators.[10] Translators cannot transpose everything in a source text to the receptor language and text because of anisomorphisms of language and asymmetries of culture, because meaning in a text is both open and underdetermined, because a text makes contradictory demands that cannot be simultaneously satisfied (for example, the demands of complex content and spare form), and because the information load associated with and implied by a source text is excessive and overdetermined, among other reasons. Translation is therefore a metonymic process, and translators make choices, setting priorities for their translations in decision-making processes that have ideological implications (Tymoczko 1999b:41–61, 278–300; Boase-Beier 2006:50–70). Translators' choices also establish a place of enunciation and a context of affiliation for the translator and the translation. The result is that choice in translation inevitably involves values, ethics, responsibility. At the same time because cultures are heterogeneous and include different perspectives on values and responsibility, translations are always potentially controversial, potentially the subject of conflict and contestation.

These aspects of translation are nowhere more evident than in translations with an activist edge.

One interesting facet of the subject at hand is that like translation, resistance—or activism in general—is also a metonymic process: a translator cannot resist, oppose, or attempt to change everything objectionable in either the source or target culture. The ideological aspect of translation is heightened because translators make choices about what values and institutions to support and oppose, determining activist strategies and picking their fights, even as they also make choices about what to transpose from a source text and what to construct in a receptor text. Activism in translation thus stands at the intersection of two metonymic systems: the normal metonymies of translation and the metonymies of activism itself, particularly in situations where the social antagonist is not necessarily predefined or well defined. Resistance and activism in translation are therefore complex acts involving complex textual constructions and complex social positioning. Translators must choose what (if anything) to resist or undertake in situations where a social antagonist is not necessarily obvious. Translators' strategies for accomplishing their social or ideological goals are legion, highly localized in time and space, shifting as culture shifts, a subject to which we will return in the conclusion of this volume. Translators and interpreters shape their words and their texts to the needs of the moment. To a large extent the partisanship of the translator results from partiality in translation—by definition an inescapable aspect of the metonymics of any process of translating—and partiality in resistance or any activist endeavor. Such partiality is not a defect, a lack, or an absence in translation; it is a necessary element of the task of the translator to make choices and to decide which specific parts of a text and a culture to transpose, to represent, to construct in the target text. Partialities are what differentiate translations, enabling them to participate in the dialectic of power, the ongoing process of political discourse, and strategies for social change. This flexibility makes the act of translation inescapably engaged and committed, either implicitly or explicitly, even when translators do not set out to be activists.

Calls for action in translation have not always fully recognized these complexities. Some scholars have assumed that the object of resistance is known; others have been prescriptive in the extreme about specific textual strategies to be privileged in activist translations (perhaps because of pretheoretical assumptions about values or about the object of resistance).

In *The Translator's Invisibility*, for instance, Venuti promotes a resistant strategy that he calls "foreignization," which "enables a disruption of target-language cultural codes" and registers "the linguistic and cultural differences of the foreign text," exerting "ethnodeviant pressure" on the values of the target culture (Venuti 1995:42, 81; cf. 2008:34, 68). He argues that such a strategy is effective in combating the cultural dominance and cultural enclosure of readers in the United States. Generalizing such arguments beyond their immediate cultural context is extremely difficult, however. Although at times foreignization may be an appropriate resistant technique in dominant cultures such as the United States or in countries (whether dominant or not) that have a history of cultural enclosure (such as France), it is not at all suited to subaltern cultures that are already flooded with foreign materials and foreign linguistic impositions (often from the United States and other Eurocentric cultures) and that are trying to establish or shore up their own discourses and cultural forms. Foreignization has also been rightly criticized as an elitist strategy, more appropriate to a highly educated target audience than to a broad readership or a cultural situation in which the normal education level is more modest than it is in Europe and the United States.[11]

In *Metaphors We Live By* (1980), George Lakoff and Mark Johnson demonstrate that metaphors and their associated image-schemas permeate language, structuring how people conceive of common activities and common concepts, often in ways that are implicit and preconscious for speakers. Such metaphors frequently undergird discourses in academic fields as well. In translation studies the concept of resistance is obviously such a metaphor, accessing the prestige of discourses about resistance established in conflicts such as World War II, and the metaphor itself reveals some of the difficulties of conceiving of activist translation as resistance. The metaphor *resistance* presumes the existence of a specific powerful opponent that exerts force in particular directions. The metaphor suggests that it is the function of activists to oppose the opponent's force so as to deflect or thwart (i.e., resist) the actions that the force initiates and the directions that the power wishes to move in and to impose on others.[12] The metaphor of resistance thus implies reaction more than action. Despite (or perhaps because of) the popularity of the metaphor of resistance in European languages, it is important to understand that resistance is a reactive view of activism rather than a proactive one: initiative largely rests with the principal power in the situation, and activists attempt to stop those initiatives. Although widely used and fully appropriate in some contexts, nonetheless the metaphor implicit in translation as *resistance* seems to be problematic as the foundation for conceptualizing political and ideological agency and activism in translation in general: it is unnecessarily restrictive with regard to initiative, limiting translators to a more passive role than is required or desirable.

The second metaphor used widely in the debate about activism and agency in translation studies is associated with the English word *engagement*. The term derives from words meaning 'to be under a pledge' (from Old French *gage*, 'pledge'). The history and usage of the words *engage* and *engagement* imply commitment, involvement, participation, mutual pledges and promises, making guarantees, assuming obligations, exposing oneself to risk, entering into conflict, becoming interlocked or intermeshed, and action undertaken by more than one person (*OED* s.v.). As a term and metaphor for activism, the concept engagement suggests a much more proactive stance than resistance does. Engagement implies a wide range of enterprises that activists initiate rather than reactions or oppositions to an external powerful force (as in resistance). Engagement also suggests activities based on commitments to specific principles, as well as undertakings involving solidarity with other people. The metaphor seems to lend itself much more easily to forms of activism involving choice and action than does the metaphor of resistance. At the same time it also implies a broader and more flexible concept of power: in this concept of activism, power is not simply seen as "top down" but as inherent in many types of transactions and all levels of society (cf. Tymoczko and Gentzler 2002:xvii–xxi).

The concept of activism as engagement—particularly engagement taking textualized forms such as translation—is associated in postwar thought with the concept of *littérature engagée* (engaged or committed literature), widely promoted in the mid-twentieth century by Jean-Paul Sartre and others in his circle, but also advocated by various Marxist writers, notably those outside the Soviet bloc. Calling for "a literature of *praxis*" and using phrases such as "to speak is to act" and "words are loaded pistols," in the postwar period Sartre advocated using writing "to help effect certain changes in the Society that surrounds us" (1988:36, 38, 255). Sartre believed that change could be achieved by developing a literature that would disclose the world (1988:65), that would be "moral and problematic" (1988:235), that had the duty "to take sides against all injustices" (1988:229). He argued that "literature is in essence a taking of position" and that a writer's every word "has reverberations," as do a writer's silences (1988:224, 252). All these characteristics could be claimed for engaged translations as well.

Sartre's arguments are inspiring, yet when translators or scholars advocate engagement as a form of activism in translation, I believe that it is important to envision something much more proactive than the activities touted by advocates of *littérature engagée*. I take this view of engagement in translation for a number of reasons. First, the effectiveness of literary works or other textual forms that aim merely at attitudinal shifts in the receiving audience is very difficult to assess and less certain to achieve actual political or societal results than other forms of activism have been. Attitudinal shifts are notoriously difficult to correlate with social change; they are also conspicuously volatile and subject to reversals or ironic finales. It seems especially dubious at present to argue for the transformative value of changing the attitudes of a small avant-garde after a century of repression, suppression, and even extermination of cultural elites. From the annihilation of intellectuals in the Nazi death camps to China's Cultural Revolution, from the neutralization of leftists and the disruption of art of all sorts during the McCarthy period in the United States to massacres of the educated classes in various African countries after the end of colonialism, we should understand that such hopes of attitudinal shifts are often badly misplaced. Pogroms and purges of progressives and of the left as a whole convulsed virtually every continent in the last century, wiping away gains associated with attitudinal change. Such repression continues unabated today in many places in the world, and freedoms of speech and of the press are currently under general attack everywhere. Engagement as a metaphor for activism in translation can aim at more direct and more powerful forms of action than mere attitudinal shifts.

Before leaving the question of how to conceptualize agency in translation, let us also consider the word *activism* that I have been using as an umbrella term for social interventions of various types. *Activism* is a relatively new term in English, as is *activist* used as a noun, in common circulation only since the middle of the twentieth century. An index of their recent lexical status is the absence of these words from the Compact Edition of the *Oxford English Dictionary* published in 1971. *Activism* gained currency in the 1960s and 1970s, largely to refer to the diverse large social protests that occurred around the world during the period. Public gatherings of civil rights movements, demonstrations against colonialism and imperialism, protests against occupiers of nations, antiwar marches, feminist demonstrations, political protests, and rallies for causes of all types have been a common part of the social and political landscape since that time throughout the world. Manifestations of these sorts have been referred to as *activism* in English for decades, but the term has come to be used for many other forms of political involvements as well, most of which are considerably less dramatic than such massive demonstrations and their associated political causes.

Why did this general English-language term for public political involvement gain currency after World War II? In answering the question it's worth considering what demonstrators and political activists were called in earlier times. If we look back to the end of the eighteenth century and thereafter, it is notable that people we would call activists were referred to either in general terms (agitators, reformers) or in more specific ones (rebels, revolutionaries, Decembrists, abolitionists, nihilists, anarchists, socialists, communists, Bolsheviks, Boxers, populists, and so forth). That is, before World War II specific movements were recognized as involved in activities (often disruptive ones) that were intended to advocate for or demand social change, but their claims were often viewed as limited and particularist in orientation. Implicitly such groups were represented as promoting a specific political or ideological stance and as contesting and challenging the legitimate authority of a government or an established social order, whether that authority was based on the divine right of a king, the expedience of victory in armed struggle, or voluntary federation.[13]

These attitudes seem to have shifted after World War II, with a different view of the relationship between the people and government implied and discernible in the concept of activism itself. Indeed it may be that the concept arose in response to the events of the war: activism can be seen as standing in contrast to the shame and opprobrium associated with the passivity of individuals and populations dominated by the occupying armies of the Third Reich and Japan, as well as collusion with the policies and programs of Axis countries.[14] It may also be that the recognition and valorization of a concept like activism was entailed in the judgments at Nuremberg, suggesting that all human beings are ultimately responsible for the morality of their own actions and those of their societies and nation-states. The Nuremberg decisions imply that a person cannot hide behind the power of authorities, orders from "above," social rules, or unjust laws as a means of explaining or exculpating his actions and acquiescences. The postwar period denied passivity a legitimate position in the face of injustice.

Behind the very concept of activism, thus, I discern an implied sense that each person has an inherent responsibility for social conditions, a fundamental conception that each person is accountable for the state of society, the maintenance of the social contract, and justice at home and abroad. Where views of society that dominated before World War II—and that still hold sway in some countries—saw social responsibility as more limited to those in power, since the middle of the twentieth century there has been a widespread and growing consensus that all individuals are implicated in the social order and that they are socially and morally accountable for the common weal. With this accountability has come an enabling perception of empowerment as well, celebrated in stories of personal resistance and engagement in the face of adversity, ranging from narratives about the many individuals who opposed or mitigated oppression during World War II to those about heroes of civil rights movements and more. Discourses in translation studies related to activism participate in these broader shifts in attitude regarding social responsibility.

The perspectives on social responsibility that emerged after World War II and that serve as a framework for current activism can also be read backward in time. They are useful for assessing the work and positionality of socially engaged translators and translation movements before the modern period. The concept of activism highlights the ways translation has been used instrumentally to further large programs of social change, the affiliations translators have had with other social activists, the extent to which translators acting alone have had programmatic motivations for their translation choices, and so forth. Thus, the projects of German translators such as August Wilhelm Schlegel and Friedrich Schleiermacher at the turn of the nineteenth century or the programs of translators in China such as Yan Fu, Lin Shu, and Lu Xun at the turn of the twentieth century can be set in a new light using the concept of activism.[15] These translators were all engaged in translational activities aimed at language reform, cultural change, and nation building. They were acting out of what we would call activist motivations to improve their societies, helping their cultures take new directions and adapt to new conditions. In all these situations—as in the eighteenth- and nineteenth-century case studies in this volume—translation is instrumental, a means serving larger political and ideological purposes. It is important to note that many of these early translators are explicit about their programmatic motivations and purposes in their writings about translation; these statements read in light of the modern concept of activism take on new meaning.

In exploring the nexus of translation and activism, translation in postcolonial contexts is frequently invoked as a paradigm for translation studies discourses, not least because postcolonial theory has shaped views of ideology and power in literary and cultural studies as a whole.[16] Colonialism on the one hand and postcolonial responses on the other have often served to epitomize oppression and resistance respectively. Not surprisingly this volume contains chapters focused on translation in postcolonial contexts. Studies of colonialism have identified mechanisms by which colonizers have used translation as a means of imperial control and expropriation. Still others have shown that activist translators in colonized nations have effectively advanced cultural nationalism, self-determination of peoples, and national independence.[17] As with resistance during World War II, the oppositions and polarizations in postcolonial cultures and the asymmetries of power are generally sufficiently clear to make the object of resistance and the goals of activism manifest and even self-evident.

Postcolonial translation studies are particularly interesting because of the centrality of ideology in postcolonial cultures. Postcolonial contexts also underscore the importance of the material constraints on translation, including constraints exerted by those in power. Moreover, translation in postcolonial contexts exemplifies in rather clear ways the oppressive and coercive aspects of discourse and the temptations of collusive involvement in discursive fields that can deflect and undermine resistance. The asymmetrical power relations in postcolonial cultures are pertinent as well to the mechanisms of both censorship and self-censorship that circumscribe resistance and activism in translation.[18] Despite all these barriers to action, the historical record of translation in postcolonial contexts reveals the manifold possibilities for creative resistance and engagement on the part of translators.

Sustained exploration of postcolonial translation has illuminated activism and activist practices in translation, challenging some fundamental received conceptions about translation. Postcolonial studies make it clear that translation does not usually take place between two equal cultures as a means of free exchange or transfer of information, and they show that translation is not simply or even primarily a question of communication. Translation in postcolonial contexts lays bare the constructivist aspects of translation. Dominant models assume that a translator must "know" the two languages and cultures involved, but postcolonial contexts challenge this view, showing that translation has a fundamental epistemological dimension: it does not merely reflect existing knowledge, it can also precede knowledge and construct knowledge, much of which becomes the foundation of representations. Translation can be a mode of discovery used to preserve, create, or amass knowledge, and in this role it can have marked political and ideological dimensions, becoming a mode of spying or intelligence gathering used for purposes of domination, or, by contrast, a mode of counterespionage, resistance, and rebellion.

Postcolonial situations set in high relief the fact that activist translations are not uniform and consistent. Seldom can postcolonial translations be usefully defined or discussed in terms of the binaries that translation studies has relied upon—literal vs. free, formal-equivalence vs. dynamic-equivalence, adequate vs. acceptable, or domesticating vs. foreignizing—nor do they generally fall on a continuum between such polarities. Instead postcolonial translations are complex, fragmentary, and even self-contradictory, as translators position their work through a metonymic process to achieve strategic ideological goals, prioritizing particular aspects of the source texts for specific activist effects relevant to the immediate context. Such metonymies are essential to the ability of translations to participate in ideological struggles, to be engaged and partisan, and to be agents of resistance and activism generally, as we have seen. Thus, paradoxically, the polarization of postcolonial cultures facilitates theoretical insight into the process of activist translation by setting in sharp relief the significance of the featural, functional, and contextual aspects of translators' metonymic choices.

Postcolonial translations also indicate that a translation is not merely a text but an act, where sometimes (though not always) the function is as important as the product itself. Because of extreme political mobilization, fidelity in translation is not always of paramount importance in postcolonial situations with their asymmetries of power and imperative political complexities. Translation as an act generally has a very public dimension in most postcolonial contexts. Far from being invisible, postcolonial translators are almost inevitably prominent cultural figures, highly visible and publicly engaged in the creation of discourses and representations and in the enactment of resistance to oppression. Thus, translation in postcolonial cultures answers the calls to action in translation studies urging translators to be visible, but postcolonial translators often go far beyond mere visibility to become actors in history themselves. Several essays in this collection epitomize these features of activism in postcolonial translation.

Finally, consideration of actual translations in postcolonial situations illuminates the ironies that can result from activist translation movements. Case studies demonstrate not only possibilities for the activist use of translation and necessary conditions for the success of resistance, but the limitations of success as well. An example is the highly effective movement of cultural nationalism in Ireland at the turn of the twentieth century that involved translations of early Irish literature into English, which we will return to in the conclusion of this book. Led by prominent Irish cultural figures, the translation movement was an important element in securing (partial) independence for Ireland and establishing the Irish state; it helped to demonstrate the existence of an independent Irish culture and had an important impact on identity formation at the time. Ironically, however, the skewed nationalist representations of early Irish culture in translations (regarding heroism and sexual purity, among others) helped achieve independence but later also contributed to a problematic mythos about Irish identity, some of which was written into Irish law, making cultural configurations in the independent Irish state among the most regressive and repressive in Western Europe, particularly for women. The representations of heroism were also later resuscitated to validate an ethos of violence in Northern Ireland that both the IRA and the Unionists subscribed to during the Troubles in the second half of the twentieth century. In a sense Ireland became a victim of its own translational self-representation and self-construction. In such cases postcolonial translation studies stand as a warning about the unintended consequences of activist translation, as well as the dangers of implicit and explicit collusion with hegemonic values.

These characteristics of postcolonial translations are relevant to many cases of activist translation, but valuable and instructive as postcolonial translation studies are, they have limited use in modeling activism, engagement, and resistance in translation overall. The social models underlying postcolonial theory are not fully applicable to all situations

of conflict, coercion, or oppression. Although some writers think of postcoloniality in existential or ontological terms, it is best seen in terms of a
particular configuration of political circumstances involving factors such
as conquest and dispossession; the subjection of a local culture within an
empire or an imperial network (that is, dominance by a political, economic,
linguistic, and cultural "center"); the presence and interface in the colonized setting of two or more languages and cultures, of which at least one
antedates the advent of imperialist conquest; and the absence of self-
determination, instantiated not only by lack of choice of leadership and
autonomy of the polity but also by the absence of an independent army or
the right to bear arms. Obviously this is merely a suggestive list, not one
meant to be definitive or complete: postcolonial situations differ significantly in their characteristics. Nonetheless, as is clear from this list, the
problems of postcoloniality are not precisely those of people in diaspora,
of minorities within a pluralistic society, or of women who are oppressed
the world around, nor can postcolonial studies be used as a framework
for many types of international conflicts. By lumping such divergent cases
together, we actually learn less about conditions of oppression, contestation, and the possibilities for resistance, engagement, and activism;
conclusions about the data become less reliable as well. In part postcolonial theory has become popular because it has filled a theoretical gap
since the fall of the Soviet Union and the consequent diminished confidence in Marxist analyses. Though postcolonial theory cannot serve as a
model for all cases of activist translation, it nonetheless remains a relevant springboard for many considerations. The trajectory of translation
studies indicates, however, that new theories of power are needed, as
are new theories of activism. Such theories must be more flexible and
more applicable to a broader range of cultural contexts than postcolonial
theory can be.[19]

Consideration of concrete case studies such as those in this volume
often permit the contours of new theories to emerge. Indeed a goal of this
collection is to contribute to the development of a better theory of activism
in translation, not merely to illuminate specific historical examples. The
choices of translators, the partial and partisan nature of activist translations,
the roles of resistant translations in target cultures, the nature of translators'
engagement and activism, the ethical problematics involved in activist
translation, and the usefulness of paradigms offered by postcoloniality are
some of the pragmatic and theoretical issues that this collection addresses.

These concerns are fundamental to understanding how translations change societies and they set the stage for further inquiry about translators who undertake activist endeavors.

If translations are primarily facts of receiving cultures, as Toury asserts, then the following questions are relevant to readings of the studies in this volume. What cultural, ideological, and social changes in target cultures are promoted by specific translation movements and specific translators? What is resisted and opposed in any particular translation? How are resistance and opposition enacted? What other forms of activism do translators and translation movements interact with and participate in? To whom are translators committed and with whom do they engage? What constitutes engagement for specific translators and translations? To what extent are particular translations and translation movements successful in changing their receptor cultures and to what extent do they fail or become coopted? In what ways do translators collude with the very system they are trying to change? What range of activist translation strategies can be discerned? Are particular strategies privileged by activist translators? Are there strategies that further activist goals most effectively? What limitations are there to activist translation?

The answers to these questions in the studies that follow indicate the myriad ways that translation, resistance, and activism intersect, and in the final chapter of the book we will turn to some of the conclusions that can be drawn from the collection as a whole. Though many questions remain to be explored, the essays in this book confirm that translation constitutes a distinct and significant impetus for literary, cultural, and political change, with translations often at the leading edge of a society, particularly in contexts of cultural contestation. The studies in this volume delineate the initiative, resourcefulness, responsibility, and courage of translators, their willingness to put themselves on the line for social change. The essays indicate the wide range of purposes that translation can be put to, as well as the wide variety of activist translation strategies that can be effective. In wartime such critical aspects of translation have long been recognized and translation has been seen as essential to security and cultural survival. In times of peace, by contrast, it is easy to stereotype and dismiss translation as a secondary activity, a process that can be undertaken by anyone with a good bilingual dictionary. The essays here are reminders that in peace as in war, translation always has a potentially radical and activist edge, that it is driven by ethical and ideological concerns, and that it participates in

shaping societies, nations, and global culture in primary ways. Both translation and activism allow us to see that another world is possible. Together
they can change the world.

Notes

1. A brief history of the development of translation studies is found in Tymoczko (2007:15–53). See also sources cited.

2. As exceptions to Toury's statement, for example, translations can be determined to have a significant impact on the source culture in cases where the very fact
of having work translated into a dominant world language raises the prestige of an
author in the home culture. This sort of effect contributed to the rising fame of Jorge
Luis Borges, Gabriel García Márquez, Julio Cortázar, and other writers of the Latin
American Boom after their works were translated into French and English and received a positive reception in France and the United States. Translations are also primary facts of a source culture when the source culture itself sponsors translation as
part of its political program; such was the case in the Soviet Union and the People's
Republic of China when there was enormous state-sponsored translational output
into languages of countries that were ideological targets.

3. The English word *translation*, for example, has as its first meaning the concrete sense of moving things through space, including objects such as the relics or
bones of saints and cultural phenomena such as learning and power. Its meaning was
extended to the activity of interlingual translation relatively late, probably in the four-
teenth century. Cf. Halverson (1999), Tymoczko (2010). Alternative conceptual metaphors for translation found in a number of non-Indo-European languages are discussed in Tymoczko (2007:68–76).

4. The Cold War prioritized developing forms of machine translation in part so
as to make intelligence gathering a cost-effective process; to do so it was essential to
reduce the ambiguous linguistic and cultural aspects of translation to manageable
and reliable protocols. Clearly political and ideological agendas were to the fore in all
the postwar approaches to translation. It is telling that even W. V. O. Quine (1959:171)
uses the term *manual* to refer to different translation protocols in his arguments about
indeterminacy. On the anisomorphisms and asymmetries of language see Nida (1964)
and Catford (1965) which are obviously texts of their time.

5. An excellent overview of the development of descriptive studies is found in
Hermans (1999).

6. Accordingly, systems analyses of translation studies challenge all branches of
literary studies as they are currently conceived in university settings. It is obvious that
literary disciplines must expand their concept of any particular literary system to include texts that have been translated into the language(s) of the receiving culture and
that have played significant roles in the shaping of the literature.

7. Cf. Venuti (1995:12). Note the criticisms of Venuti in Pym (1996:168–69),
however, who points out that the much larger book trade in the United States means
that numerically far more translations are actually produced in English than in
Italian.

8. A simple linguistic anisomorphism is the contrast between the binary system *yes/no* in English and the threefold system *oui/non/si* in French. Differences in color concepts illustrate cultural asymmetries. See Nida (1964), Catford (1965), Bassnett (2002), and sources cited for additional examples and theoretical implications of both linguistic anisomorphisms and cultural asymmetries.

Landmark studies of shifts in translation that go far beyond linguistic necessity are found in Hermans (1985); Lefevere (1982, 1992); and Lefevere and Jackson (1982).

9. See Venuti (1995:307–13; 2008:265–77) for his call to action. The influence of cultural nationalism on Canadian translation is surveyed in Brisset (1996); "woman-handling" of texts by feminist translators is canvassed in Simon (1996), von Flotow (1997), and sources cited; and the cannibalistic or anthropophagic program of Brazilian translators is discussed in Vieira (1994, 1999). See also Gentzler (2008).

10. For example, see Levý (1967).

11. These and other criticisms are taken up in Pym (1996), Lane-Mercier (1997), Hatim (1999), Tymoczko (2000a), Shamma (2005), and sources cited.

12. The *Oxford English Dictionary* (s.v.; henceforth *OED*) offers the following definitions of the word *resistance*: (1) "the act, on the part of persons, of resisting, opposing, or withstanding"; (2) "power or capacity of resisting"; (3) "opposition of one material thing to another material thing, force."

13. Note that in the United States the emergence of a general term like *activism* would have been favored by experiences during the Cold War, notably those associated with the House Un-American Activities Committee and the McCarthy period. During that period labels like *communist* or *socialist* were used to attack, discredit, and silence concerned citizens and social movements demanding change in general. Widespread distrust of specific labels resulted. I am indebted to Ann McNeal (personal communication) for this observation.

14. Discourses stressing the problems of passivity in the face of oppression can be found in the nineteenth century as well, notably in colonized countries. The contrast between passivity and activity in Ireland, for example, lies behind a political discourse about the "paralysis" of the Irish, lambasting the Irish themselves for having been subdued and kept in thrall by a very small English force. This discourse of paralysis was popular among nationalists in the last third of the nineteenth century and the early twentieth century; it is signaled, for example, in the opening story of James Joyce's *Dubliners* as well as his letters about the stories, indicating that he saw Dublin as the center of paralysis of his country (cf. Joyce 1996/1916:9, 253, 262). Similar discourses are represented as part of Nigerian responses to colonialism in Chinua Achebe's *Things Fall Apart*.

15. On activist readings of Chinese translators, see Cheung (forthcoming). I am also indebted to an unpublished essay by Xuefei Bai.

16. The temporal scope of the term *postcolonial* varies in postcolonial studies, with some using the term to refer to conditions after the end of colonialism and others using it to refer to conditions after the inception of colonialism. I am using the terms *postcolonial* and *postcoloniality* in the latter sense. Cf. Robinson (1997:13–14).

17. On colonialist translation see Cheyfitz (1991), Niranjana (1992), and Fitzpatrick (2000). Tymoczko (1999) offers an extended case study of postcolonial activism. Both colonialist translation and postcolonial resistance are discussed in Spivak

(1988, 1993); Rafael (1993); Dingwaney and Maier (1995); Bassnett and Trivedi (1999); Tymoczko (2000a); Simon and St-Pierre (2000); Hung and Wakabayashi (2005); and Hermans (2006).

18. Studies on topics related to censorship and self-censorship are found in Merkle (2002) and Ní Chuilleanáin et al. (2009).

19. More extensive consideration of these issues is found in Tymoczko (2007:189–220).

MONA BAKER

Translation and Activism: Emerging Patterns of Narrative Community

> What matters at this stage is the construction of local forms of com-
> munity within which civility and the intellectual and moral life can be
> sustained through the dark ages which are already upon us.
>
> ALASDAIR MacINTYRE, After Virtue

T HIS article begins the exploration of some of the ways in which translation and interpreting may be embedded in a variety of projects that are set up outside the mainstream institutions of society, with agendas that explicitly challenge the dominant narratives of the time. More specifi-cally, the essay outlines a narrative framework within which the work of communities of translators and interpreters who are actively involved in social or political agendas may be explained and critiqued. As I argue, narrative provides a basis for shared language and values, thus enabling the mobilization of numerous individuals with very different backgrounds and attributes around specific political, humanitarian, or social issues.

Numerous amorphous groups of individuals of various backgrounds have long participated in translating and interpreting a range of narratives that challenge the dominant institutions of society. Examples of organizations that continue to draw heavily on the services of such committed translators and interpreters include Peace Brigades International (www.peacebrigades .org/), Front Line Defenders (www.frontlinedefenders.org), Habitat Interna-tional Coalition (www.hic-net.org), and Gush Shalom, The Israeli Peace Bloc (www.gush-shalom.org/english/), among many others. In addition to these groups, a pattern of committed, strongly politicized communities is emerging within the world of professional translation and interpreting itself. I refer here to the part spontaneous, part planned conversions of pro-fessional translation and interpreting communities into political/activist groups. Examples include Translators for Peace (www.traduttoriperlapace.org/),

23

Babels (www.babels.org/), Translators and Interpreters Peace Network (www.saltana.com.ar/pax/paxbabelica.htm), and ECOS (Traductores e Intérpretes por la Solidaridad; www.ecosfti.tk/).

In between the amorphous groups of professional and non-professional translators who service a broad range of humanitarian and activist organizations on the one hand and committed communities of professional translators and interpreters with a clear political agenda on the other, there is a vast range of different types of groupings and associations, including some with less clearly defined agendas. One such group is Translators Without Borders/Traducteurs Sans Frontières, an offshoot of Eurotexte, a commercial translation agency based in Paris. Promoted as a not-for-profit association set up to provide free translations for humanitarian organizations, especially for Doctors Without Borders (Médecins Sans Frontières), Translators Without Borders is nevertheless used by Eurotexte as a selling point for the agency, thus arguably commodifying the very idea of establishing political communities of action within the professional world of translation. I return to Translators Without Borders at the end of this essay, where I draw on Walter Fisher's narrative paradigm to assess the moral implications of its ambivalent position as a commercial-cum-activist community.

I begin with an outline of the theoretical framework that informs my understanding of the emergence and practices of various activist groups in the field. These, I argue, are ultimately motivated not by any intrinsic attributes of the individuals who constitute each group but by a sense of identification with a "story" or set of "stories" around which the group gathers. They are, in other words, held together by their willingness to subscribe to the same, or a very similar, set of narratives. The account offered here acknowledges the power of narrative to instigate and maintain a sense of common identity and its potential as a basis for political action.

Narrative in Social and Communication Theory

> People act, or do not act, in part according to how they understand their place in any number of given narratives. (Somers and Gibson 1994:61)

The notion of narrative has attracted much attention in a variety of disciplines and has accordingly been defined in a variety of ways. Many scholars, especially in literary studies and pragmatics, tend to treat narrative as an optional mode of communication, often contrasting it with argumentation or exposition. In the work of social theorists such as Margaret Somers (1992, 1997) and communication theorists such as Walter Fisher (1984, 1985, 1997), by contrast, narrative is conceived as the principal and inescapable mode by which we experience the world. Thus, Margaret Somers and Gloria Gibson write that "everything we know is the result of numerous crosscutting story-lines in which social actors locate themselves" (1994:41).[1] Narratives in this view are public and personal stories that we subscribe to and that guide our behavior. They are the stories we tell ourselves, not just those we explicitly tell other people, about the world(s) in which we live. Jerome Bruner further argues that narrative is "a form not only of representing but of constituting reality" (1991:5). It follows that a given narrative, in the social and communication theory sense, is not necessarily traceable to one specific stretch of text but is more likely to underpin a whole range of texts and discourses without necessarily being fully or explicitly articulated in any one of them. At the same time, there are very specific, detailed narratives that are fully articulated within the confines of a single text or group of texts, though even these will ultimately be embedded in and informed by broader narratives that cannot be located within individual stretches of language.

Somers and Gibson (1994; cf. Somers 1992, 1997) distinguish between ontological, public, conceptual, and meta narratives. *Ontological narratives* are personal stories we tell ourselves about our place in the world and about our own personal history. They are interpersonal and social in nature, but they remain focused on the self and its immediate world. *Public narratives* are stories elaborated by and circulating among social and institutional formations larger than the individual, such as the family, religious or educational institutions, a political or activist group, the media, and the nation. As examples of public narratives, Somers and Gibson mention stories about American social mobility or the "freeborn Englishman" (1994:62). A more recent example might be the numerous and competing public narratives of the war on Iraq. What happened? Why did it happen? Who is responsible? Is it motivated by a bid (however misguided) to make the world a safer place or by imperialist interests in Iraqi resources?

Somers and Gibson define *conceptual narratives* as "concepts and explanations that we construct as social researchers," and they go on to argue that "the conceptual challenge that narrativity poses is to develop a social analytic vocabulary that can accommodate the contention that social life, social organizations, social action, and social identities are narratively, that is, temporally and relationally constructed through both ontological and public narratives" (1994:62–63). It seems to me, however, that it is both reasonable and productive to extend this definition to include disciplinary narratives in any field of study. Thus, conceptual narratives can be more broadly defined as the stories and explanations that scholars in any field elaborate for themselves (and others) about their object of inquiry. Some of these stories or conceptual narratives can have considerable impact on the world at large, while others remain limited in scope to the immediate community of scholars in the relevant field.

A good example of a particularly pernicious conceptual narrative that has exercised considerable influence beyond its immediate disciplinary boundaries is Samuel Huntington's *The Clash of Civilizations and the Remaking of World Order* (1996). A political scientist based at Harvard University until his death in December 2008, Huntington classified world civilizations into distinct groups, namely Western, Eastern Orthodox, Latin American, Islamic, Japanese, Chinese, Hindu, and African civilizations, each with "inherent" cultural characteristics (mostly conflicting with "good" American values); and he predicted that culture would replace ideology as the principal cause of conflict in the twenty-first century. In a more recent book, *Who Are We? The Challenges to America's National Identity* (2004), Huntington looked at North American society through the same neoconservative cultural prism and elaborated a narrative of an internal clash of civilizations, arguing that the new war is between the country's white majority and its growing Hispanic population. In an earlier article on the same theme published in the influential journal *Foreign Affairs* in 1993, Huntington explicitly argued that "in this emerging era of cultural conflict the United States must forge alliances with similar cultures and spread its values wherever possible. With alien civilizations the West must be accommodating if possible, but confrontational if necessary."[2] Huntington's *Clash of Civilizations* was a major reference point for George W. Bush's U.S. administration, and the narratives it spawned have been directly linked to the official public narratives related to the events of 11 September 2001 and the wars on Afghanistan and Iraq. Every discipline, including translation studies, elaborates and thrives on its own set of conceptual narratives; and Huntington's narrative stands as an example of the role narrative plays in such contexts.

Finally, Somers and Gibson define *meta narratives* or *master narratives* as narratives "in which we are embedded as contemporary actors in history. . . . Our sociological theories and concepts are encoded with aspects of these master-narratives—Progress, Decadence, Industrialization, Enlightenment, etc." (1994:63). An obvious candidate for a more recent meta or master narrative is the public narrative of the "War on Terror," which is aggressively sustained and promoted through a myriad of national and international channels; thus, it is rapidly acquiring the status of a super narrative that cuts across geographical and national boundaries and that directly impacts the lives of the entire world population. The choice of *terror* rather than *terrorism* is significant here and offers a good example of the discursive work required for the successful circulation and adoption of narratives.[3] *Terrorism* refers to one or more incidents that involve violence, with localized and containable impact. *Terror,* by contrast, is a state of mind, one that can rapidly spread across boundaries and encompass all in its grip. To qualify as a meta or master narrative, a narrative must have this type of temporal and physical.breadth, as well as a sense of inevitability or inescapability. *Terror* indexes such features much better than *terrorism.*

Clearly narratives do not travel across linguistic and cultural boundaries and do not develop into global meta narratives without the direct involvement of translators and interpreters. What is significant at present is that growing numbers of professional and non-professional translators and interpreters are actively setting out to elaborate alternative narratives that can challenge the oppressive public and meta narratives of our time.

Assessing Stories: Fisher's Narrative Paradigm

The test of each story is the sort of person it shapes. (Hauerwas and Burrell 1989:185)

The version of narrative theory I have chosen to adopt in my research assumes that no one stands outside all narratives and that narrative constitutes reality rather than merely representing it. This might suggest that there can be no criteria for assessing individual narratives. But our embeddedness in narratives clearly cannot preclude our ability to reason about individual narratives. If it did, we would have no basis for establishing communal identity, given that narrative theory also stresses that "narratives, along with the values they prescribe . . . form the basis of communities large and small, and thereby define who we are" (Hinchman and Hinchman 1997:238).

Walter Fisher's influential narrative paradigm (1984, 1985, 1997) helps to explain why our embeddedness in narratives does not mean that one story is as good as another or that we passively internalize rather than actively choose and elaborate the narratives we subscribe to.[4] Fisher argues against the conceptualization of human beings as simply rational and instead suggests that people are essentially storytellers who "creatively read and evaluate the texts of life and literature" (1985:86). As both storytellers and audience, we make decisions on the basis of good reasons, but what we consider good reasons is determined by our history, culture, experience of the world, and, ultimately, the stories we come to believe about the world in which we live.

Two points are worth highlighting here. First, within this framework there is still a rational basis for assessing the stories that shape our understanding of the world, but rationality in Fisher's model is redefined as "narrative rationality." Fisher writes that narrative rationality "is determined by the nature of persons as narrative beings—their inherent awareness of narrative probability, what constitutes a coherent story, and their constant habit of testing narrative fidelity, whether the stories they experience ring true with the stories they know to be true in their lives" (1984:7–8). I discuss the two criteria of coherence and fidelity in more detail below and attempt to apply them to translation in the final section of this article.

Second, the notion of "good reasons" suggests that assessing narratives in order to position ourselves in relation to them does not just depend on how well they "fit" with our experience of the world in factual terms. *Good* here has a moral import as well, as Fisher indicates: "All forms of human communication function to influence the hearts and minds of others—their beliefs, values, attitudes, and/or actions. The concept of good reasons coincides with the assumption that human beings are as much valuing as they are reasoning beings. The fact is that values may serve as reasons, and what we usually call reasons are value-laden" (1997:314). Fisher points out, however, that we need specific guidance in the form of features that narratives must display (rather than merely the effects they may have) in order to decide "whether or not they are deserving of our adherence" (1997:315). This is what coherence and fidelity, the two basic principles that define narrative rationality and that embody the concept of good reasons in Fisher's paradigm, allow us to do.

A narrative may be "tested" in relation to three types of coherence: structural or argumentative; material; and characterological. Structural coherence relates to internal consistency—whether or not the narrative reveals contradictions within itself. Material coherence is a question of how a narrative relates to other narratives that cover the same issue and that we are familiar with. More specifically, a narrative can be tested with respect to the "facts" it might downplay or ignore, the counterarguments it chooses not to engage with, and so forth. Characterological coherence assumes that the reliability of any narrative depends very largely on the credibility of its main characters as well as the characters narrating it. If the decisions and actions associated with a character change significantly "in strange ways" (Fisher 1997:316) or contradict each other, we inevitably question the credibility of the character and, hence, the narrative in question. Fisher indicates that "Coherence in life and literature requires that characters behave characteristically. Without this kind of predictability, there is no trust, no rational order, no community" (1997:316). Hence, once we decide that a given person is trustworthy, honorable, courageous, and so on, we are prepared to "overlook and forgive many things: factual errors if not too dramatic, lapses in reasoning, and occasional discrepancies" (Fisher 1997:316).

In addition to testing for coherence, we also test narratives for fidelity. Here, the focus is on assessing (a) the elements of a narrative that may be regarded as its reasons (i.e., examining it largely from the perspective of traditional logic: patterns of implicature and inference, representation of the facts, etc.) and (b) the values that the narrative promotes. For Fisher good reasons are "those elements that provide warrants for accepting or adhering to the advice fostered by any form of communication that can be considered rhetorical" (1987/1989:107). He stresses, however, that the concept of good reasons "does not imply that every element of rhetorical transaction that warrants a belief, attitude, or action—that any 'good reason'—is as good as any other. It only signifies that whatever is taken as a basis for adopting a rhetorical message is inextricably bound to a value—to a conception of the good" (1987/1989:197).

Assessing the values explicitly or implicitly promoted by a narrative means asking what effects adhering to it would have on the world, on our ability to maintain our sense of self respect, and on our relationship to others. As Fisher argues, we ultimately have to ask "even if a prima facie case has been made or a burden of proof has been established, are the values fostered by the story those that would constitute an ideal basis for human conduct?" (1997:317). It is this ability to judge narratives on the basis of their moral implications and the values they promote that ultimately guides human behavior and allows communities to gather around a given narrative or set of narratives.[5]

Fisher's narrative paradigm has two principal strengths in the current context. First, because it privileges moral values, it explains why activist communities can form across boundaries of nation, color, gender, profession, and almost any other division one can think of, without any motivation of personal gain—indeed, often at great personal risk to individual members of the community. Second, the narrative paradigm goes beyond explaining why communities emerge and unite around narratives. It specifically anchors this process in the notions of narrative rationality and good reasons, which imply considerable agency on the part of individuals and communities. As storytellers we do more than "choose" from prevalent narratives in our own societies. If we judge the moral consequences of these narratives negatively, we can look elsewhere for "better" narratives or even elaborate narratives of our own. This is precisely what communities of activists, including those forming within the professional world of translation, attempt to do—they organize and select narratives on the basis of "good reasons," looking beyond the dominant narratives of their cultures, often selecting counter narratives or elaborating new ones.

It is worth pointing out that much of the impetus for narrative research in general, including Fisher's work, comes from a belief among theorists working in this area that the unexamined assumptions of narratives "conceal patterns of domination and submission" (Mishler 1995:114), which exclude the experience of large sectors of society while legitimating and promoting those of the political, economic, and cultural elite. There is also general agreement in the literature that narrative both reproduces the existing power structures *and* provides a means of contesting them: "If stories can be constructed to wall off the senses to the dilemmas and contradictions of social life, perhaps they also can be presented in ways that open up the mind to creative possibilities developed in ways that provoke intellectual struggle, the resolution of contradiction, and the creation of a more workable human order" (Bennett and Edelman 1985:162). More specifically, narrative theorists acknowledge that undermining existing patterns of domination cannot be achieved with concrete forms of activism alone (such as demonstrations, sit-ins, and civil disobedience) but must involve a direct challenge to the stories that sustain these patterns. As language mediators, translators and interpreters are uniquely placed to initiate this type of discursive intervention at a global level.

The narrative paradigm, then, and narrative theory more generally offer a framework that "generate[s] a sense of what is good as well as what is strictly logical in the stories that people might adopt" (Fisher 1997:317), explaining how individuals and communities can exercise sufficient agency to imagine that "another world is possible," to use the well-known slogan of the World Social Forum, serviced by the translators and interpreters in Babels. I suggest we might rewrite this motto in the present context as "another narrative is possible."

Narrative Communities in Translation Studies

> An elaborate network of translators, called Babels, volunteers from all over Europe, sat in little boxes translating the cries against imperialism, capitalism, colonialism and occupation into English, French, Spanish, German, Turkish, Kurdish, Arabic and a plethora of other languages including Euskera. (Kattan 2004, reporting on the European Social Forum)

Fisher suggests that "communities are co-constituted through communication transactions in which participants co-author a story that has coherence and fidelity for the life that one would lead" (1997:323), and he goes on to propose two types of community. The first type is created by concession or conformity: members of the community adhere to a story because it provides justification for a way of life that leads to success or survival. The second type is created by election or conversion; one becomes a member of such a community because the story that brings its members together provides an "honored perception of oneself" (1997:323).

There is no shortage of examples of communities formed by concession or conformity in the world of translation. Whether in professional or academic circles, most countries today boast several professional and academic associations that provide different types of platforms for conducting communication transactions to support such communities. But it is the emerging pattern of communities "by election or conversion" that arguably responds to the most urgent needs of our time, because these have the potential to function as foci of resistance and to sustain "civility and the intellectual and moral forms of community . . . through the dark ages which are already upon us" (MacIntyre 1981:245).

Members of these translation communities recognize that the concrete experiences of our lives cannot be changed without simultaneously changing the narratives that underpin them. Such translators also recognize that the intersections between the narratives of "our" lives and those of "other" peoples in other parts of the world are much denser and more heavily mediated today than at any other time in history. Today's conflicts reverberate across the planet and, almost without exception, are played out in the international arena. The Middle East and Chechen conflicts, for instance, cannot be resolved by appealing only to local constituencies in the United States, Israel, Palestine, or Russia, to suggest obvious examples. Competing narratives of such conflicts circulate in all the widely spoken and many of the less widely spoken languages of the world—largely in and through translation.

Already a number of communities "by election or conversion" are operating in the world of professional translation and interpreting, as I noted at the beginning of this article. For example, Traduttori per la Pace/ Translators for Peace (www.traduttoriperlapace.org/) describes itself as "a free association of translators from all countries and of all nationalities . . . established . . . in order to publish, as far as possible in every language and by whatever channel, every message against: war in general; and in particular, against the use of war as a means of resolving international disputes." The association is based in Italy with some 300 members, mostly Italian; Italian is the main language of the discussion group. It was founded in 1999 at the start of the war in Kosovo. One of the founding members, Andrea Spila, explains the origins of the group as follows.

> [Translators for Peace was established] with the intent of translating articles and documents which did not appear in the Italian press at the time. Five years (and many wars) later we are working in a different way. Our activity is mainly to help civil society organizations to spread their peace message and we help them by translating their documents/websites etc. and by supplying interpreters for conferences, meetings etc. We also translate documents we believe people should know, for example we translated the documents of the neo-con organization Project for a New American Century because it describes exactly what is happening now, i.e. US supremacy worldwide by means of preventive war.[6]

ECOS, Traductores e Intérpretes por la Solidaridad (Translators and Interpreters for Solidarity; cicode-gcubo.ugr.es/ecos), was set up in 1998 by members of the staff at the Faculty of Translation and Interpreting at the University of Granada, Spain, and is still based there. The association offers volunteer translation and interpreting for NGOs, social forums, and other non-profit organizations, but most of its work originally came from NGOs in Granada, including anti-cancer groups, the Granada section of the

Human Rights Association of Andalusia, and AKIBA (the association of support for Black Africa). The aim of ECOS is "to work for a better quality of life for certain social sectors, and to struggle against the injustices of the established system" (Jerez et al. 2005). Its founders also believe that "translators and interpreters must be trained for society and not just for the market" (Jerez et al. 2005). In addition to volunteer translation and interpreting, members of the association also organize talks to raise awareness about contemporary social questions, including fair trade and the situations in Iraq and the Middle East. Since 2003 ECOS has been working with Babels in some international venues, including World Social Forum events.

Babels (www.babels.org/) is a larger and more structured community of volunteer translators and interpreters. Its activist profile is broader than that of Translators for Peace and other existing associations in the field. The group's agenda is not restricted to the issues pertaining to war, and both the range of activities undertaken and the locations of activity are more varied. Moreover, the composition of the group itself is broader, with members in many different parts of the world. The plural form Babels is meant to "underline the supranational character of the association," as their website indicates. Babels was set up in September 2002 by a group of activists linked to the French branch of the alternative globalization network ATTAC, to meet the translation and interpreting needs of the European Social Forum (ESF) in Florence.[7] The group's debut in Florence featured 350 volunteer translators and interpreters working without a budget and without even basic facilities such as computers and telephones (Hodkinson and Boéri 2005). The success and dedication of the group and their effective participation in the conferences opposing the G8 in Evian and Annemasse in May and June 2003, however, convinced the Paris ESF organizers to give them decent facilities and the relatively large sum of £200,000 to prepare for the next forum. This investment seems to have paid off because the Paris ESF held in 2003 was serviced by more than 1,000 "Babelitos" drawn from a volunteer pool four times that number. By the time the London ESF was held in October 2004, the Babels database included over 7,000 volunteers representing 63 languages (Hodkinson and Boéri 2005; Boéri and Hodkinson 2005).

Babels has now been considerably expanded to meet the translation and interpreting needs of organizations identified with the Charter of Principles of the World Social Forum. There are national coordination centers in France, Italy, Germany, the United Kingdom, Spain, Greece, Hungary,

Turkey, Russia, the United States, Brazil, Korea, and Japan, and their website mentions "a facility for linguistic coordination for Arabic," but it is not
clear what this facility consists of.[8] In addition to unpaid translation and
interpreting work, the tasks undertaken by Babels volunteers range from
"giving (moral and material) support to interpreters" to developing linguistic tools that are available to anyone. Babels is perhaps the best example to
date of a carefully planned, equitably structured, and highly politicized international community of translators and interpreters; indeed, it explicitly
describes itself as a "player in the 'anti-capitalist' debate."[9] The group is also
committed to "orchestrating a conscious process of 'contamination' in which
the excellent language skills of the politically sympathetic trained interpreter interact with the deeper political knowledge of the language-fluent
activist to develop a reflexive communications medium organic to the social
forum movement" (Hodkinson and Boéri 2005). In other words Babels
does not see itself as a low-cost service provider for the social movement
but rather as an active member of that narrative community with a key role
in elaborating the narrative vision of the World Social Forum.

Clearly the groups discussed above do not simply come together on
the basis of national or other such static affiliations, nor are they motivated
by personal ambition or profit. These are communities created by "election,"
to use Fisher's term. Translators and interpreters come together in these
groups willingly to volunteer their time, to invest emotionally and intellectually in projects designed to undermine dominant discourses, and to elaborate more equitable and peaceful narratives of the future. What we make of
their efforts depends on our own narrative location and on how we judge the
coherence and fidelity of the narratives they elaborate about themselves.

Coherence and Fidelity in the Narratives of Activist
and/or Volunteer Translation Organizations

Narrative theory allows us to examine communities of these types and their
work from at least two different perspectives. In the first instance it is possible to examine the type of narratives these groups elaborate and to ask how
they mediate those narratives, both in terms of the selection of material to
be translated and the specific modes of translation adopted. Questions such
as the following are productive in this regard. What type of texts do members of such activist communities select for translation? Do they embellish
certain narratives in order to give those whose voices are suppressed and

marginalized a better chance of being heard? Do they frame narratives with which they disagree strongly, such as the Project of the New American Century, in specific ways in order to undermine and expose their underlying assumptions? Do they omit or add material within the body of the text or do they rely on paratexts to guide the reader's interpretation of each narrative? Do interpreters in the social fora reveal their own narrative location through such factors as tone of voice, pitch, or loudness?[10]

For example, with regard to the issue of marginalization, Robert Barsky (1996) argues that the nature of the asylum system is such that it systematically works against claimants, however valid their claims might be. He describes how interpreters working within this system often elaborate a claimant's statement, supplement it with details they learned prior to the hearing, and improve it stylistically and rhetorically. Interpreters working for disempowered claimants who are ill served by their lawyers and the system as a whole may at times mediate "the gap between the claimant's competence in matters of self expression . . . and the requirements of the Refugee Board" (1996:54); indeed, one of the functions they fulfill "can be to quite simply tell a good story" (1996:57).

In terms of translation and activism, a systematic examination of interventions of this type in the output of committed communities of translators, using a theoretical framework that makes it possible to transcend narratives of neutrality and objectivity, would be a worthwhile and illuminating endeavor. I suspect it might demonstrate, for instance, that direct textual manipulation of the type that preoccupies many theorists of translation is relatively rare. In fact the accuracy of translation in this context becomes even more important, because blatant interventions can be used against the translators to brand them as "biased" and hence "untrustworthy," which would have repercussions for the credibility of their own narratives and the narratives they set out to promote, undermining their characterological coherence (in Fisher's terms, as outlined above). Instead we may well find that accuracy acquires an additional value in this context and that much of the "political" work is done through the selection of material to be translated and through various methods of framing the translation, including paratexts, timing of the release of translations, where translations are placed, and so forth.

A second line of inquiry informed by narrative theory involves examining the relevant translation communities' own narratives for coherence and fidelity, using the framework outlined by Fisher above. The point here is not to use the theory to "expose" the incoherence or hidden agendas of a narrative, in the tradition of critical discourse analysis, for instance. Rather, what narrative theory and Fisher's narrative paradigm in particular allow us to do is to retrace our steps and articulate our own reasons for wishing to subscribe or refrain from subscribing to a given narrative, while acknowledging that someone with a different set of values might reach a different decision for equally "good reasons" (as understood in terms of the narrative paradigm itself). A brief analysis of the narrative of one of the communities I mentioned earlier, Translators Without Borders, serves to illustrate the potential for this application of narrative theory.

Aligning itself with what has been dubbed the "sans frontièrisme" or "without borderism" movement (Fox 1995:1607; DeChaine 2002:355), Translators Without Borders or Traducteurs Sans Frontières (www.tsf-twb.org/) consists of a group of volunteer translators and interpreters who provide free translations for organizations they deem deserving, including Doctors Without Borders, Reporters without Borders, Amnesty International, and Handicap International. In some respects this is a very different type of community from Babels and Translators for Peace. As mentioned in the introduction to this article, Translators Without Borders is an offshoot of Eurotexte, a commercial translation agency based in Paris, with offices also in Lisbon.

Fisher's principles of narrative coherence concern the way in which a story hangs together. Perhaps most relevant in this context is structural coherence, which to my mind would test negatively in the case of the narrative of Translators Without Borders because of a lack of internal consistency. This inconsistency results from the conflict between humanitarian and commercial agendas consequent on the identification of Translators Without Borders and Eurotexte. The Eurotexte site features several prominent links to the Translators Without Borders site, often collapsing the distinction between a commercial organization and a not-for-profit community of volunteer translators. For example, Translators Without Borders is listed as a "partner," together with Viva Translations in Lisbon and Eulogia (currently a dead link), on the Eurotexte site. Similarly, the Translators Without Borders site features a link to Eurotexte on the main page and, after outlining the group's services to several humanitarian organizations, informs us that "many Eurotexte translators and staff volunteer their time for these important translation jobs so that translations can be provided free to humanitarian NGOs."

The narrative of Translators Without Borders is also structurally incoherent in another respect, as a consequence of its dependence on and overlap with the Eurotexte narrative. Translators Without Borders, listed under the rubric "Success Stories" on the Eurotexte site, espouses humanitarian and political ideals that are arguably at odds with Eurotexte practices. Lori Thicke, managing director of Eurotexte and founder of Translators Without Borders, addresses these ideals in an undated speech to the Italian Federation of Translation Companies, which she begins with a powerful reminder of the atrocities committed in Chechnya, Palestine, and Kosovo.[11]

> A man in Chechnya says, "A ground-to-ground missile killed my two sons in the market in Grozny. They weren't fighters—they were just there to buy some jeans." The Palestinian girl who at first is too afraid to talk to the visitors, whispers, "I don't think we're going to come out of this alive." On a forced march to the border a mother in Kosovo cries as the soldier takes aim, "Not him, he's not even 15!"

Thicke goes on to ask, "If there's no money for translations, who will tell their stories?" This is a valid question and an admirable call for intervention. Yet at the same time the Eurotexte site proudly lists among its top clients numerous companies that are directly or indirectly implicated in the very atrocities that communities like Translators Without Borders are meant to be bringing to our attention. These include General Electric, the subject of an intense boycott campaign by various peace groups between 1986 and 1993 because of its involvement in the production and sale of nuclear weapons. As a major U.S. defense contractor, it is now back on the boycott lists of several anti-war groups.

Similar criticisms could be leveled at other clients that Eurotexte proudly lists on its site, including L'Oréal, as well as its subsidiary Lancôme. Apart from its dismal record on animal testing, L'Oréal established Israel as its commercial center in the Middle East in 1995 and in 1998 received Israel's Jubilee Award, for organizations who have done most to strengthen the Israeli economy. L'Oréal is on the boycott lists of various solidarity groups set up precisely to respond to the kind of fear and oppression opposed by the humanitarian organizations that are served by Translators Without Borders. At best, then, Eurotexte/Translators Without Borders may be accused of taking only a superficial interest in the plight of the groups it presumes to defend and of failing to look into the wider context of the tragedies it purports to oppose. At worst Eurotexte knowingly and cynically exploits both oppressor and oppressed to further its own commercial success.

In Fisher's framework, fidelity ultimately ranks higher than coherence. Structural incoherence of the type outlined above in the narrative of Translators Without Borders can in principle be explained and even justified from the perspective of narrative fidelity. As I explained earlier, narrative fidelity allows us to test a story in relation to its reasons as well as the values it promotes. In terms of reasons, one could argue that Eurotexte has not misrepresented its links with Translators Without Borders and has not sought to mislead by omitting facts about how the two organizations relate to each other. Eurotexte can only gain by its links with Translators Without Borders; thus, the "reasons" for its particular narrative being what it is are logical and justified. For Eurotexte, doing good comes at a price. The ability to use Translators Without Borders as a selling point at the same time as keeping its own operation focused on making money ensures in turn that Translators Without Borders can continue to enjoy a stable platform even as Eurotexte continues its associations with clients like General Electric and L'Oréal. In her speech Thicke explicitly maintains this duality, stating, "I'm sure I don't have to convince you of the importance of humanitarian work. If you didn't believe in it, you wouldn't be here today. But we're in business. We all need to make money. Good works are often a luxury we can't afford. Or can we? The great news I have for you today is that good works not only help the world: they can also be good for business. Much as I believe in good works, I'm a businesswoman, through and through" (www.eurotexte.fr/downloads/TSFspeechRiminiEurotexte.pdf).

Apart from indirectly securing a financial basis for its activities by promoting its sponsor as a responsible agency, however, it is not obvious how the aims of Translators Without Borders are served by being commodified to enhance the image of Eurotexte. It is this element of the commodification of the humanitarian work of the group that (for some like myself) undermines the narrative of Translators Without Borders, particularly in light of Fisher's fidelity principles. Here, we ask what kind of worldview is promoted by the narrative under examination, and what cultural values it directly or indirectly gives credence to. This is a question that requires us to think beyond the immediate narrative and its impact on a temporally and spatially circumscribed situation or environment. It requires us to think in terms of global and long-term effects. One could argue, for instance, that the narrative of Translators Without Borders ultimately sustains and justifies an ethics of consumerism through the commodification of human grief. By blurring the boundaries between commercial and humanitarian agendas, the narrative accommodates itself to the established "cosmetic" use of good causes by big business to improve its image and deflect attention from its less savory practices. Finally, the Translators Without Borders story feeds into hegemonic cultural narratives of social responsibility that are ultimately designed to make the donors feel good about themselves rather than directly address the needs of the recipients. This is evident in Lori Thicke's article, published in *Multilingual Computing and Technology*, where she explains the attraction of the humanitarian exercise as follows: "Giving away translations for a worthy cause is a win-win scenario. Eurotexte feels good about it. The translators feel good about it, and they see Eurotexte as an agency that really cares—which we do. And last but not least, our customers consider this to be a point of distinction" (2003:4).

In the final analysis, as Lewis P. Hinchman and Sandra K. Hinchman point out, "we extend or withhold allegiance to communities depending on our rational judgments concerning the narratives on which they are based" (1997:238). Fisher's narrative paradigm, as I have tried to demonstrate with the narrative of Translators Without Borders, offers us a framework not only for making rational judgments but also for assessing narratives in terms of fidelity and, thus, their ethical import.[12] It differs from other approaches such as critical discourse analysis in that it does not set out to expose or undermine other narratives as such but to assist us in articulating and re-flecting upon our own values, our own narrative locations. In other words it targets—and exposes—the values of the assessor more so than the weak-nesses or strengths of the narrative being assessed. This is vitally impor-tant because self-reflexivity is seen as the most effective means of resisting the normalizing, totalizing effect of narratives and our inevitable embed-dedness within them.

Conclusion

Faced with an increasingly polarized and violent world in which the oppor-tunities for remaining "neutral" are continually being eroded, translators—like most professional groups—are finding it difficult to position themselves individually and as a group in relation to various narratives that circulate around them and among them. Today, the worldwide web has become a symbolic space in which peace activists and marginalized groups who wish to challenge dominant discourses can elaborate and practice a moral order in tune with their own narratives of the world. Translation enables such groups to elaborate their alternative narratives across national and linguistic boundaries, to create an international community bound by a similar vision of the world and unhindered by linguistic frontiers. At the same time, the professionals who provide these translations are beginning to organize themselves in various ways in order to elaborate their own narratives and play a distinct role as translators in shaping an alternative vision of the world.

As communities of activists in the translation world continue to form and develop their profiles, narrative theory enables us to critique not only their translation practices but also their own narratives about themselves. In the process we reflect on *our* own values and narrative locations. This is an important line of research to pursue, as I demonstrate here, not least because developing a critical stance toward the stories circulating among members of a community—and articulating and reflecting on our own values and principles of assessment—may ultimately help members of the community in question to avoid sustaining the very narratives they set out to challenge. At the same time a narrative theoretical framework helps us as analysts to clarify the basis on which we engage with activist work and professional groups in the field.

Notes

1. For an alternative view see Novitz (1997:156), who argues that "there is no good reason for denying the existence of so-called prenarrative facts, or for insisting . . . that all experience and knowledge must be mediated by or derived from, narrative."

2. See www.foreignaffairs.org/19930601faessay5188/samuel-p-huntington/the-clash-of-civilizations.html; last consulted 16 March 2005; emphasis added.

3. I am grateful to Maria Pavesi of the University of Pavia in Italy for alerting me to this distinction.

4. For a detailed discussion of Fisher's narrative paradigm, see Baker (2006, chap. 7).

5. A full critique of Fisher's narrative paradigm is beyond the scope of this article. For example, Fisher's account fails to explain the power and attraction of evil stories such as *The Silence of the Lambs*. For critiques of his paradigm, see McGee and Nelson (1985), Warnick (1987), Kirkwood (1992), and Baker (2006, chap. 7).

6. Personal email communication, 22 November 2004.

7. The World Social Forum is an activist meeting place for networks of social movements, NGOs, and various civil society groups who are "opposed to neoliberalism and to domination of the world by capital and any form of imperialism, and are committed to building a planetary society directed toward fruitful relationships

among Humankind and between it and the Earth" (Charter of Principles, www .forumsocialmundial.org.br/main.php?id_menu=4&cd_language=2; accessed 21 July 2006). The first meeting of the World Social Forum was held in Porto Alegre in 2001.

8. Babels is a highly self-reflexive group which in some respects seems to be constantly reinventing itself. In other words it deliberately works at retaining its character as "a project in the making." As such any details provided about the workings of the group or the nature of the coordinations it sets up (national, project based, event based, etc.) are always provisional. For a detailed discussion of Babels, see Boéri (2008, in progress).

9. Babels Charter, www.babels.org/article.php3?id_article=21; accessed 21 July 2006.

10. For an extended model of textual analysis informed by narrative theory and applied to the work of translators and interpreters, see Baker (2006). In Baker (2009) I draw on the same theoretical framework to outline a research agenda for studying communities of the type discussed here.

11. The complete text is found at www.eurotexte.fr/downloads/TSFspeech RiminiEurotexte.pdf; accessed 21 July 2006.

12. A sobering example of the dangers of accepting big business narratives of doing good uncritically is a story recounted in Williams (1991) and summarized in Ewick and Silbey (1995:219–20). An African American woman, Patricia Williams, tells her story of being locked out of Benetton one Saturday afternoon by a salesperson who refused to buzz her in. This is the same Benetton "whose advertising campaign appropriates images of racial and ethnic diversity to sell the sweaters they wouldn't give Williams the chance to purchase" (Ewick and Silbey 1995:219).

GEORGES L. BASTIN, ÁLVARO ECHEVERRI,
and ÁNGELA CAMPO

Translation and the Emancipation
of Hispanic America

ALTHOUGH it is true that history recalls and recounts events and facts, these accounts are never fully devoid of underlying ideologies and, hence, subjectivities.[1] The Venezuelan historian and writer Arturo Uslar Pietri makes the following observation:

> Where can we find the history of Latin America among all those partial and partialized views? This is a task that still needs to be done. The historiography of Latin America is like a set of deforming mirrors. Depending on where you stand, the reflection changes, giving one the impression of looking at a different person each time. (1991:114).[2]

These realizations are of utmost importance when studying the pre-independence period and the first years of the new republics in Hispanic America (1785–1835). On the one hand historical discourses tend to reflect ideological positions that portray the views of a specific social group, Eurocentric positions for the most part in this particular field. On the other hand the first documents produced to report the happenings of the time were registered by people who were in most cases simultaneously actors in and reporters of the historical events.

Translators, like other actors in history, do not function in a vacuum; rather they are social beings and as such espouse ideologies and identities that are particular to their social contexts. Román Álvarez and M. Carmen-África Vidal note:

Translators are constrained in many ways: their own ideology, their feelings of superiority or inferiority towards the language in which they are writing, the text being translated, the prevailing poetical rules at that time, the very language in which the texts they are translating is written, what the dominant institutions and ideology expect of them, the public for whom the translation is intended. The translation itself will depend upon all of these factors. (1996:6).

Moreover, in translation studies, just as in other fields, the gathering and analysis of historical data correspond to specific research agendas that have ideological and political biases. At the same time, translation can act as a lens providing an alternate perspective on the materials of history, a perspective not unlike those of literary analysis or anthropology that can serve as a corrective to other approaches to history.

This essay looks at the role of translation in the emancipation movement in Hispanic America. Translation is considered here as a form of activism in the *pragmatic* sense of the term, a subversive *activity* used by a repressed group struggling to resist domination, the *criollos* (those of Spanish descent born in the colonies) resisting the oppression of the Spanish Crown in the case at hand.[3] Such translation activity clearly has important ideological significance and repercussions. In this essay, therefore, resistance and activism are not viewed as ideological positioning expressed primarily through the choice of formal textual strategies, as conceived by translation scholars such as Luise Von Flotow (1997), Susan Bassnett and Harish Trivedi (1999), Lawrence Venuti (1995, 1998), and Gayatri Spivak (1993).

The Written Word in Hispanic America during the Age of Independence

The emancipation process in Hispanic America began in the last two decades of the eighteenth century and ended between 1810 and 1835 for most countries. It represents the efforts of Hispanic Americans to put an end to three centuries of Spanish rule on the continent. The earliest insurrections occurred among the Indian and slave populations throughout the region—the Catari in Bolivia (1780), the Tupac Amarú in Peru (1780–81), and the comuneros in Colombia (1780), among others. Although these risings were significant, they never had an impact on the continent as a whole. They were forms of resistance involving small numbers of people interested in righting specific wrongs and were local in their purview. In addition, the social groups leading these movements were usually the least empowered of American society: the Indians, slaves, mestizos, and mulattos.

By contrast the wars of independence that occurred in the first three decades of the nineteenth century stemmed from both internal and external pressures exerted on the criollo elite of the society. External pressures included the expulsion of the Jesuits from Latin America in 1767; the influence of Enlightenment philosophy; the example of the Revolution of the United States and the subsequent independence of the new republic; the French Revolution; and the Napoleonic invasion of Spain in 1808. Internal pressures included the economic problems typical of the colonial system (such as dependence on imports, absence of industry, and lack of large-scale agriculture) and the heavy burden of taxes levied by the Crown on the inhabitants of the colonies.

From a sociopolitical perspective Javier Ocampo Lopéz cites the prevalence of nepotism among peninsular officials regarding appointments to administrative positions in the colonies (1999:83) as a significant cause of discontent; such discrimination against Americans was in fact the immediate cause of criollo resistance. In spite of their economic clout, the criollo elite had little hope of participating in the administration of the colonies as a result of new policies laid down by Spain concerning the appointment of peninsular agents.

> . . . by the eighteenth century the criollos had become the hacienda owners; they owned slaves and paid Indians, but political power was still out of their reach. . . . The peninsular elite had acquired the right to administer the colony in the name of the king and to accumulate wealth that would enable them to enjoy luxury and ostentation upon their return to the metropolis. (Ocampo 1999:69).

In addition to the economic elite, a kind of intelligentsia had also begun to emerge from the shadows of the inquisitorial controls. This generation of educated criollos—a product of the Spanish Enlightenment—was well versed in the democratic and liberal ideologies of the eighteenth century. In spite of their commercial and intellectual power, however, criollos found it increasingly difficult to overcome the discrimination and abuse perpetrated by the Spanish government. The inferiorization of everything that was American was one of the reasons behind their quest for independence (Sariola 1972; Lavallé 1993, 2002). The first sign of resistance from criollo

Hispanic Americans was in fact their adoption of the Enlightenment ideals of freedom, equity, and democracy.

Books and written documents during this period were essential in shaping and consolidating the revolutionary mentalities intent on emancipation. Measures taken by the inquisitorial authorities to control the production, marketing, and circulation of books applied to the Spanish metropolis as well as to the colonies. Controls were instituted initially in the main ports. Every ship was inspected by both civil authorities searching for banned merchandise and representatives of the Inquisition looking for any printed material contrary to the teachings of the Catholic Church. On land printers and booksellers were under close and constant scrutiny by the authorities. Public and private libraries were subject to the same scrutiny. The Inquisition also established a system for denouncing those who possessed, sold, exchanged, had access to, or shared books and ideas banned by the authorities.

Control by the Inquisition was only partly successful. Applying these measures along the coastal areas of South America was almost impossible. In Venezuela, for instance, proximity to the English and French islands of the Caribbean facilitated the smuggling of various goods to South America and made possible the influx of people of many different origins and with many different views. By the end of the seventeenth century, the production of books and other printed materials completely overwhelmed the capacity of the authorities to exercise control; the ever growing number of written documents, moreover, made the task of expurgation impossible (Pardo Tomás 1991:344).

The relative failure of these controls partly explains the presence of banned books in the libraries of educated criollos, including writings by John Adams, Jean le Rond d'Alembert, Francis Bacon, Buffon, Étienne Bonnot de Condillac, the Marquis de Condorcet, René Descartes, Denis Diderot, Benito Jerónimo Feijóo, Claude Adrien Helvetius, Thomas Hobbes, Thomas Jefferson, John Locke, Gabriel Bonnot de Mably, Montesquieu, Thomas Paine, Guillaume Thomas Raynal, Jean-Jacques Rousseau, Emmanuel Sieyès, Adam Smith, Voltaire, and other thinkers associated with the political, literary, and scientific ferment of the century. Although such books did not circulate freely across Hispanic America, the ideas they conveyed were frequently discussed in *tertulias* (the social, artistic, literary, and political gatherings of educated criollos), cafés, and, later, public places, before trickling down to the lower classes. An article published in 1806 in the *Diario de México*, the first daily newspaper that was entirely Mexican, notes: "Although the less educated people do not read the journals and other public papers (they are blissfully unaware of their existence), the useful information contained in these documents is spread unknowingly by the enlightened" (Rodríguez 1998:61). Nonetheless, the Inquisition made the dissemination of knowledge and the free flow of ideas difficult. Indeed, ideas reached Latin America at a slower pace than the rest of the Western world because of both the geographical distance and controls imposed on printed material. These impediments notwithstanding, the written word gave form and permanence to the liberal ideas of the century, transcending the immediacy and evanescence of the spoken word. By its mere physical existence, the written text exemplifies permanency and authority, conveys a stronger sense of historical veracity, and allows for broad circulation and dissemination.

As long as the philosophical and political ideas of the eighteenth century remained the privileged prerogative of the elite, any significant change in the administration of the colonies remained a remote possibility. The leading figures of the independence movement understood that in order to make contemporary revolutionary ideas accessible to a larger group of people, they needed to move from the orality of the tertulias to writing.

According to Benedict Anderson (2006:65), liberalism and the Enlightenment were instrumental in the increasing resistance of Americans against the metropole. Nevertheless, these intellectual movements did not play a role as determinant in the emancipation process and the creation of an "imagined community" as that played by the constant travels of criollo functionaries and the work of provincial printmen in the colony. By creating a readership that could relate to the same political and social reality, early regional periodicals performed this essential function. If initially some periodicals were compilations of commercial news and announcements of social events, most were born under the incipient republics, and as they developed, they mainly devoted themselves to the political and ideological education of their readership. They published political news about the chaos of the metropole after Napoleon's invasion, official resolutions adopted by newly established local governments and legislative assemblies, reports of local conflicts and wars, and ideological perspectives and positions from abroad. As the political ideas that shaped the emancipation era were produced in languages other than Spanish (principally English and French), if the criollos wanted to create a community that related to such ideas, including Enlightenment and republican ideals, they had to make those ideals available in Spanish through translation. In his insightful essay Anderson does not refer to the role played by translation in the use of print to spread ideas and create community. The present study is intended precisely to rectify this omission.

Translation as Resistance and Activism

In the early eighteenth century, Spanish authorities tolerated a certain amount of freedom of the press, allowing the most influential members of criollo society access to the printing press. The result was the creation of the first periodicals called *gacetas* (gazettes), as we have seen, notably the *Gaceta de México*, which was published in 1722, 1728–1739, and 1784–1809, and the *Gaceta de Lima*, which appeared between 1745 and 1800. By the turn of the nineteenth century, many other periodicals were in circulation throughout the rest of the continent. These periodicals were readily available because of their novelty and the absence of any coherent legislation regulating their circulation. This situation made it possible to publish works by leading authors of the time, including French and English philosophers. As Jaime Rodríguez (1998:58) points out, some texts by these authors appeared in the gacetas as complete translations and others as summaries.

Thanks to political and diplomatic exchanges and the proximity of French and English territories in the Caribbean, some wealthy Spanish Americans became familiar with the liberal ideas of the century, but the lack of written documents in Spanish gave such ideas little weight and authority. The emerging liberal and democratic philosophy developed orally as part of folklore, reaching even the lowest levels of society. In his biography of José María Vargas, Laureano Villanueva relates how new philosophical ideas spread in Venezuela: "[Vargas] devoted his spare time to reading and commenting on the works of Jean-Jacques Rousseau . . . ," and "late at night, he worked on the translation of the *Contrat social*, reading it to his friends later in secret meetings" (1986:3).

Revolutionary songs also played an important role in the years before independence, making it possible to include less favored social groups in the emancipation process. Music provided a means for the lower classes to articulate their discontent with the colonial administration. In fact, revolutionary songs such as "La Carmagnole" and "La Marseillaise" were frequently sung in the Spanish colonies. Unlike "La Marseillaise," which was never translated into Spanish, a comparative analysis of the Spanish and French versions of "La Carmagnole" clearly shows how a translator can be resistant (Bastin 2004, Bastin and Díaz 2004). As Armas Ayala affirms, Americans displayed prolific ingenuity and wit in musical creations intended to criticize and ridicule the colonial authorities. Music was for the common people what books were for the "cultivated." Nonetheless, the "non-cultivated" also had indirect access to books; ideas overheard in public places and in the privacy of the masters' homes were potentially as influential as the actual reading of an entire book (Ayala 1970:134). Smuggled books, travel abroad by wealthy criollos, and contact with travelers, former slaves from the Antilles, and others helped attune Hispanic Americans to the new ideas and issues of the time. By the end of the eighteenth century, they had attained enough intellectual and administrative maturity to yearn for independence, and, as Anderson (2006) puts it, an imagined and sovereign, though limited community had taken shape.

Case Studies

Case studies of resistant and activist translations from the period in question underline the decisive role translation played in the independence and creation of the first republics in Hispanic America. The following cases are a small sample of the many that need to be investigated, for there are numerous documents and translators to be identified and considered as historical objects of study with respect to the topic at hand. Here we look at Spanish translations of the following texts: La Déclaration des droits de l'homme et du citoyen (Declaration of the Rights of Man and of the Citizen) of 1789 in 17 articles, translated into Spanish by Antonio Nariño in 1794; La Déclaration des droits de l'homme et du citoyen of 1793 in 35 articles, translated into Spanish by Juan Picornell in 1797; the Spanish translation of the *Lettre aux Espagnols américains* written by the Peruvian Jesuit Juan Pablo Viscardo and translated from French by Francisco de Miranda; Manuel García de Sena's book titled *La independencia de la Costa Firme justificada por Thomas Paine treinta años há* (The Independence of the Costa Firme Justified by Thomas Paine Thirty Years Ago; 1811), which includes Spanish translations of excerpts from various works by Paine, as well as translations of the United States Declaration of Independence and the Constitution of the United States; and García de Sena's Spanish translation of John M'Culloch's book, *A Concise History of the United States, from the Discovery of America till 1807* (1807), published in

1812 as *Historia concisa de los Estados Unidos: Desde el descubrimiento de la América hasta el año de 1807.*

Published between 1789 and 1812, these translations are central elements of the ideological bedrock of emancipation in Hispanic America. They fostered ideas and textual models for those who led the revolutionary movement in the Spanish territories in Hispanic America. What is important in these translations is not their literary or aesthetic value but rather their teleological force and the way translators and readers utilized them to serve their own agendas in that specific historical context. Exploring these aspects of the translations is the primary focus of the discussion here. Our discursive approach seeks not "to determine whether a translation transforms and thus— as conventional wisdom would often have it—betrays an original text, but rather the question becomes one of defining how such a transformation is carried out and the conditions which make it possible" (St-Pierre 1993:82).

Translation helped to introduce into Spanish-speaking American countries a version of ideas that had already served to transform other societies in the Western world. Concerning the interculturality of translations and translators, Anthony Pym asks whether the history of translation should focus on translations or translators (1998:182–83). He argues that independently of their linguistic competence, translators can be considered members of an interculture. They occupy a space created by the intersection of the two cultures they mediate between. In the case of the translations considered in this essay, the men who translated the texts were certainly bilingual but to say that their role as translators makes them members of an interculture, in Pym's terms, would be an overstatement. With regard to the translations considered here, the act of translation and the translated texts per se as forms of resistance and activism played a more important role than the translators as agents. Indeed, more than the translators themselves who in these cases translated principally on occasion, the very essence of their subversive activity and the existence of the translated texts were instrumental in reforming and reconstituting the receiving culture.

The 1789 Version of the Déclaration des droits de l'homme et du citoyen

On 26 August 1789 the General Assembly of the French Revolution promulgated the Declaration of the Rights of Man and of the Citizen, a document in

17 articles. After the publication of the Declaration, the Tribunal of the Inquisition of Cartagena banned it from circulation in the Spanish territories in an edict of 13 December 1789. By 1790, in the aftermath of the French Revolution, this edict enabled Spanish authorities to tighten their controls over printed material and ideas originating in France. This did not, however, prevent the Colombian Antonio Nariño (1765–1823) from translating and publishing the first Spanish version of the Déclaration des droits de l'homme et du citoyen.

Nariño had held important official positions in the Virreinato (the Viceroyalty) of Nueva Granada: treasurer, accountant, mayor of Bogotá, and lieutenant in the king's army. In criollo society he was recognized as a compulsive book collector and seller. Published in Bogotá in 1794, Nariño's translation of the Declaration into Spanish was a two-page, word-for-word document. His decision to translate and publish this document was prompted primarily by his liberal ideas and his Masonic affiliation and secondarily by his business acumen. He was convinced that his text would capture the interest of a select readership. Although the document is his only translation, he is one of the few individuals in history to bear with equal honor the titles of general, president, and translator.[4] In translating the text Nariño overtly subverted the prohibition against circulating the Declaration. According to Javier Ocampo, the translator and editor printed one hundred copies of the document; only two or three copies had been sold when a purchaser and friend warned Nariño of the implications of his act (1999:171). The translator then decided to burn the remaining copies, but he was nonetheless prosecuted by the colonial authorities and given a penalty intended to serve as a deterrent in a society that was becoming more and more disgruntled with peninsular authorities: imprisonment in exile. Nariño somehow managed to escape and, as did many others before and after him, began a campaign in Europe to gain support for the cause of independence. He later returned to Colombia and joined the revolutionary movement.

Pym considers translators as "active effective causes, with their own identity and agenda" (1998:160). In the case of Nariño, it is more relevant to concentrate on the act of translation itself and the content of the translated text as forms of resistance and activism. This translation provided Spanish-speaking American society with a written document legitimating the desire for independence.

The ideas enunciated in the Declaration of the Rights of Man were to become guiding principles for founding the new states. The importance of

Nariño's act is commensurate with the tensions it created in colonial society. First, it consolidated the revolutionary spirit that became manifest in conspiracy, secret criticism, satire, and pamphleteering. Second, the translator provided Spanish-speaking Americans with a document that was in itself the embodiment of principles for a new kind of polity and political organization, as well as the materialization of rights that until then existed only as hearsay oral accounts of events occurring in distant lands. In response the Spanish authorities started an arbitrary "witch-hunt" against conspirators, bolstering the resolve of criollo society to fight for independence. This period witnessed the division of the society into traditionalists on the one hand and advocates of enlightenment ideas on the other (Ocampo 1999:177).

The translated Declaration took on a new dimension following the independence of various Latin American countries. Nariño's text, the Spanish translation of the Constitution of the United States, and, of course, Picornell's version of the second Declaration (see below) were used as guiding documents for drafting the first republican constitutions across Hispanic America. The translation of the Déclaration des droits de l'homme et du citoyen of 1789 is therefore considered the first clear act of overt ideological and political resistance by the dominant Hispanic American elite against the Spanish authorities in the New World. It gave Spanish Americans a "road map," a model of the type of political entity to strive for. Several translations akin to Nariño's were published in the following years. The goal of all these translations was to provide a philosophical and political foundation for legitimizing independence, as well as a corpus of legal texts for creating the new republics. Picornell's translation of the second Declaration of the Rights of Man (1793) lent impetus to this endeavor in Venezuela in 1797.

The 1793 Version of the Déclaration des droits de l'homme et du citoyen

In the heat of the Reign of Terror (1793–94), a second Declaration of the Rights of Man and of the Citizen was drafted to be appended to the 1791 French constitution. Although its 35 articles emphasized the welfare of society over individual rights, it recognized freedom as a natural right. It was also drafted in more violent language completely attuned to the bloody atmosphere of the times. Article 35, for example, recognizes the legitimacy of insurrection to overcome the oppression of any government.

The translation into Spanish of the 1793 version of the Declaration of the Rights of Man was carried out in Venezuela in 1797. It had come by way of Madrid two years earlier. On 3 February 1795 (the Day of Saint Blas), an insurrection in Spain known as the San Blas conspiracy, designed and led by Juan Picornell (1759–1825), was to take place in Madrid to overthrow the monarchy and establish a republican government. An eminent pedagogue and, like Nariño, a Mason, Picornell had been influenced by the French Revolution. Translation was an activity common to the architects of the conspiracy, including José Lax, Bernardo Garasa, and Juan Pons Izquierdo.[5] The vital force of this revolutionary enterprise was the translation of documents issuing from the political turmoil in neighboring France. The Venezuelan historian Casto Fulgencio López writes that "the conspirators gathered in José Lax's house to translate books and speeches from the neighboring republic" (1997:32). Picornell was aware of the power of translation and its capacity to introduce subversion into the receiving culture. His friendship with the Abbot Marchena, the translator of Rousseau's writings into Spanish (Schevill 1936), is evidence that his involvement in translation was no accident. Picornell's translation work was clearly a purposeful activity. For him texts had a definite role to play in social change. Picornell's dream was to bring about a Spanish version of the French Revolution, and he saw translation as a means of enlightenment to inspire Spaniards about the greatness of democracy as understood by the French revolutionaries.

After the failure of their coup, Picornell and his accomplices were imprisoned and sentenced to death. Their sentences were later commuted to life imprisonment in the colonies. From his cell in La Guaira, Venezuela, Picornell was able to stoke the desire for emancipation in important members of Hispanic American society. Among those who joined him in his revolutionary efforts in America were Pedro Gual and José María España. These two are associated with the Gual y España conspiracy of July 1797, the most significant and most carefully orchestrated plot conceived by the criollos to overthrow the Spanish government in America prior to the wars of independence.

During the few months that Picornell was imprisoned in La Guaira, he indoctrinated a group of influential criollos who facilitated his escape the same day the Gual y España revolt was to take place. As with the earlier plot in Madrid, this conspiracy also failed. Picornell had to escape to Guadeloupe, where he pursued his revolutionary activities. On this Caribbean island he published the texts prepared in La Guaira: *Derechos del hombre y del ciudadano, con varias máximas republicanas y un discurso preliminar, dirigido a los americanos*; the book was published with a fictitious imprint, "Madrid Imprenta de la Verdad, año de 1797." The work includes the Declaration of the Rights of Man, some republican maxims, a speech, and two revolutionary songs. The conspirators printed two thousand copies and distributed them all over America. As historians have recognized, Picornell and his collaborators adapted most of the documents used in the Saint Blas conspiracy in Madrid for their Hispanic American readership.

Picornell's contribution to this set of translations was confirmed in José María España's confession to his prosecutors on 3 May 1799: "When Picornell arrived in Curaçao from Guadeloupe in November 1797, he took with him a printing press with the purpose—in his own words—of printing the papers of the revolution. He also had some copies of the book titled 'The Rights of Man and the Citizen' and . . . two songs titled 'American Carmagnole' and 'American Song'" (qtd. in C. López 1997:239). Irrespective of the identity of the translator, this text in itself constitutes the blueprint for the republics that were to be established in the new century. Its importance for the first constitutional documents of Venezuela has been rightly demonstrated by Pedro Grases (1981b, 1997). According to C. López, Picornell's "political and philosophical doctrine not only signaled the beginning of the independence movement, it ensured the continuity of the movement and its survival until the birth of the [Venezuelan] Republic; it served as the legal foundation for the [Venezuelan] Declaration of Independence and the first Venezuelan constitutions" (1997:60).[6]

The Translation of Viscardo's "Lettre aux Espagnols américains"

By a royal edict of Charles III of Spain, all members of the Order of Jesus were forced to leave the Spanish territories in the Americas in 1767. Among the five thousand Jesuits who left was the Peruvian Juan Pablo Viscardo y Guzmán (1748–98). At the age of 21, Viscardo arrived in Modena, Italy. Managing to keep informed of relevant events in America, he traveled in Europe and attempted to secure England's support for Indian and slave uprisings. These efforts failed because England was negotiating peace with Spain. Disappointed with English indifference, Viscardo ultimately died in London in 1798, leaving his papers to Rufus King, U.S. minister to the English court (Vargas Ugarte 1964:70).

Viscardo wrote extensively from his exile in Europe, denouncing the abuses of the Spanish Crown in the Americas and telling the world about the greatness and richness of his continent (Bastin and Castrillón 2004). In Florence between 1778 and 1791, he wrote a letter in French of some 30 pages with the goal of having it ready for publication on 12 October 1792, the date marking three hundred years of Spanish presence in the Americas.[7] Historians such as Mariano Picón-Salas consider Viscardo's "Lettre aux Espagnols américains" (literally, "A Letter to the American Spaniards") to be "the first and most widely distributed pamphlet championing the cause of revolution for independence" in Hispanic America and historically "the first declaration of independence" (1994:226). The letter is composed in three parts: the first is an accusation, similar to, though much longer than that in the Declaration of Independence of the United States; the second part is a philosophical justification of independence based on a text by Montesquieu; and the third part is an exhortation to Hispanic Americans to fight for their independence (Bastin and Castrillón 2004).

The Spanish translation of Viscardo's letter is the work of the Venezuelan Francisco de Miranda (1750–1816), one of the most important figures in the emancipation of Hispanic America and generally acknowledged as "El Precursor." Miranda had traveled extensively in the United States and Europe, had firsthand experience of the new republic after the independence of the United States, and had participated actively as a general in the French army during the French Revolution. Through his friend Rufus King, Miranda inherited Viscardo's writings and in 1799 published the original French text of Viscardo's letter in London, giving a fictitious place of publication, namely Philadelphia. As editor he added a preface and some footnotes to Viscardo's text, materials that were also included in Miranda's Spanish translation of the letter published by Miranda himself in London in 1801. This text became the bible of revolutionaries in Hispanic America as a result of Miranda's efforts to make it known everywhere in Europe and the Americas, first in French and Spanish and later in English as well.[8] The significance of this translation is recognized principally because of the striking intertextuality between Miranda's text and "La carta de Jamaica," written by Simón Bolívar in 1815 and one of his most important political texts. Luis Navarrete goes so far as to suggest that Viscardo's letter may have served as a model for the one written by Bolívar (1994:125).

An analysis of the translation shows that the translator succeeded in making it as accessible as possible to Spanish-speaking readers. The teleological nature of the text justified its "domestication."[9] The Americans were addressed and depicted in the text, and they needed to identify with it. To achieve this goal it was essential to bring Viscardo's letter to them in their own language. Some manipulations of the text are worth considering because they make the translator's agenda explicit. As mentioned above, Miranda added an editor's note and several footnotes to both the original French publication and the Spanish translation. The editor's note is a short presentation of the author and the manuscript. The purpose of the note, however, is far from innocent and impartial. Miranda's subjectivity and political intentions are quite manifest.

> Ce legs précieux d'un Américain-Espagnol à ses compatriotes, sur le sujet, le plus grand et le plus important qui puisse s'offrir à leur considération, est imprimé conforme au manuscrit de la main de l'Auteur même; et on pourra s'apercevoir au style, que c'est un étranger qui, s'exprime dans la langue Françoise sans aucune sorte de prétention. C'est D. Juan Pablo Viscardo y Guzman, natif d'Arequipa dans le Pérou, ex-Jésuite, mort à Londres, au mois de Février 1798, qui en est l'Auteur. On fera connaître dans la suite le reste de cet intéressant manuscrit sur l'Amérique Méridionale. (Viscardo 1799, editor's note)

> Este precioso legado d'un Americano Español a sus compatriotas, sobre el objeto más grande y más importante que se puede ofrecer a su consideración, esta impreso conforme al manuscrito de la mano del autor mismo; y se podra conocer por el estilo del original que es un extranjero que se explica en la lengua francesa sin ninguna especie de pretensión. El autor es Don Juan Pablo Viscardo y Guzman, nativo de Arequipa en el Perú, ex-Jesuita muerto en Londres en el mes de Febrero de 1798. En lo sucesivo se hara conocer el resto de sus interesantes manuscritos sobre la América Meridional. (Viscardo 1801, editor's note)

> This precious legacy of a Spanish American to his countrymen, on the greatest and the most important subject that could be put to their consideration, is printed according to the manuscript written by the author himself; and it is possible to see from the style that he is a foreigner who has expressed himself in the French language without any pretension. The author is Don Juan Pablo Viscardo y Guzmán, native of Arequipa, Peru, a former Jesuit who died in London in February 1798. In the following pages, we will introduce the rest of this interesting manuscript about South America.

The choice of words in the first sentence shows that in Miranda's view translators are not merely instruments of communication. First, there is the value judgment conveyed by the use of the adjective *precioso* (precious) to describe the text, and the use of the word *legado* (legacy) makes the text the property of all Spanish-speaking Americans. Of greater interest from an ideological and sociolinguistic point of view is the use of the adjective of nationality in Viscardo's title of the original French text, "Lettre aux Espagnols americains" (later translated by William Burke into English as "A Letter to the Spanish Americans," in Burke 1808/1976)). Although Miranda titled the Spanish translation "Carta derijida a los Españoles Americanos," (literally, "Letter Addressed to the American Spaniards"), in his editor's note he refers to Viscardo as "un Americano Español" ("a Spanish American"), defining a distinct and separate identity for his compatriots and shifting their affiliation. This exemplifies the resistance of the criollos to their inferiorization (Lavallé 1993, 2002). The language used here is a manifestation of resistance, the kind of resistance translators can exert by manipulating the linguistic code to reflect their own agendas. This translation strategy clearly illustrates the nascent desire of revolutionary criollos to be recognized not as Spanish people born in America but as Americans first with only secondary or contingent affiliations to Spain. Note that Miranda's term is anticipated even more strongly in Picornell's title: Discurso dirigido a los Americanos," where he omits the Spanish connection altogether.

Miranda used the translation of Viscardo's letter not only to introduce readers to the original author and his text but also and perhaps primarily to nurture his own project of independence, a goal he thought he had attained in view of the reception of his translation in the Spanish colonies. Several historians have corroborated the dissemination and influence of the text in Europe and in the colonies in the first decade of the eighteenth century (cf. Batllori 1953:153–57; Navarrete 1994:127). Picón-Salas argues that in fact Viscardo's text was successfully disseminated as a significant weapon of propaganda (1994:226).

The period was notable for conspiracies and espionage affecting all the economic and military powers of the time. Miranda was involved in planning an armed invasion of Venezuela in 1806. He obtained the economic support of the English but he was not allowed to procure arms or men in Europe (Parra-Pérez 1992:100). In New York he bought weapons and recruited a group of men who were for the most part of good social standing but ruined and in search of glory and fortune. In preparation for the invasion, Miranda wrote a proclamation in New York in which he appropriated Viscardo's arguments to justify his military actions. In this document he also included the complete text of Viscardo's letter and instructed the religious and the civil authorities of Venezuela to make the public aware of it by posting it on doors and by reading it once or twice daily at mass and other public gatherings (Batllori 1953:150–51). Miranda's military expedition to Venezuela was a complete failure. Although he succeeded in disembarking his troops on Venezuelan soil at Vela de Coro on 3 August 1806 and in seizing control of some territory, he lacked the military might required to guarantee the security of the very people he had come to liberate. Moreover, although widely read, his translation did not convince a significant number of his compatriots to join the rising, and he was forced to flee Venezuela. Departing from the same location where he had just landed, Miranda left Venezuela on 7 August 1806.

Back in Europe, Miranda promoted an English version of the letter. In 1808 one of his supporters, the journalist William Burke, published a book titled *Additional Reasons for our Emancipating Spanish America*, to which Burke appended his own English translation of Viscardo's letter. Aware of the interest of the *Edinburgh Review* in American matters, Miranda seized this opportunity to make Viscardo's thought more available to English-language readers. With the help of James Mill, in 1809 Miranda published a 34-page essay in the *Edinburgh Review* based on Viscardo's letter, justifying once again the independence of Hispanic America. The first two pages of this article are dedicated to Viscardo's letter and the other 32 pages are devoted to the emancipation of Hispanic America (Batllori 1953:154).

Viscardo's letter struck a deep chord with Spanish-speaking Americans during the critical years of the struggle for independence. Early evidence can be found in the Venezuelan declaration of independence (1811), the content of which was much influenced by Viscardo's ideas. In the same year the *Gaceta de Caracas* reproduced the full text of the declaration. By then William Burke had taken up residence in Caracas and was using this paper to make constant references to the Jesuit's legacy (Batllori 1953:157). The letter was also reprinted frequently in English, Spanish, and French in the first years of the twentieth century, as historians interested in the ideological foundations of the independence movement recognized Viscardo's letter as one of the most influential documents of the time.

The Writings of Thomas Paine and John M'Culloch

In 1803, after fighting in the Valles de Aragua in Venezuela under the command of the Marqués del Toro (Simón Bolívar's father-in-law), Manuel García de Sena (1780–1816) took up residence in Philadelphia with his brother Domingo. In 1810 he began translating excerpts of several works by Thomas Paine into Spanish, publishing them in 1811 in Philadelphia under a single title, *La independencia de la Costa Firme justificada por Thomas Paine treinta años há: Extracto de sus obras, traducido del inglés al español* (The Independence of the Costa Firme as Justified by Thomas Paine Thirty Years Ago: Excerpts from his works translated from English into Spanish by D. Manuel García de Sena).[10] In this book García de Sena included Spanish translations of excerpts from the most influential works of Paine, as well as translations of the Constitution of the United States, the United States Declaration of Independence, and the constitutions of various former colonies. He subsequently translated John M'Culloch's *A Concise History of the United States, from the Discovery of America till 1807* (1807) into Spanish as *Historia concisa de los Estados Unidos: Desde el descubrimiento de la América hasta el año de 1807*, in which he also incorporated a revised version of his first translation of the U.S. Declaration of Independence (Grases 1981a:400), publishing the volume in Philadelphia in 1812.

García de Sena used his translations as political tools to champion the cause of emancipation. His choice of Paine's texts is quite significant. He excerpted the most general texts and the ones most applicable to Hispanic America. In the texts selected he omitted all references to contemporary conditions in North America, considering them of little interest to his compatriots (Grases 1981a:404). To his translations he added personal comments such as ". . . para la mejor comprensión de los lectores americanos" ("to enable [Hispanic] American readers to better understand"; Grases 1981a:405). He also addressed a delicate aspect of U.S. culture: the role of the church, specifically the prohibition against priests holding public office. García de Sena not only translated this prohibition, he explained its reasons. This aspect of the separation of church and state in the United States was particularly important to confront in adapting European or North American models to Hispanic America, where most political leaders feared opposing the church and excluding it from the new duties of the state. The following excerpt of a letter written by García de Sena to his brother Ramón in December 1810 attests to the importance of the issue: "Convinced after reading [the translation] that it does not contain a single word contradicting our religion, I hope it can circulate freely among my countrymen" (qtd. in Grases 1981a:406).

To further his strategy García de Sena added paratexts of his own to the translation of Paine's texts, including a dedication and some footnotes. He dedicates his work to the "americanos españoles" ("Spanish Americans"), choosing the same expression Miranda used in the foreword to Viscardo's letter. This illustrates the high degree of intertextuality found in revolutionary texts of the period. García de Sena also adds a footnote to his translation of the U.S. Declaration of Independence at the point where the original text enumerates the atrocities of the English king:

> A todo esto [las atrocidades del Rey de Inglaterra] puede añadir en favor de los americanos del Sud, y con relacíon a los últimas gobiernos de España en Europa: Ellos nos quieren gobernar sin más derecho que el que tenemos nosotros para gobernarlos a ellos. (1949:156)

> To all this [the atrocities of the King of England] it is possible to add the following in favor of the South Americans in relation to the most recent Spanish regimes in Europe: they want to govern us without having any more right to that than the right we have to govern them.

In his translation of M'Culloch's book, García de Sena also adds a dedication to "los americanos españoles" ("the Spanish Americans"), exhorting them to continue the struggle. The goal of this long dedication is twofold. First, the translator recognizes with full "professional humility" his linguistic shortcomings.

> Pero me ha animado al fin la consideración de que ni lo fastidioso del estilo ni los muchos defectos que se encuentran en la traducción, serán capaces de desfigurar los hechos que me propongo transmitir al español para aquellos a quienes no sea posible obtenerlos de otro modo. (qtd. in Grases 1981a:398)

> But I decided to translate [the book] as I felt that neither the stylistic deficiencies nor the numerous defects in the translation would distort the facts that I intend to transpose into Spanish for those who would otherwise have no access to them.

García de Sena thus anticipates Grases's modern critical assessment that the Spanish text of the translation is by no means a model of stylistic perfection (1981a:398). The translator clearly indicates he has focused much more on the content of his translation than on its wording. This illustrates that the contents of the translations rather than discursive or textual strategies are here the primary site of resistance, contrary to arguments about resistance in (literary) texts proposed by Venuti (1995, 1998), for example.

Second, García de Sena urges his compatriots to remain united in order to take their rightful place in the community of nations. He concludes his dedication with the following exhortation.

> ¡Que el Nuevo Mundo todo le dé al Viejo una lección de virtud! Cuánta felicidad cuando de las tierras frías del Labrador al rincón más apartado de la Tierra del Fuego, solo se asistirá a congresos de los que se pueda decir con dignidad: "¡Ojalá este gran monumento elevado a la Libertad sirva de lección a los tiranos y de ejemplo a los oprimidos!" (qtd. in Grases 1981a:404)

> Let the whole New World teach a lesson of virtue to the Old World! Rejoice then when from the cold lands of Labrador to the most distant tip of Tierra del Fuego, there will be congresses everywhere. Then we may say with dignity, "May this great monument erected to liberty serve as a lesson to tyrants and an example to the oppressed"!

De Sena's political agenda, as his dedication shows, is clearly not that of a timid, invisible, and transparent translator.

Both the selection of texts and the censorship exerted by García de Sena (on everything contrary to his Catholic beliefs, as well as aspects of the original texts that were not directly applicable to the situation in Hispanic America) confirm the hypothesis that politically committed translators use their translation work to serve their goals of resistance and activism and to promote their own political agendas. The translations by García de Sena were neither requested nor sponsored: they were self-initiated undertakings. García de Sena's objectives were neither philanthropic nor economic, they were clearly political: to demonstrate the legitimacy of independence for Hispanic America and the potential benefits of independence for his compatriots, using the sociopolitical and economic situation of the United States as a model. Such efforts by the translator were not in vain when one considers the historical significance of his translation of the Constitution of the United States, in particular, included in his volume of translations from Thomas Paine. Grases has documented the circulation of this translation throughout Latin America and its traces in the first Venezuelan constitutions. Five thousand copies of García de Sena's translation of Paine's work were printed, most of which were shipped to Venezuela, with the remainder going to Vera-cruz, Cartagena, Havana, and Puerto Rico, where they became required reading (Grases 1981a:410–20). In fact, on Venezuela's independence day, 5 July 1811, it was García de Sena's translation of the Constitution of the United States that was read before the newly created Venezuelan congress (Grases and Harkness 1953:56).

Conclusion

The interest of translation scholars in postcolonialism outside Europe and North America is gaining momentum as demonstrated by the activities of translators and translation scholars in the developing world. This growing interest bodes well for Spanish-speaking America, but it has not yet been significant enough to impel descriptive studies of translation history in this part of the globe beyond the mere archaeological stages of its development, even though, admittedly, archaeological data on facts and events do help define the agendas of translators and researchers.

The examples discussed above demonstrate once again that translation is not an impartial and objective activity. The translators discussed—Nariño, Picornell, Miranda, and García de Sena—were textual and cultural mediators committed to their personal goals and those of the communities dedicated to the liberation of Spain's American colonies. The original texts were only "pretexts" for the greater enterprise of communicating and massively disseminating ideas to which they were profoundly committed. In the translators' agendas, therefore, translation was a means, not an end.

These specific cases related to Hispanic America clearly illustrate how vital the study of translation history is to explain the sociopolitical facts of communities and nations. Latin American translators made a significant contribution to its history. The political imprint they left on their translations can be paralleled with influences exerted in other times and other places. The translations of Shakespeare by Michel Tremblay and Michel Garneau, deemed to give Quebec a sense of renewed identity at the time of the "Révolution Tranquille," come to mind (Brisset 1990). A parallel can also be drawn with the Irish translators such as Augusta Gregory or Mary Hutton who helped effect the independence of Ireland (Tymoczko 1999). Such renditions are quintessentially subjective, political, resistant, activist. Tremblay and his fellow Canadian translators and the Irish translators became historical actors, not unlike García de Sena and the others discussed here.

The Brazilian concept of *anthropophagia* (anthropophagy; Andrade 1928) is also relevant to the cases discussed here.[11] Although developed during the modern period, such a concept seems to have motivated translators such as García de Sena, as well as their Hispanic followers including Andrés Bello, José Martí, and Jorge Luis Borges, whose translation work is characterized by appropriating strategies as well (Bastin, Campo, and Echeverri, 2004). In this regard Diego Saglia notes, "The concept and practice of appropriation may thus reconfigure the status of translation as the production of texts that are not simply consumed by the target language and culture but which, in turn, become creative and productive, stimulating reflections, theorizations and representations within the target cultural context" (2002:96).

The history of translation in Hispanic America is for the most part unknown to the rest of the world and, even more discouraging, to Hispanic Americans themselves. Many Latin American translation scholars and professionals are more at ease talking about Perrot d'Ablancourt, Walter Benjamin, or John Denham than about Francisco de Miranda, Manuel García de Sena, or Andrés Bello. The cause is, of course, a somewhat xenophile attitude on the part of many Latin American scholars, rooted in a long tradition of a Eurocentric orientation in Latin American culture as a whole. Moreover, the Eurocentric manner in which translation studies as a field has developed compels Latin American scholars to study European or North American issues, as well as to adopt foreign models to explain local matters, because this is the only means of participating in translation studies discourses. The time has come to study translation using local models (whether inspired by literary criticism, sociology, or philosophy) as the most appropriate way to interpret local realities. This may be the way for Hispanic American scholars to develop their own form of resistance within the field of translation studies, and it may be a model for other local groups of scholars to utilize as well.

Our research has focused primarily on the importance that translation played in the independence period when the rising Hispanic American elite used it to subvert Spanish domination, highlighting a genuine Latin American way of translating. At the same time translation also served the goals of the criollo elite to establish and consolidate their domination and control over the less empowered social classes and ethnic minorities in Spanish-speaking America. Translation certainly fueled the impetus for emancipation, but it also gave the controlling minority the means to perpetuate the social inequalities that continue to be characteristic of Hispanic America. Such an ironic outcome of translation leading to both emancipation and oppression, to both resistance against and collusion with established structures of power, remains to be studied. It is in many ways representative of the heterogeneous position of translators as historical and social agents.

Last but not least, the cases discussed above are only a few among many more to be uncovered and studied in order to characterize the profound influence that translation exerted on the history and fate of Hispanic America. Although limited, these case studies demonstrate one significant feature in translation history, namely that a sociological rather than an anthropological approach is needed to understand how translation has influenced the course of history. It has been clearly shown that content rather than textual strategy is the focus of resistance and activism in translation in the case studies considered here and, moreover, that the message of the translated text and its reception rather than the identity of the translator are the main issues to be considered even when translators are visible agents of history.

Notes

1. This study took shape within the framework of a research project funded by the Social Sciences and Humanities Research Council of Canada (SSHRC). Additional information can be found at www.histal.umontreal.ca.

2. Unless otherwise noted, all translations are our own.

3. Anderson (2006:47) offers a useful definition of *Creole* (*Criollo*) as a "person of (at least theoretically) pure European descent but born in the Americas (and, by later extension, anywhere outside Europe)."

4. In 1811 Nariño was appointed president of Cundinamarca, a province of Nueva Granada, Colombia, where the capital Bogotá is located. He was general in the revolutionary army during the period 1813–14.

5. José Lax was a teacher of the humanities and an official translator; Bernardo Garasa was a lawyer and literary translator; Juan Pons Izquierdo was a teacher of French and the humanities and sometimes referred to as co-translator of the Declaration (Grases 1997:32).

6. Including the federal constitution in 1811, the constitution of the province of Barcelona in 1812, and the constitution of the province of Angostura in 1819.

7. Viscardo probably chose to write in French because it was the language of diplomacy and culture in Europe at the time and very widely known by educated people in the Americas as well, as he himself exemplifies.

8. On the English version of the letter, see below. See also the facsimile of the second English edition (1810) with an introduction by D. A. Brading in Viscardo (2002).

9. On the distinction between domesticating and foreignizing translations, see Venuti (1995, 1998).

10. The term "Costa Firme," literally the 'firm coast', refers to the northern part of South America, mainly Venezuela. Our work is based on the 1949 edition of the volume.

11. On anthropophagy and translation see also Vieira (1994, 1999).

ANTONIA CARCELEN-ESTRADA

Covert and Overt Ideologies in the Translation of the Bible into Huao Terero

DESPITE being a broadly documented sociolinguistic phenomenon of twentieth-century evangelization, the immersion into Western culture of the Huaorani (an indigenous people in the Ecuadorian Amazon whose language is Huao Terero) has resulted in research focused mainly on the socio-anthropological issues that the communities have faced since contact, leaving a gap in understanding the linguistic phenomena per se. This is surprising since the condition of the Huaorani people today is principally the consequence of linguistic colonization by the Summer Institute of Linguistics (SIL), a process that started in the 1950s and officially ended in the late 1980s. The work of these linguist missionaries resulted in tension over power from several sectors related to this group, tension that continues to the present. The strategies used by SIL missionaries constitute a significant case study in translation. To delineate the linguistic implications, here I first outline the specificities of the interactions between the Huaorani and various groups, and the systemic agony that has resulted. Among the groups are the Huaorani, SIL, the national government of Ecuador, various oil companies, the Amazon's Kichwa communities,[1] the Parque Nacional Yasuní (Yasuní National Park), other ecological organizations, the tourism industry, and lumber dealers. I then attempt to set SIL and the Huaorani people in dialogue, hypothesizing that the latter translated their bodies as the former translated the Bible, with consequent divergence between actions and intentions in both systems. The temporal, semiotic, and intentional miscommunication between these two groups unveils different levels of ideology and significant ethical problems. I argue that the disconnect between the actions and intentions of the Huaorani is a native strategy for cultural survival that we can trace elsewhere. By contrast the SIL slippages seem to have ideological connections that perhaps constitute yet another battle of the Cold War. Finally, this essay will fill some of the gaps in understanding the linguistic aspects of translating the Bible into Huao Terero by discussing specific aspects of the strategies of the SIL translation process.

The Huaorani people descend from the Abishira, inhabitants of colonial Ecuador. There is documentation of at least 400 years of Huaorani auto-exclusion; the culture was in flight from the atrocities of European colonists, missionaries, and, later, rubber hunters (Fuentes 1997:93). The Huaorani occupied a region of approximately 20,000 square kilometers (two million hectares) in the hinterlands of the Napo and Curaray rivers, land that sits above the richest oil pools of Ecuador. Such attractive resources made their solitude vulnerable to increased intrusion of global interests in the twentieth century. The group remained isolated in the central Amazon region of Ecuador until 1958, when SIL missionaries made peaceful contact with the Huaorani for the first time. Prior to that date on repeated occasions the Huaorani had killed all strangers who attempted any contact (Rivas Toledo and Lara Ponce 2001; Fuentes 1997; Kimerling 1996; Kane 1995; Liefeld 1990; Elliot 1958).

Before analyzing the interaction between SIL missionaries and the Huaorani cultural system, it is necessary to detail the other systems that have been involved in this process. There are myriad interest groups wishing to access Huaorani resources. Indeed, relations between the Huaorani and other groups tend to be defined by the desires—cast as "needs"—of other groups for a given Huaorani resource. Conversely, such a desire or "need" defines the view that any specific cultural group or system has of the Huaorani. Each system interacting with the Huaorani translates the image of the Huaorani into their terms, and that translation is to a large degree shaped by the perspective of the vested interests of the outside groups.

In these complex systemic relationships, every group has its own understanding of the meaning of the Huaorani. The Kichwa communities of the Ecuadorian Amazon "needed" the land inhabited by the Huaorani, who would attack with spears anyone attempting to enter. Before the 1950s the Huaorani were translated into a canonical image shaped by indigenous Kichwa peoples, also known as *Canelos* (people from the *canela*, or cinnamon, forest) and *Naporuna* (people from the Napo River) by the mestizo national society. The Kichwa were the first group to create a stereotype of the Huaorani, which has served as a model and been reproduced in other spheres. The schema in Figure 1 below indicates that (apart from the Huaorani) Kichwa groups are among the most peripheral elements of the cultural system diagrammed. Prior to 1956 the name given to Huaorani Indians was *Aucas*, meaning 'savages' in Kichwa; the term was transferred—translated in the physical sense—from Kichwa into Spanish and from Spanish into English (Rivas Toledo and Lara Ponce 2001; Fuentes 1997; Kimerling 1996; Kane 1995; Liefeld 1990; Elliot 1958).

In the Kichwa language, *Auca* also means 'not baptized' (*tucui llactacunapi*), that is, a person not adapted to manners (*mana chican llactacunapi yacharic runa*; Fuentes 1997:94). The Kichwa to this day refer to the Huaorani as not knowing anything, as killers, and as thieves (Fuentes 1997:36). This Kichwa image has been reproduced by others, introducing Kichwa stereotyped norms to other systems in Figure 1 below. Paradoxically this Kichwa image is the *opposite* of Huaorani self-representation: *wao*, written *huao* as a result of Kichwa phonetic transcription, means 'human person' (Costales, qtd. in Fuentes 1997:94); by contrast for the Huaorani, the rest of the world is *cowudi*, or cannibals.

Under Spanish colonialism the distance from the legitimate authority and the power of the king, among other pragmatic factors, called for supervision of the natives by missionaries, colonizers, and the military. After Ecuador's independence, the national government functionally replaced the structures of the Spanish colonial system with similar institutions. In republican times, military officers and a new group of settlers (or *colonos*) failed to control marginal populations. In 1953 Ecuadorian President Plaza placed responsibility for the uncooperative native populations—the internal Others—in the hands of a new set of missionaries, including SIL (Fuentes 1997:129–31). The Huaorani people were never part of the colonial history of Ecuador, yet today they feel the persistence of colonialism in many ways.

The national government of Ecuador accepted the Kichwa stereotype of the Huaorani and imposed it on the national imaginary still in force today (Fuentes 1997:55). The introduction of the Huaorani stereotype to national spheres began in the 1950s. Savages were counterproductive for the emergence of a modern nation. During the Cold War, Ecuador was still a nation-state at the beginning of its modernization, and it needed U.S. academic knowledge, scientific development, and international recognition as a capitalist state. Moreover, Ecuador, like other nations, sought a homogenous and coherent cultural identity (Fuentes 1997:55). Conversely it was in the interests of the United States to expand its influence in the Americas during the Cold War to avoid communist sympathies, and native populations were particularly vulnerable to communism in North American views. In this context the activities of SIL and other missionary groups can be viewed as an extension of anti-communist controls in Latin America (Stoll 1985:30–36, Rivas Toledo and Lara Ponce 2001:29).

After first operating in a somewhat ad hoc manner, in 1941 SIL came under the sponsorship of the University of Oklahoma (www.sil.org/sil/history.htm, accessed 17 July 2007). The university's institutional backing allowed SIL to be welcomed as a legitimate scientific and linguistic organization by the Ecuadorian government, as a partner in the modernization project (Ziegler-Oetro 2004:52–55, Fuentes 1997:132), and as a representative of American capitalism. Cooperation with SIL seemed to hold the promise that other groups would recognize the newly crafted Ecuadorian identity.

On 10 April 1990 the government of Ecuador recognized 612,560 hectares as the legal property of the Huaorani, the largest indigenous territory in the country (Rival 2002:154; Rivas Toledo and Lara Ponce 2001:36). The land had been occupied by the Huaorani for centuries, but it had been mostly abandoned after 1974 when various Huaorani families moved into Tihueno, a protectorate founded in 1969 by SIL to concentrate Huaorani populations. However, the Huaorani began to repopulate the forest during the 1980s and had never abandoned ownership of their land. Thus, they fought for recognition during the period when other indigenous groups were pressuring the government for territorial and cultural rights. In 1990 a massive indigenous march paralyzed the country for weeks, causing the government to negotiate with indigenous communities. The government of Ecuador issued a title of collective property of the indigenous reserve to the Huaorani people as a placating measure. Despite the Huaorani's legal ownership of their land, however, they do not control the underground rights of their territory, because their title reads, "the adjudicated will not impede or make difficult the mineral and hydrocarbon exploration and/or exploitation" (Narváez, qtd. in Rivas Toledo and Lara Ponce 2001:37). As a consequence the Huaorani cannot interfere with the oil exploitation in their own territory.

By keeping the Huaorani as legal holders of title to the land but controlling the rights to oil development, the Ecuadorian government ultimately retains possession of Huaorani territory. According to Eric Cheyfitz, a title is one essential aspect of the Western concept of property ownership (1997:46), but the right of property ownership and the right of possession are two distinct rights; moreover, "when to this double right the *actual* possession is also unified, then, and then only, is the title completely legal" (Blackstone qtd. in Cheyfitz 1997:47; emphasis added). Thus, Huaorani populations have been dispossessed of their territory. Even their legal rights are not always respected by other parties with interests that conflict with theirs. Besides the dispossession of the wealth of their land, the Huaorani were also assigned legal ownership of only a quarter of their original territory of more than two million hectares. One might conclude that in practice the Ecuadorian paternalistic regime protects its "children" by controlling land use and providing them with what the state as a father considers fair. Alternatively, one could say that the paternalistic government retains all rights as legal guardian over its children and disposes of the children's property. In such circumstances legal title is merely nominal. The government's paternalism recognizes the territory solely as a nominal legal inheritance rather than a legitimate patrimony to be fully enjoyed by the Huaorani.

The Ecuadorian government assigned the petroleum development rights for Huaorani territory to foreign oil companies. The development rights were distributed to incoming groups according to their place and power in the bigger system considered in this study. In 1937 the government assigned exploration and exploitation rights to the Royal Dutch Shell company, and a Texaco-Gulf consortium soon followed (E-Shen 1999:15). By 1969 the oil companies had become the de facto possessors of the Huaorani lands because oil development entailed exclusion of natives from lands in operation. This political configuration echoes arrangements during the period of Spanish colonialism when indigenous lands together with their inhabitants were given to Spanish colonists to manage, resulting in a form of indentured servitude of the native population. The Huaorani escaped enslavement during the colonial period because of their auto-exclusion from colonial society, but their auto-exclusion not only marginalized them collectively during republican times, it also excluded them from the construction of "official" history. Paradoxically, the lack of colonial experience thus made the Huaorani vulnerable during the twentieth century in the cultural systems of the Amazon, the nation, and the world.

A major factor to be considered in the Huaorani power struggles of the 1950s and 1960s is SIL. SIL missionaries brought the gospel to remote corners of the planet by rendering the Bible into a plain, simple, and flowing message that would function in indigenous languages. To the missionaries, translating the Bible into indigenous languages around the world saved souls (Elliot 1958:23). At the same time they appeared to be conscious of the cultural damage they were causing; for instance, Peter Fleming, a missionary who attempted contact with the Huaorani, wrote in his diary, "It is *easy* to see how the availability of even so simple a tool as the machete can profoundly alter a culture" (qtd. in Elliot 1958:157, emphasis added). While SIL missionaries were trying to save people, they were also aware of the cultural impact of their work, which raises questions about their ethical stand.

Elisabeth Elliot's *Through Gates of Splendor* (1958) gives an insider's perspective on the first missionary contact with the Huaorani via the so-called Auca Mission. James Elliot, Elisabeth's brother, was the first SIL missionary to show an interest in contacting the Huaorani. He shared this thought with his good friend Peter Fleming, who came along on the mission. In 1952 the two missionaries spent some time in the Ecuadorian capital, Quito, learning Spanish, reading the Spanish Bible, and analyzing how the Bible had been translated. They also learned about the national perceptions of Protestant missionaries (Elliot 1958:26). After mastering Spanish the missionaries moved to Amazonian Shandia, where they learned Kichwa. This linguistic progression is fundamental for understanding the power gradients in the entire cultural system discussed in this essay: from the beginning the SIL approach to Huaorani language and culture was doubly mediated, first through Ecuadorian Spanish culture and language, then through the culture and language of the Ecuadorian Kichwa.

Fleming summarized the evangelization process as having three fundamental steps: to reduce Huao Terero to writing (Liefeld 1990:213); to translate the Bible in a manner applicable to the lives of the Huaorani; and to prepare teachers equipped with linguistic materials for literacy programs (Liefeld 1990:183). This process was first carried out on Amazonian Kichwa populations in the early 1950s, a step which served as an antecedent to the Huaorani project. The evangelization of the Kichwa spread closer and closer to the Huaorani territory, an encircling motion already planned by the missionaries in 1952 (Liefeld 1990:120). The Protestant Sunday services were fully translated into Kichwa by 1956.

The linguistic aspects of the evangelization of the Kichwa served as a preliminary exercise for Elliot and Fleming, but the Kichwa phase provided more than linguistic information. From the Kichwa community, the missionaries learned important details about Huaorani culture and social structures. Such structures were initially understood only from the perspective of the Kichwa, outsiders to the Huaorani community. However, as the evangelization progressed further east from Shandia, the missionaries had an important breakthrough. They met Dayuma, a self-exiled Huaorani woman who had escaped her group years before and who had worked for Carlos Sevilla, owner of the farm El Capricho. Dayuma was central for understanding Huaorani culture and their way of life.

In the 1950s the Kichwa of the Napo River (the Naporuna) continued as an indentured labor force, a legacy from the Spanish colonial system. Dayuma, working on Sevilla's farm among Kichwa workers, was taken to be one of them. Once identified as a Huaorani, she became an essential source of ethnological information about her ancestral group, informing the missionaries, for example, that the Huaorani did not experience family violence (Elliot 1958:102). By contrast family violence is a characteristic cultural trait of Kichwa communities, which Dayuma had witnessed. Another Huaorani cultural characteristic she identified was that they never got drunk because their *chicha*, a manioc beverage, was not fermented. By contrast most Kichwa communities ferment their corn or manioc chicha with saliva, resulting in an alcoholic drink. Other information included the fact that Huaorani families lived in clans of approximately 30 people, that the women worked with manioc and cotton while men shaped lances and sharp points, and that the Huaorani could recognize human beings individually by the sound of their footsteps (Kane 1995).

Moreover, the missionaries learned that if they could create family ties through affiliation with a Huaorani individual, they could reach the group safely (Liefeld 1990:227). They also learned that the Shell Oil Company had given the Huaorani gifts and had received a vine-woven basket in return as a result of attempts at contact via airplanes (Elliot 1958:98). Dayuma also told the missionaries about various Huaorani legends, including a story of fire that fell from heaven and spread throughout the world, burning all the trees (1958:103). These legends were later helpful in translating the Bible into Huao Terero. As we will see, some biblical passages were replaced by Huaorani stories or adapted to their oral tradition in order to convert the Huaorani to Christianity. Dayuma also taught James and Elisabeth Elliot the basics of her language.

While Kichwa was being reduced to writing, a similar method was used with Jívaro, the language spoken by another Amazonian community. Missionary Roger Younderian prepared visual dictionaries for the Jívaro people, which included a column of drawings (mostly objects), a column indicating the Jívaro sounds for these objects as transliterations in the Roman alphabet, and a third column with isolated syllables that could be learned by heart in the future (Elliot 1958:40). These primers constituted the first textbooks for the alphabetization program, later also used among the Huaorani (Elliot 1958:80). Younderian also worked with other resistant communities; for instance, he flew 50 miles to the eastern Amazonian jungle to meet the Atshuara peoples. The first contacts with these groups followed the pattern used by Shell, namely airplane drops. Airplanes had been a popular means of contact, and drops of goods had been perfected by the military during the twentieth century, particularly during World War II. Younderian had served in the U.S. Army Air Forces during World War II, and it is possible he was trained in airdropping techniques.

The airplane drop method was chosen for the first Huaorani contacts. In 1956 the Auca Mission began with gift drops that, according to Dayuma, the Huaorani believed came from the stomachs of the airplanes wounded by their lances (Elliot 1958:134). The flights did not always target the same clans (Elliot 1958:137–42). The missionaries chose different Huaorani *malocas*—oval houses typically found in the Amazon. Whatever the location, the routine was always the same: on Sunday mornings the missionaries flew low enough for the people to distinguish the airplane as the gifts were dropped; then they would fly lower and scream Auca phrases through loudspeakers; and finally even lower so that the Huaorani could see the faces of the missionaries printed on enlarged pictures. The phrases were simple: *Biti miti punimupa, biti miti* (I like you, I want to be your friend, I like you). On succeeding trips the missionaries saw some people wearing their gifts. Nate Saint recorded in his diary: "May the praise be His, and may it be that some Auca, clothed in the righteousness of Jesus Christ, will be with us as we lift our voices in praise before His throne" (qtd. in Elliot 1958:145). The gift-drop procedure was costly. The missionaries accelerated the process by leaving the gifts in the treetops to force the Huaorani to chop them down until a big enough clearing was formed for a landing area. Peter Fleming wrote in his diary: "These fellows will be dressed like dudes before we get to see them on the ground" (qtd. in Elliot 1958:164). The first landing day was scheduled. The Huaorani received an invitation in sign language from the missionaries. The missionaries wore headdresses, placed small airplanes on a landing area nicknamed Palm Beach, carried more gifts, and spoke Huao Terero, the language of the Huaorani. In return, the Huaorani killed all five missionaries. The Huaorani thought Roger Younderian, Jim Elliot, Peter Fleming, Nate Saint, and Ed McCully were cannibals and killed them out of fear (Liefeld 1990:13).

The self-styled martyrdom was an enormous success for SIL. It increased SIL's membership and contributions, channeled new sources of income for the expansion of its activities, and secured free publicity, including a ten-page illustrated article in *Life Magazine*. The martyrdom was an essential catalyst for the translation of the Bible into Huao Terero because the event inadvertently created a family tie that allowed for nonviolent contact. Dayuma's brother had been killed by Nate Saint at Palm Beach (Kimerling 1996:177).[2] We have seen that absent a secure family connection, any stranger would be killed without warning. According to the Huaorani definition of family structure, however, if two people killed each other, the members of each family became immediately related. Therefore, Rachel, Nate Saint's sister, and Dayuma were "blood sisters" or sisters of "peace after revenge" (Rival 2002:158). Dayuma was free to return to her people at any time, and she could bring her new sister along (Kimerling 1996:177). Rachel Saint, trained by the Wycliffe Bible Translators (Kimerling 1996:176, Kingsland 1980:36), became the leading translator in the first project to translate the Bible into Huao Terero, the Gospel of St. Mark.

After the martyrdom the missionaries became culture heroes and self-appointed authorities on the Huaorani in the wider world (Fuentes 1997:133). Various missionaries "translated" the Huaorani image to the outside world, propagating the view of the Huaorani as "ignorant savages," "primitive people," and "stone age people" (Fuentes 1977:12). Regarding the Huaorani people who had relocated to the town of Tihueno, Judith Kimerling, for example, points out that Rachel Saint "spoke to the newcomers about Christian love, but in conversations with [Rosemary] Kingsland, she qualified them as 'garbage'" (Kimerling 1996:181).[3] Olive F. Liefeld, widow of Peter Fleming, wrote that she "couldn't believe God would allow the sacrifice of five men for only fifty Indians" (1990:206). Thirty years after the first encounter, Liefeld's image of the Huaorani had not changed: they were still just "Indians," despite the fact that they were dressed, baptized, and their souls saved. One sees the depths of the missionaries' stereotyping of the Huaorani in such statements. These stereotypes clarify the ambivalent missionary ideology, one stated in their daily work and a more hidden one expressed in the slippages of their inner thoughts. This ideological contradiction highlights another ethical problem in this case study.

The martyrdom legitimized SIL's "custody" of the Indians, and SIL was given control of the Huaorani "protectorate" by the Ecuadorian government. Access to the Huaorani by any other people was mediated by Rachel Saint until she left the area in the late 1980s (Kane 1995:86). SIL governance of the Aucas, aimed at "saving" them and "teaching them how to live" (Rivas Toledo and Lara Ponce 2001:29), was later followed by the oil companies doing business in Ecuador. SIL established a hierarchical relationship in which the missionaries were dominant and the Huaorani became dependent on a group of outsiders as suppliers, providers, benefactors, and gift givers. After the successful SIL mission, when oil companies were able to undertake large-scale exploration and drilling in Huaorani territory, the oil companies replicated the missionaries' function as goods givers in a symbolic exchange for the land's oil. The oil companies perceived the Huaorani through missionary lenses as "uncivilized savages," but most importantly as an obstacle to transnational economic development in zones of "needed" high petroleum density (Rivas Toledo and Lara Ponce 2001:26).

Prior to the SIL protectorate of the Huaorani, the natives had managed to expel Royal Dutch Shell. In 1937 Shell was the first company granted rights to prospect and drill for oil in the Ecuadorian Amazon. Ecuadorian soldiers and Naporuna workers, however, became increasingly reluctant to serve Shell as they saw many co-workers killed by Huaorani spears. Shell left in 1948. When Texaco began its operations in 1964, the SIL mission had cleared the land of hostile natives, enabling petroleum exploitation (Stoll 1985: 311). Significantly, it was revealed in the 1990s that Texaco had directly funded SIL by means of "blank checks" and other resources, including planes and facilities (Kimerling 1996:180, E-Shen 1999:15). In 1964 Texaco received exploitation rights to 1,413,450 hectares of land from the Ecuadorian government (Rodríguez Guerrra 2002). Soon afterwards Texaco started pumping oil from its first well, Lago-Agrio-1, at a rate of 2,640 barrels per day. The company's role with respect to the Huaorani became that of father—a "giver"—who decides what its beneficiaries ought to need or receive. Like the Ecuadorian government and SIL, Texaco adopted a paternalistic stance toward the Huaorani.

One might say that the Huaorani communities asked the company to "give them" goods and services, and the foreigners who were the distributors of the goods became the de facto leaders of the people. In a sense the forest as provider was replaced by the oil company as the source of life, food, and shelter. Since the conversion of the Huaorani by SIL missionaries, every incoming new system to that region of the Amazon—including NGOs and ecological organizations—has interacted with the Huaorani as benefactors. Consequently an acceptance of outside leaders has driven the Huaorani into an identity crisis. Moreover, this permanent mediation has resulted in a radical dissociation from the national population and government (Rivas Toledo and Lara Ponce 2001:56). For example, as I discovered from personal experience in the area, if an Ecuadorian mestiza such as myself wants to interact with Huaorani people, she must acquire a permit from the oil company in order to circulate in Huaorani territory; she must also pay a fee to the Huaorani community (which rarely reaches actual Huaorani families) and bring enough clothes and food to care for the group for the duration of her stay.

The concessions of the Ecuadorian government to the oil companies are not exploitative of the Huaorani alone. Since 1974 the national government of Ecuador has received only 25 percent of Texaco's income from Huaorani oil despite the contracted partnership that granted 62 percent of benefits to the government (Rivas Toledo and Lara Ponce 2001:49). Meanwhile, major pollution problems have resulted from the exploitation, including those caused by routine airplane spills and the construction of the Via Auca, a road built by Texaco during the 1970s to facilitate oil operations and transportation. Joe Kane refers to this damage as the "worst case of toxic contamination in the entire Amazon" and compares it to other oil disasters, concluding that Texaco's damage was "one and a half times as much oil as the *Exxon Valdez* spilled off the coast of Alaska" (1995:5). According to Kane, Texaco spilled 16.8 million gallons of raw crude oil on the 27 occasions its pipeline broke, and 4.8 million gallons of untreated toxic waste went directly into the watershed every day from 1972 until 1989 (1995:70). In 1993 the Huaorani brought a collective suit against Texaco in federal court in New York as a consequence of the pollution. The Second Circuit Court of Appeals affirmed a five-billion-dollar judgment related to the pollution;

Texaco by contrast had claimed that twelve million dollars would be enough to clean up the Amazon (Kimerling 1996:190, Kane 1995:251). Moreover, Texaco seems to have "forgotten" to take actions it had agreed upon; instead the oil company covered the waste pits with dirt, created a canal connecting cesspools directly to the river, and dug new holes to bury waste (Kane 1995:193).

Other groups have made their own additions to the image of the Huaorani. Elliot states that "the Aucas have constituted a hazard to explorers, an embarrassment to the Republic of Ecuador, and a challenge to missionaries" (1958:96). These translations of the image of the Huaorani echo the Kichwa perception of the Huaorani as savages. This image is clearly operative in the film *End of the Spear* (2005), where the Huaorani are portrayed as stereotypical savages who attack the beautiful and kind-hearted missionaries. For the tourist industry, by contrast, the group's "savage nature" is a plus, an occasion for further exploitation. Tourist companies have made enormous profits by selling the image of the Huaorani savage, packaging tours for evangelical groups, anthropologists, adventurers, peace advocates, and scientists (Rivas Toledo and Lara Ponce 2001:90). The image sold is the one tourists pay to see. None of these companies is run by Huaorani entrepreneurs. The benefits, once again, are diverted from Huaorani territory. Kane describes tourist brochures promoting river trips to see the Aucas, "naked savages" wearing only earrings (1995:16). However, the Huaorani people he actually encountered did not resemble those pictured in the brochures. The Huaorani in town were dressed, had shoes, and were undifferentiated from the Naporuna or colonos from the coast.

The image of the Huaorani as savages also appeals to various Western watch groups claiming to know what is best for the natives (Rivas Toledo and Lara Ponce 2001:30). Yasuní National Park authorities also consider them an "aggregate value" to the ecological park. In 1979, after a long study undertaken by the United Nations, this park was superposed on the Huaorani ancestral territory. The study concludes that the park had "4 types of forest, 621 species of birds, 173 species of mammals, 11 species of amphibians, 107 species of reptiles, and 385 species of fish" (Rivas Toledo and Lara Ponce 2001:40), but does not mention the human populations that live there. NGOs and scientific organizations, including CARE, Cultural Survival, the Nature Conservancy, the Natural Resource Defense Council, Wildlife Conservation International, the Sierra Club, the World Wildlife Fund, and a dozen others, were or are involved in letter-writing campaigns, boycotts, lawsuits, and grants in the name of the Huaorani (Kane 1995:10). These organizations act on behalf of the Huaorani for this people's "benefit." Dichotomies such as oil vs. jungle, abundance vs. poverty, and local vs. global continue to lure "guardian" organizations to become involved with and speak on behalf of the Huaorani.

The opening of Huaorani territory as a result of evangelization has also brought a new wave of colonos, generally Ecuadorian mestizos, who have moved to the Amazon as new settlers. These settlers look for employment either in the oil fields or in agriculture, and lately they have organized networks of lumber exploitation and drug dealing. Because they do not receive free land from the government as colonos had in the past, they have married Huaorani individuals as a means of acquiring property (Ziegler-Otero 2004:38), often unaware that the Huaorani land cannot be appropriated because it is communal property. Other resources that have attracted colonos are gold, which has motivated a migration trend since the 1980s, and wood for the lumber industry, which deforests some 2,000 hectares of Huaorani land each year with little profit for the natives (Rivas Toledo and Lara Ponce 2001:86, Cleary 1990:1). Today, the deforestation has taken a new twist, as forest has been replaced by cocaine plantations run by the drug industry.

In this context it is not possible to give a comprehensive survey of all the various interests, cultural groups, and cultural systems interacting with the Huaorani people. Figure 1, however, gives an idea of the complexity of the systemic interactions, and, from a Western standpoint, represents a tentative hierarchy of those interacting cultural systems.

Contrary to what one might conclude from Figure 1, the relationship between the Huaorani and other groups is not merely a top-down power relationship. Rather there is a two-way flow; herein lies a hidden form of translational resistance taking the form of silence and invisibility. It is a particularity of the Huaorani to silently resist outsider cultural impositions. This practice is consistent with indigenous politics of difference elsewhere that seek recognition apart from constructs that project illusory homogenous national identities. Indigenous groups in Peru, Bolivia, Ecuador, and Guatemala, for example, claim to have survived culturally by keeping the secrets of their ancestors from reaching outsiders despite their seeming assimilation to Western cultural standards. This cultural strategy of survival through silence has been revealed to the world and become widely known through the writing of Rigoberta Menchú about the descendants of

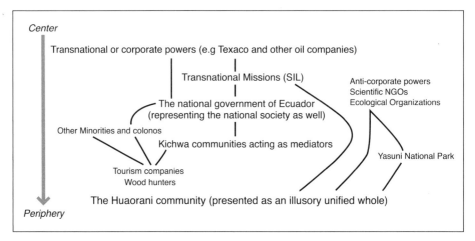

Fig. 1   Systems in interaction with the Huaorani from a Western perspective

the Mayans. Menchú believes that the hardships her people endure must be overcome with the presence of their ancestors and that by hiding their true identity, the people have resisted Westernization and obliteration for five hundred years (Menchú 2005/1985:220, 245). The deep cultural transformations endured by the Huaorani have likewise taught them to keep their secrets to themselves while superficially appearing to be whatever the observer wants to make of them. Silence is the strongest Huaorani weapon to resist encroachment, just as it has been for the descendants of the Mayans now fighting under the motto "we are still here."

While playing at being converts performing whiteness, the Huaorani in fact use their position to get as many goods and services from outsiders as possible, even as they organize to expel cultural Others in the near future with the help of still other outsiders. The Huaorani disguise themselves to conform to the perception of Others. In their "illiterate" culture, the body is their text and temple; the sacred and the secret reside within themselves. Here lies the difference between Huaorani covert and overt ideologies, the one they hide and the one they perform. The Huaorani perform for the Other in order to get what they have determined is needed in terms of their inner symbolic values. Thus, they follow their own rules, resisting impositions from the outside world. Kane describes how Quemperi, one of the founders of ONHAE (Organización Nacional de Huaorani Asociados del Ecuador), perceived strangers in his land: "he spoke of killing Ecuadorian soldiers for their machetes, Peruvian soldiers for their boots, oil workers for their food and T-shirts, Quichua for daring to cross the Napo River into Huaorani land" (Kane 1995:35). Performing the role of pacified peoples, they will not literally kill strangers, but by accepting their objects they are symbolically killing them as their grandparents did in fact. The Huaorani are not savages, but they act out of a different system of cultural logic in situations of cultural interface. The problem is that no one in the groups interacting with the Huaorani knows what form this covert ideology takes, what their needs are, or who they are. This lack of transparency at the moment of interaction is yet another ethical problem to note in this case study.

Some echoes of their covert ideology have reached less marginal discourses. For instance, some suggest that the Huaorani accept tourists and marriage outside their kinship groups so as to gain independence from SIL (Ziegler-Otero 2004:72), even though traditionally exogamy is perceived as a "wild" marriage (Rival 2002:140). The Huaorani think the Kichwa are "pale impostors" (Kane 1995:66) and yet they intermarry with them. They have also learned the norms of Western culture and know that by wearing their necklaces of jaguar teeth, their string bags, and their reed tubes filled with blowgun darts, they can move closer to the center of the layered cultural system that marginalizes them and thus win power in their own way. The Huaorani exercise an absolute power by commanding the linguistic and semiotic environment. They manipulate language and symbols by releasing themselves to the Others and resisting the Others with Huaorani logic and axiology. In this sense the cultural hierarchy of the intricate interlocking systems illustrated in Figure 1 fails. Instead, there is a deeper symbolic triumph of the Huaorani, who in this light can be perceived as being at the center of the system and manipulating the actions of outsiders. Although economically the hierarchy prevails as diagrammed, the Huaorani cultural victory is steady and silent. After long silence other postcolonial indigenous groups gained relative independence and wide recognition in the late twentieth century when conditions were ripe for organizing. I believe the Huaorani are following the same path.

Outsiders perceive reflections of their own images through many Huaorani performances, but such performances are images of texts that remain mistranslated or unverifiable. The Huaorani have displayed their bodies as mirrors, not as subjects. Feathers, necklaces, spears, and nudity can be used as a guise to fight corporate powers at the center of their own power. Moi, a Huaorani witness in the lawsuit against Texaco and another founding leader of ONHAE, testified in a New York courtroom wearing the most exotic outfit possible. He later told Kane, "your world wants me to wear this" (Kane 1995:8). This is an example of silent subversion. What at first seems to be consensual subjugation is instead the enactment of "escaping the social dominant order without leaving it" (Gentzler 1996:124). The Huaorani adhere simultaneously to two sets of contemporary cultural norms.

Research on the Huaorani thus far seemingly presents diverse viewpoints reflecting different cultural positions, but it is an illusory unmasking of "the" Huaorani image. Moreover, work thus far has failed to present an inside Huaorani response to the different systems interacting with theirs. Even if the diachronic axis of the cultural systems being investigated has certainly changed, a presupposed victory of Western culture over the ancestral Huaorani system seems hasty. We can see a change in the diachronic axis of Huaorani society in terms of cultural forms adapted to the West. Nonetheless the cultural focus remains unknown and some dare say even "untouched": Frances Herkovitz asserts that the missionaries "did not manage to definitely alter [the Huaorani's] cultural focus but only their cultural forms" (qtd. in Fuentes 1997:39).

Their cultural focus has been kept secret within the Huaorani people, producing a cultural silence for outsiders. To remain culturally alive, many indigenous populations like the Huaorani have opted to hide their habitus, defined by Pierre Bourdieu as a "system of durable, transposable dispositions, structured structures predisposed to function as structuring structures, that is, as principles which generate and organize practices and representations" (1990:53). In this sense, there is a secret way of passing on values, cultural practices, and representations. More important, the habitus implies "the system of dispositions—a present past that tends to perpetuate itself into the future by reactivation in similar structured practices . . . —is the principle of the continuity and regularity" (1992:54). In other words, Huaorani cultural survival is a continuity that comes from the past to the present and future and that needs to be kept secret, while superficially the body operates in the ways the outsiders expect it to operate, not at the levels of dispositions, but at that of behaviors. Cultural forms (behaviors) and foci (dispositions) can thus be effectively distinct. This is why a leader of the Huaorani and the people in general "had learned to play all the angles: ONHAE, the church, the Company, *cowode* like me" (Kane 1995:92) in an attempt to protect ancestral cultural continuity.

In investigating translations of the image of the Huaorani—and we cannot deal with the image of the cowudi translated by the Huaorani because we have no voices to express that side of the equation—we encounter a problem of representation already addressed by Gayatri Chakravorty Spivak in "Can the Subaltern Speak?" (1988). Analyzing Marxist rhetoric, Spivak underscores a problem of representation as having two different levels: a level of representation as "speaking for" that I associate in the present study with the unrepresented, untranslated, and *unvertreten* ('non-substituted') voice of the Huaorani; and a level of representation as "re-presentation" that I associate with the represented, translated, and *darstellt* ('translated' as represented, depicted, pictured, and allegorized) superficial image of the Huaorani (1988:275). The superficial image of the Huaorani has been interpreted in a variety of ways, as each system interacting with them has desired. This image has been constructed artistically and philosophically, but the Huaorani dispositions are unattainable.

The silence of the Huaorani is an overt form of resistance. It can also be seen as located at the center of the system of systems we are exploring here. They are the ones who have the power to remain "untouched" by Western culture. The Huaorani weapon of resistance is the ambivalence between "self" and "Other." Such a hypothesis dismembers the diagram in Figure 1 of the system of cultural systems. From this viewpoint the power is either in Huaorani hands or it has not yet been realized and seized. I suggest that a single center does not exist. Some important questions follow from this perspective. How do the Huaorani hold onto their power while giving away their land, their resources, and their cultural forms? How can we consider their image or text as untranslated?

One hint at answers to these questions with their paradoxes of power can be found in an examination of the process that produced the translation of the Bible into Huao Terero as it has been described by Kimerling (1996) and Kingsland (1980). They indicate that the translating took place in groups, a common practice in Bible translation, enlisting the aid of native speakers. Catherine Peeke, a Wycliffe translator, guided most of the Huao Terero rendering of the New Testament with the help of Tamanta, the son of one of the Huaorani men who killed the five missionaries in 1956. Most of the translation process was conducted orally. The missionaries told Bible stories and changed them in response to the reaction of the Huaorani listeners. For example, after telling a Bible story, the SIL missionaries asked if the Huaorani had heard of something similar. If a match was found, the missionary replaced the Bible story with the Huaorani tale (Kingsland 1980:122). Such a method circumvented having an intolerably high information load which results from telling a new story (cf. Tymoczko 1999:47). Ironically in this process the SIL linguists appear to be subordinate to the Huaorani voice that interpellated them.

We see here the hybridization of the Bible, the emergence of literary postcolonialism through the interaction of a "signifier of authority" and the originality of native cultural response (cf. Bhabha 1994:105). The missionaries' attempt at fixation of meaning establishes their position as authorities in presence and creation, a transparency disturbed by the visibility of difference (Bhabha 1994:111). This ambivalence leaves room for subversion in the act of undecidability, an empty space that calls authority into question, because symmetry between colonizer and colonized has been broken (Bhabha 1994:117). In this act of translation the Tagaeri, a group of dissident Huaorani people still self-exiled in the deeper jungle, were formed. They did not return to a pre-contact Huaorani way of life, but re-presented themselves as the hybrid text, the Huao Bible, phantoms of colonialism, reminders of difference. Here the source text (the Bible) in a sense became less than an echo: rather, biblical remembrances are echoed in Huaorani stories told by Huaorani people. This process of intralingual translation is more a process of selection and edition of Huaorani stories with an introduction of Christian elements to them than a translation of a source text into a target language. Christian concepts were also assimilated to Huaorani concepts. For example, the concepts Heaven and Paradise were rendered as 'the Forest', a generous place that will feed future generations (Kimerling 1996:175). "Happiness" was translated as "another serving of Chicha and we laugh" (Kimerling 1996:176).

The extreme level of dynamic equivalence in this translation process compels the "translation" to be so culturally evident to the target audience that the source message itself disappears. It is important to note that the approach of the SIL translators constitutes a limiting case of Eugene Nida's (1964) translation theory of dynamic equivalence. For Nida translation happens at the level of the image and not at the level of the text (1964:147). He stresses the importance of the target language and its connection to the original through a particular subject (empathy) while reading the words and body language of all the characters as "mimicry" of the author (1964:151). When Peeke told Bible stories, she was looking at the words and body language of her audience. She was looking for "centrifugal" meanings for her stories, that is, meanings for the audience in the margins of or even outside the written source text (cf. Nida 1964:147). Those marginal meanings could potentially even be different from or opposite to more central meanings in the Greek and Hebrew biblical stories.

In terms of understanding the message of the Bible, this method of generating a target text poses a theoretical problem for Bible interpretation by further generations of Huaorani or even for a synchronic perception of the Bible by Huaorani communities that were not part of this initial oral process. The translation method explained above is based on what W. V. O. Quine calls occasion sentences (1959:150).[4] The group of Huaorani that SIL worked with orally explored its own myths and "assented" to a meaning that was successful in replacing a certain passage of the Bible, but this assent was possible only in the particular context in which it was elicited by the missionaries. Nevertheless, that assent was generalized by the translators as standing sentences rather than as occasion or contextually bound utterances. Moreover, the Bible translators adopted a different form of language, namely written language, for enshrining the translations. This method pre-supposes a future "assent" from people in different temporal and contextual circumstances, not to mention simultaneous assent from other Huaorani groups that were not part of the translation process, thus further shifting the translation from the occasion sentences to presumed standing sentences. Although Huaorani myths are standing sentences within the Hua-orani communities, the acquired biblical connotations are contextual and occasional, associated with the translation process. Potentially the occasion sentences could even displace the standing meanings of the Huaorani myths after an initial assent as a result of usage of the Bible translation. In fact it is possible—and this was probably the translators' hope—that after time had elapsed and the Christian paradigm had become ubiquitous, Huaorani myths could be fully displaced, not only in their meaning but altogether as narratives.

Such a conspicuous form of dynamic equivalence implies a commit-ted but cursory attempt at assimilation. Although meaning was extracted from an ad hoc group of Huaorani participants, the missionaries assigned a permanence to those meanings for biblical passages by writing them down in a canonized, valorized form. The Huaorani were thus incorporated into a collective Christian structure, but the process was fast and superficial. Here Paul de Man's observations are relevant; he asserts that characteristics of reality do not respond to "a question of ontology, of things as they are, but of authority" (1978:19). A meaning generated in a specific context and a Bible translation generated by occasion utterances were imposed on the rest of the Huaorani population, thus asserting the authority of the missionaries and constituting the words of the missionaries as an absolute truth for the native communities (cf. Fuentes 1997:132). By translating the Bible into traditional stories belonging to the specific Huaorani community that SIL worked with, the missionaries created a text in which new information is scarce and redundancy is abundant. The critical spirit of translation as a way that newness enters the world as metaphors, as Homi Bhabha (1994) observes, a spirit one might expect particularly in the case of translating sacred texts, vanishes completely in a common-sense use of signs in this translation process. The missionaries attempted to insert the new text in the receiving culture without eliciting any type of resistance. The native groups could then embrace Christianity as natural, assimilating its religion and ways of life rapidly, albeit superficially.

Norman Fairclough's (1989) analysis of discourse is pertinent to this matter. Discourse is not ideology-free; in fact, ideology in discourse plays an active role in achieving consent or acceptance of new information by an audience, for "ideology is most effective when its workings are least visible" (Fairclough 1989:85). The translation method used by SIL to generate the Huao Terero Bible is a case of the immersion of missionary ideology using the common-sense notions of the Huaorani system as a vehicle for becoming a legitimate power, emptying their own linguistic actions of conspicuous ideology. Fairclough argues that "invisibility is achieved when ideologies are brought to discourse not as explicit elements of the text, but as the background assumptions" (1989:85). The missionaries' ideology is invisible in that it remains shielded behind Huaorani mythologies, with the latter conspicuous as elements of the discourse. Nonetheless, the textualization of the myths with Christian connotations delineates the interpretation of the text in the future. This translation method is a subversive way to inject Western, Christian ideology into Huaorani communities. Despite the use of the Other's imagery, it is a form of "ontological legerdemain," to invoke Paul de Man's terminology (1978:25), that allows SIL missionaries to strengthen their own image and authority and to violently impose their axiology on remote communities throughout the world.

Huaorani ideology is also invisible and at play in hidden ways in this translation process. Appearing to comply with missionary requests about Christian ways of life, the people are silent about their intentions, interpretations, and dispositions, and their covert ideology is even more invisible than that of missionaries. Thus, according to Fairclough's thesis, the Huaorani ideology is more effective. In fact, this sort of strategy has been successful in the survival of indigenous populations since colonial times, as we have seen. The long-range power of the Huaorani hidden ideology remains to be seen with time.

At the same time the translation itself is not a case of Huaorani resistance. Huaorani resistance resides in the group's ability to manage silence. The written and the spoken word can be lenient to violent Western impositions. In fact, Western imposition can take over all the superficial domains it pleases. But the Huaorani will not allow the cowudi to represent them by substitution, but only by recreation. Moreover, we must ask about the status of the translation itself. If the Bible rendering in Huao Terero is not a rendering of the Bible, then what is it? This gray zone where ideologies interact in a language game of translation remains to be explored in the future.

In terms of translation and resistance, it is important to consider the active role of the target culture members, as the Huaorani reassert their own image—this time themselves as subjects—into the Others' framework. They use the disguise desired by the other, they even at times objectify themselves as a joke, mocking the other. This is why the asymmetrical relationship between the Huaorani and the missionaries—asymmetrical in terms of the disparate identity of the hermeneutical imagery of both parties involved in this case—cannot be considered a unilateral imposition by SIL upon the poor savages. We have in front of us an agony of systems and a fight for power.

This study of the translation of the Bible into Huao Terero exhibits distinct translation strategies of different texts. In the Ecuadorian Amazon, Huaorani people create a visual text of their bodies that lacks meaning. Huaorani meaning is protected in the depths of silence, waiting for the right time to emerge culturally from the margins, as other indigenous groups have done since the second half of the twentieth century. Transnational native silence remains latent until possibilities arise that allow resistance to be overt again. By contrast SIL missionaries from the (white) United States created a text from Huaorani stories to slowly shift the axiological elements of Huaorani sacred beliefs. From oral to written, from myths to Bible, Huaorani communities seem to have passively accepted

Western cultural impositions. What we are witnessing is a severe case of miscommunication, where neither party is willing to engage in meaningful conversations, but where ethics and ideology are at stake.

One must not celebrate indigenous victory too rapidly in this interaction. Huaorani leaders are highly fragmented and dispersed, which makes organizing the people a difficult enterprise. Moreover, the Huaorani still have to discover technologies that might enable them to join a transnational and global indigenous fight. For example, Chiapas indigenous communities benefited tremendously from globalization and technology networks that enabled them to take off in an international field. Technology and watch groups have maintained the Chiapas in the international community awareness, while nation-states have increasingly become weaker in the context of globalization. The Huaorani plight has the potential to forge a direct link with the global, bypassing the national, in part because the Huaorani have always been excluded from national life and politics in Ecuador but also because at present the so-called glocal is more effective than the national in terms of funneling and organizing resources.[5]

By 1965 the translation of the Gospel of St. Mark was completed (Kingsland 1980:122). By 1981 some 20 percent of the Huaorani protectorate was able to read this Gospel (Rival 2002:210). The SIL translation of the Old Testament into Huao Terero was almost finished by 1989, a year before SIL left Ecuador. Some young Huaorani people still live in sin. Oil is still exploited and the forest is endangered more than ever. National society in Ecuador in general ignores the continued use of translation to further exploit the Huaorani people, which is why the study of translation and resistance takes on such urgent importance in this case.

Coda

The research for this study derives from secondary sources. I have made repeated attempts to engage in dialogue with SIL, but they have refused to give me any useful information about the translation of the Bible into Huao Terero. In the winter of 2006, therefore, I began to learn Huao Terero and went to Huaorani territory in order to find the SIL Bible in use. I spent several weeks in a maloca with a Huaorani clan to learn more about these issues. In the Amazon community I visited, the Huao Terero Bible had never been heard of; only Spanish Bibles were in use.

After returning to the United States, I contacted SIL for help again in vain. After I contacted a lower-level worker at the information desk, the employee took up the task of finding this text that was nowhere to be found. In December 2008 I was given the name of a researcher who had worked with the Huaorani at the time the New Testament translation was completed who still had a couple of copies of the work. I continue to wait for a copy which the researcher said would be forthcoming, so as to look at specific linguistic details, translation strategies, and basic information about publication and date of completion. My research about the SIL translation of the Bible into Huao Terero is thus an ongoing project and it is far from being concluded.

I continue to have ethical questions as well. To what extent were the Bibles translated by SIL actually published for indigenous target audiences or even produced for indigenous use as SIL leaders claimed in their 1981 annual performance report? Was the translation of the Bible into Huao Terero a cover to get oil companies into the impenetrable land of the Huaorani? Is the conspicuous absence of Huao Bibles in Amazon communities typical of SIL practices? After SIL left Ecuador at the end of the 1980s, who decided to use Spanish material in church services and schools instead of the material purportedly prepared in the native language? These questions suggest that comparative study of Bible translation during the years of the Cold War throughout Latin America and the world would be a promising enterprise.

Notes

1. This group, also known as Quichua, uses international conventions for its alphabet. According to DINEIB (Dirección nacional de educación intercultural bilingüe), there is a debate among indigenous scholars about whether dominant spelling conventions, proposed by Paul Rivet in the 1920s, are fully accurate and whether they simplify alphabetization. Here I follow current preferred indigenous spellings.

2. Apparently the Huaorani sent three people as bait for the missionaries. The missionaries welcomed two Huaorani women and a man, while other Huaorani remained hidden and armed in the jungle. When the missionaries realized they were in an ambush, one of them shot his pistol, wounding Nampa, brother of Dayuma, who was hiding in the jungle. Nampa died soon after (Rival 2002:158).

3. Rosemary Kingsland is the British author of *A Saint among Savages* (1980), the story of Rachel Saint among the Huaorani.

4. Quine (1959) makes the distinction between various types of sentences, two of which are particularly relevant here. Occasion sentences are those that have meaning in a specific context and assert something about a present situation or condition.

By contrast standing sentences are sentences that are true independent of contingent circumstances.

5. On the "glocal" as opposed to the "local" or "global" see Escobar (2008). The glocal can be characterized as contested spaces in which the ethnic and the corporate compete, aided by networks that are neither solely local nor solely global.

PUAʻALAʻOKALANI D. AIU

Neʻe Papa I Ke Ō Mau: Language as an Indicator of Hawaiian Resistance and Power

"Neʻe papa i ke ō mau" is the theme of the annual ʻAha Pūnana Leo fundraiser dinner. The ʻAha Pūnana Leo is the organization that started the Hawaiian language immersion schools movement in the late 1970s. "Neʻe papa i ke ō mau" means to move forward as one, which suggests that the donors and Hawaiian speakers in the room are moving forward as one to revive the Hawaiian language. This is true, but the image that "neʻe papa" conveys, and that it is meant to convey, is that of lava moving inexorably to the sea or of a phalanx of soldiers eating up any resistance on the way to their goal. "Neʻe papa i ke ō mau" is meant to convey the inevitable return tide of the Hawaiian language and with it Hawaiian cultural values and practices. The image reverses the idea of using language as a means of resistance and suggests that resisting the surge toward Hawaiian practices, including resisting the use of the language, is the less powerful stance.

Hawaiians have resisted the complete translation of their language and their culture into something more accessible to Westerners since the "discovery" of the Sandwich Islands in 1778. Like the Irish who were similarly colonized, most Hawaiians speak English as their first language in large part because children were forbidden to speak the language in school for decades.[1] Also as with the Irish, the language of Hawaiians has become hybridized in both directions. Hawaiian pidgin is the most obvious example, but more subtle uses of key Hawaiian concepts, such as *pono*, *kuleana*, *ʻāina*, and *mālama*, used in schools and in public discussions and debates undermine "the presence of colonialist authority, creating . . . ʻobjects of epistemological or moral contemplation'" (Tymoczko 2003b:36, quoting Bhabha 1994:156–57).

This article examines translation—or rather the refusal to translate—as a form of resistance to colonial authority in Hawai'i, as well as a way of re-imaging what resistance means. As in the example above, Hawaiian is often only partially translated. Many Hawaiian words have multiple meanings, and Hawaiian phrases are meant to carry several layers of meaning. Hawaiian speakers often only translate at the first, most literal level. In this essay I look briefly at the importance of land in structuring some deeper metaphors in the Hawaiian language and the Hawaiian sense of self, and at how those metaphors become manifest in public testimonies about land use but remain untranslated. Then I briefly discuss the use of Hawaiian in public speaking events. The first example is the testimony of Hawaiians at the Kaho'olawe Island Conveyance Commission hearings held in 1990. The second is the reaction to the Ninth Circuit Court ruling against the policy of the Kamehameha Schools giving preference to students of Hawaiian ancestry.

A Brief History of the Colonization of Hawai'i

When Captain Cook "discovered" Hawai'i in 1778, each island was a separate kingdom. Kamehameha I, who later united all of the Hawaiian islands, was an adolescent living with his uncle, Kalaniopu'u, ruler of Hawai'i Island. By 1819, the year of Kamehameha's death, the islands had been united into one kingdom, and Hawai'i had become a central trading post for whalers and for the sandalwood industry. After Kamehameha's death, his queen regent abolished the *kapu* system, effectively abolishing the Hawaiian state religion and to a large degree the basis for Hawaiian social mores (Sahlins 1981).[2] A year later Protestant missionaries arrived in Hawai'i. In 1848 missionary advisers convinced Kamehameha III to divide his land and distribute it in fee to the chiefs and commoners. This is called the Māhele, the great land "sharing" in which the Mō'ī shared title to all the Hawaiian land among himself, the chiefs, and the commoners. The Māhele still has repercussions for land use policy in Hawai'i today.

By the time King Kalākaua was elected to the throne in 1874, signaling the end of the Kamehameha dynasty, the U.S. missionaries were well established and chafing against the monarchy. They convinced Kalākaua to pass the "Bayonet Constitution" which took away most of the rights of

Native Hawaiians. His sister, Queen Lili'uokalani, ascended the throne in 1891 after his death in San Francisco. She had a stormy relationship with the U.S. sugar barons and worked to restore a constitution more favorable to the native population. Lili'uokalani was overthrown by the U.S. sugar barons with the help of U.S. Marines in 1893. A provisional government was established under the assumption that the United States would quickly annex Hawai'i. However, when it became apparent that annexation would not happen rapidly, the Republic of Hawai'i was founded, essentially as a means of governing the Hawaiian Islands and protecting the interests of the U.S. sugar barons until the political climate in the United States changed (Dawes 1968, Cooper and Dawes 1987, McGregor 1990, and Osorio 2002). By 1900 Hawai'i was a territory of the United States. It became the fiftieth state on 21 August 1959.

The Hawaiian language was widely spoken until 1896 when schools that taught in Hawaiian were closed by the Republic of Hawai'i. Within a generation almost no native speakers of the Hawaiian language remained. For almost two generations Hawaiians neither spoke their language nor were they able to fully practice their culture within a Western political, economic, and educational framework (Kame'eleihiwa 1992). It wasn't until the 1920s that Hawaiian was taught at the University of Hawai'i.

Separating Hawaiians from the Land: Violation of a Central Hawaiian Cognitive Metaphor

One of the many violent acts that colonizers perpetrate is to separate a people from their language. This can be done in different ways, but is usually done by proscribing the use of the language or abolishing the language altogether. For Hawaiians it was also accomplished by removing meaning from the central cognitive metaphors of Hawaiian existence, the separation of 'ike, thought or meaning, from 'ōlelo, the word. The clearest and most lasting way this was done was to separate Hawaiians from the land which provided the central metaphors for their existence.[3]

Lilikalā Kame'eleihiwa has documented both the Hawaiian loss of 'āina (land) and the loss of structural metaphors connected to 'āina. She analyzes cultural structures that allowed Hawaiians to give away their land to foreigners and how this led to the subsequent separation of 'ike, or the way Hawaiians think about the land, from actual land and cultural practices. Kame'eleihiwa documents how these losses of central Hawaiian metaphors mirror the physical and political decline of the Hawaiian people in the 1800s.

> Communal access to the Land, or ʻĀina (lit., that from which one eats), meant easy access to the source of food and implied a certain generosity in the sharing of resources. Conversely, private, individual ownership of ʻĀina must, by its legal nature, mean a certain denial of access to the source of food to anyone not specifically designated as the Land's rightful owner. To Hawaiians the latter behavior is stingy and anti-social, and continues to be problematic even today, 140 years after the establishment of Western-style Land tenure. (1992:9)

A culture in which shared land was the norm and in which the bounty of the land was a reflection of the king's *mana*, or right to rule, assumes that all people will work for the greater good of their godlike king. No doubt the *haole* settlers in Hawaiʻi found this assumption ridiculous, especially within Protestant frameworks that promoted individual wealth as a sign of one's personal godliness. The loss of their land meant that Hawaiians had to find new ways to define themselves and their relationships to each other. In many ways Hawaiians are still translating what it means to be Hawaiian in a modern world, and refusing to translate into English is one way to resist assimilation.

Writing about the imposition of the 1887 Bayonet Constitution on the Hawaiian Kingdom, Jon Osorio (2002) extends Kameʻeleihiwa's analysis in his documentation of the loss of Hawaiian control over the Hawaiian Kingdom's legislature and the corresponding loss of the Mōʻī's status. He discusses the changes that Hawaiians went through in a mere fifty years after 1837 that made the concept of the Bayonet Constitution possible. He asks how Hawaiians had changed from believing that their kings were descendants of gods to believing that their chiefs could be elected. He emphasizes, moveover, that the land ownership and monetary requirements for suffrage under the Bayonet Constitution effectively barred most Hawaiians from participating in elections. The latter development marks the final breakdown of Hawaiians' ability to communicate effectively within their own structural and conceptual metaphors because they no longer had political or legal control over the land of their ancestors.

> "Good government" (that is, government guided by a firm white hand) had finally been achieved. The instruments that had made it possible were the drastic changes to the power of the king, the transformation of the

legislative assembly into a body that represented the business community, and equally far-reaching change in the definition . . . of the electorate. However, it also came as the result of tremendous loss of Native confidence in themselves and a very real confusion of what it meant to be Native. (Osorio 2000:246, 248)

At this point government no longer supported the Hawaiians' view of themselves or of their place in the world. Leadership of the Hawaiian Islands had passed from Hawaiian hands. With that lack of leadership went control over the use of the land and all connection between the land and the people who had lived on it for centuries.[4] The *mana* of the land was gone, because those who imbued it with meaning no longer tended the land. But that doesn't mean that the land had lost its meaning for Hawaiians.

Ironically the Hawaiian language survived these changes. Hawaiian-language newspapers were still being published. Hawaiian songs were still being composed and disseminated. In fact, after Queen Lili'uokalani was deposed for trying to restore power and dignity to the Native Hawaiians, her followers used songs published in Loyalist newspapers, such as *Ka Maka'āinana*, to keep her abreast of their activities. Furthermore, when her supporters staged a counterrevolution, their activities were captured in songs and later published in a book called *Buke Mele Lāhui ho'omākaukau, hoākoakoa a ho'oponoponiia mai na mele ho'opukaia ma ka nūpepa "Ka Maka'āinana" a me kahi mau nūpepa e a'e* (Book of National Songs Prepared, Collected, Assembled, and Corrected from the Songs Published in the Newspaper *Ka Maka'āinana* and Other Newspapers). Amy Stillman (1989a) analyzes these songs, showing they are optimistic despite the fact that the counterrevolution was doomed before it began. During this time the language itself supported the resistance to Western rule. Although 'ike and 'ōlelo had not yet been separated, Hawaiian metaphors were changing slightly because Hawaiians were redefining themselves in opposition to those who had taken over the land and the government.

Unfortunately, once the Hawaiian language was banned from the schools in 1896, its decline was swift. Within one generation almost no one spoke Hawaiian outside of the home and within two generations few people could speak the language with any fluency. Hawai'i was a land without its 'ōlelo and, therefore, the connection to 'ike was tentative. It meant so little to be Hawaiian in the 1950s and 1960s that many Hawaiians did not even put "Hawaiian" on their children's birth certificates. This loss of self has ramifications in today's world because federal and state law provide different entitlements to Hawaiians based on blood quantum. Lacking notification of race on an ancestor's birth certificate can preclude access to certain state and federal entitlements and to the Kamehameha Schools, which require proof of Hawaiian ancestry.

Struggling for Survival: The Metaphorical Seeds of the Culture Remain

Despite the physical loss of the land and subsequent loss of sovereignty, many of the same structural patterns in and assumptions about the relationships between Hawaiians and their land and government can still be found in testimonies and petitions to the United States government regarding land use and government responsibility today. In other words when Hawaiians talk about ʻāina today, they still talk about it in terms of their traditional relationship to it (Aiu 1997). Osorio has noted that sometimes Hawaiians are talking more to each other in public hearings than to the officials present (2002:255). This means that despite the fact that colonizers create their own metaphors to describe the native peoples and their histories, traces of the native structures remain in the metaphorical landscape in much the same way that archaeological structures remain in the physical landscape. These traces need the right triggers or the right information to be seen and understood and therefore usually go untranslated.

For example, I have argued elsewhere that Hawaiians think of the land in terms of ʻohana, or family, and the metaphor ʻohana structures the way that Hawaiians talk about the land and the way that they think about it (Aiu 1997). When land is family, it has a different value from land that is thought of in purely economic terms. This relationship to the land is very deep-seated in most Hawaiians and forms a fundamental belief about who they are. For this reason Kameʻeleihiwa uses the term ʻāina rather than *land* in her writings, because it enables her to quickly use the code of a deeply felt metaphorical gestalt. Tymoczko indicates that this use of "code words" constitutes a form of double language among a colonized people and that it "destabilizes traditional rules of recognition and communicates a coded message to an initiated community" (2003b:38–39). I would argue that while Hawaiians may not all be bilingual, most do have the capability to understand Hawaiian "double language" when they hear or read culturally charged references to terms like ʻāina, pono, ʻohana, or even *Hawaiʻi*. The use of culturally laden Hawaiian terms and phrases can shift the tone of a testimony or speech because not only do the words signify their literal English translations but they are also code for native Hawaiian meanings, signifying what Hawaiians no longer have. Spoken by a Native Hawaiian, the words *land, righteousness,* and *family* do not merely signify the dominant concepts associated with the English terms; they are different and incomplete until reunited with Hawaiian practices and signifiers in the Hawaiian language, in this case *'āina, pono,* and *'ohana.*

Shifts in the use of these metaphors and gestalts when moving from references based on a Western worldview to a more Hawaiian worldview are not uncommon. Following Frantz Fanon, Tymoczko suggests that such discrepancies can sometimes lead to madness (2003b:39). I would like to suggest that it can also lead to brilliance and action as Hawaiians try to put themselves back together again. Hawaiian metaphorical gestalts help Hawaiians to 'ike Hawai'i even if they cannot 'ōlelo Hawai'i, and this reframing can lead to action, albeit action undertaken in English.

These deeply rooted metaphorical framings are aided by the elements of Hawaiian language and culture that remain firmly entrenched in common Hawaiian practices. For example, although the *hula* changed over time, the missionaries were never able to eradicate it completely. Hula continued to be practiced out of sight, particularly in rural areas, until its public performance was reinstated by Kalākaua at his coronation in 1883. Hawaiian songs accompanying the hula used Hawaiian words, even during the height of the *hapa-haole* craze in the 1950s and early 1960s.[5] Older Hawaiian songs, written in Hawaiian and transposed musically for the guitar and ukulele, remained popular among Hawaiians and others. My childhood was filled with songs sung in Hawaiian, even though I did not 'ōlelo Hawai'i. Songs were able to keep the sound of Hawaiian alive, even if the musicians or listeners didn't always understand what they were singing (Stillman 1989b). Anthems like "Kaulana na Pua" (Famous are the Flowers), written after the overthrow of Queen Lili'uokalani, have also become rallying points through time, with Hawaiians attributing different levels of meaning to the song as times and musical tastes change (Stillman 1999).[6]

The missionaries also helped to keep the language alive through their translations of the Bible into Hawaiian and through their training of Hawaiian missionaries in the Hawaiian language.[7] They also translated Christian hymns into Hawaiian. These hymns were incorporated into the services of the Hawaiian Church (Congregational) and spread to non-Congregational communities as well. Today Hawaiian church music is much beloved by Hawaiians of all faiths. Until very recently Kawaiaha'o Church in Honolulu, founded and attended by Hawaiian *ali'i* in the nineteenth century, had at least one service every Sunday in Hawaiian. This service was broadcast over KCCN, the only Hawaiian AM radio station in Honolulu. The practice has stopped because the church was not able to find a pastor who suited their needs and also spoke Hawaiian. Again, although many of the traditional metaphors remain embedded in both the Hawaiian language and English as spoken by Native Hawaiians, the relationships described by the language between Hawaiians and their god(s) is changing as the language moves into new arenas.

Hawaiians in rural areas have also retained many of their Hawaiian practices and Hawaiian ways even though Honolulu and Lahaina, the capitals, have changed drastically (McGregor 1989). It is from these rural areas that university-educated Hawaiians sought traditional knowledge during the Hawaiian renaissance in the second half of the twentieth century. Fortunately, when the Hawaiian renaissance finally came, there were still enough Hawaiians who had sufficient knowledge of old practices to build a base for the foundation of a renewed *lāhui* that could put 'ike and 'ōlelo together again. In many cases these people had kept the old relationships with the land, but had translated those relationships into English or pidgin.

In the 1970s as Hawaiian culture enjoyed a renaissance, many Hawaiians went back to school to learn their language. The State of Hawai'i became officially bilingual in 1978. Although Hawai'i is a bilingual state and although bilingual education had been ongoing since 1975, it wasn't until 1983 that the first Hawaiian language immersion preschool program was opened on Ni'ihau. Ni'ihau is a small, privately owned island north of Kaua'i, which has a permanent population of about 250 pure Hawaiians who still speak Hawaiian as their first language. Two years later Hawaiian language immersion preschools opened in Honolulu and Hilo. In 1987 the State Board of Education opened two immersion kindergartens and began to develop more extensive elementary curricula in Hawaiian. These schools do more than teach the Hawaiian language; they also attempt to teach elements of a Hawaiian worldview. Laiana Wong, a Hawaiian language instructor at the University of Hawai'i and one of the initial advocates for Hawaiian immersion schools, pointed out in a recent newspaper interview that "we don't want to . . . just offer an English curriculum using the Hawaiian language. We want the worldview to be Hawaiian as well" (*Honolulu*

Advertiser, 7 November 2005:A6). In other words he would like ʻike and ʻōlelo to reconnect.

Resistance at Kahoʻolawe: Re-placing Metaphors of ʻĀina

The island of Kahoʻolawe was claimed for the Navy in 1953 by Executive Order 10436 issued by President Dwight Eisenhower. The island was used as a live fire bombing target throughout World War II and the Korean and Vietnam Wars. In 1970, during the period of the Hawaiian renaissance and as an expression of the Hawaiian sovereignty movement, Kahoʻolawe was occupied by Hawaiians who redefined the island not as dead but as the sacred lands of Kanaloa, Hawaiian god of the sea.

According to the historian Tom Coffman, for the Hawaiian sovereignty movement Kahoʻolawe "was the really transforming event. Kahoʻolawe was different. Kahoʻolawe was special. It was such a desolate place, so damaged, and such a Hawaiian place beneath its surface that it became a metaphor" (qtd. by Gordon Pang, *Honolulu Advertiser*, 30 January 2007). Nine people landed on Kahoʻolawe initially on 4 May 1976; although seven were immediately picked up by military police, two remained on the island for two days. They hid from the Navy and explored the island before turning themselves in to authorities. According to Walter Ritte, one of the two men who stayed on the island, "It was the island that shared herself with us. It was the island that told me, 'Hey, I'm dying.' So, after that one trip, it was a total commitment not to allow that island to die" (*Honolulu Advertiser*, 30 January 2007). This "occupation" of Kahoʻolawe led to a series of similar confrontations with the United States military. Ultimately the movement resulted in a Consent Decree with the United States Navy in 1980, allowing Hawaiians to have access to the island for one weekend a month.[8]

In 1990 President George H. W. Bush established the Kahoʻolawe Island Conveyance Commission and ordered the live bombing stopped while the Commission took testimony to decide what to do. Elsewhere I (1997) have analyzed at length the metaphors of Kahoʻolawe and the 20-year struggle to get the island back into Hawaiian hands. This was achieved in 1993 when the island was land-banked for the future Hawaiian nation and the U.S. Navy was ordered to clean it of ordnance. The return of Kahoʻolawe provides a land base where the metaphors that connect ʻike and ʻōlelo can be re-placed. Those metaphors and the use of Hawaiian in the testimony heard by the Kahoʻolawe Island Conveyance Commission played an important role in the struggle to get the island back into Hawaiian hands.

One can characterize the testimony of the Kahoʻolawe Island Conveyance hearings as a struggle between competing metaphors of the land, with dominant English metaphors on one side and Native Hawaiian ones on the other (Aiu 1997). However, for the Hawaiian metaphors to be heard, either one must enter into a Hawaiian worldview or the speaker has to be able to convey the deeply held connection between Hawaiians and the land. Both are very difficult because there are so few who understand the full implications of the Hawaiian metaphors, much less the Hawaiian language.

Initially at the first hearing of the Commission, held on Molokaʻi (9 April 1991), the issue of translators never came up. However, at the second hearing in Hilo, on 17 April 1991, no translators were provided, making participation impossible for speakers who wanted to testify in Hawaiian. It is significant that a number of people wished to speak in Hawaiian even though they were fluent in English. As a result of the lack of translators and the inability of the Commission members to understand Hawaiian, one witness left the meetings rather than testify in English and several others in the audience also departed. The incident brings into question the commitment of the Commission to actually listen to Hawaiians.

Part of what is interesting about this incident is the refusal of Hawaiians to translate themselves. Although all the speakers who wished to testify were fluent English speakers, with English their language of schooling, they chose to assert their affiliation to Hawaiian values by speaking in the Hawaiian language and demanding to be translated. The demand for translation was tantamount to a demand for cultural recognition and official acknowledgment of cultural difference and legitimacy. As a condition of participation in the hearings, the resistance movement insisted on official government translation into English rather than the self-translation that had been required of Hawaiians for more than a century. As a result the Commission was forced to hold another hearing in Hilo on 8 May 1991 to give Hawaiian-language speakers a chance to testify with a translator present.

Colonized people often feel they must self-translate or they will not be heard. Certainly when Hawaiians refuse to translate, they often in fact are not heard. In the case at hand, I believe that the woman who left the first Hilo meeting never attended the second, because the list of attendees was not the same. We'll never know what she meant to say.

Despite the communication paradox inherent in the speaker's choices—either to speak a language no one could hear and understand or not to speak at all—I would argue that speaking in Hawaiian in this context was important for two reasons. First, it allowed speakers to maintain their own worldview and forced the commissioners to enter the Hawaiian worldview, rather than the other way around. Second, by forcing a Hawaiian worldview on the listeners, especially in the setting of a Hawaiian hearing, the speaker indicated that he or she refused to be translated into something more comprehensible and perhaps more palatable to English speakers. The structure of language helps to structure the world and refusing self-translation is an indication that one refuses to allow one's own structural metaphors to be replaced. The issue of language, its deep meanings, and its importance for the individual and the community are all forced to the forefront.

Even when speaking in English, speakers sprinkled Hawaiian throughout their testimony. For example, at the Oʻahu hearings (25 April 1991), ʻEkela Kaniaupio testified in Hawaiian first and then in English; even in the English portion of her testimony she cited Harry Mitchell telling her "ka waiwai ʻo ka ʻāina, ka waiwai ʻo nā kupuna" (Aiu 1997:133). Literally the quote means "the wealth of the land, the wealth of the kupuna," but it means more than that. First of all, the reference to Uncle Harry Mitchell indicates he was a *kupuna*, literally a grandparent, but the term means a respected elder. Hawaiian familial terms don't differentiate absolutely between one's nuclear family and one's extended family. In this speech the reference to Uncle Harry Mitchell serves in itself as a metaphor or gestalt for the Kahoʻolawe movement and evokes an important type of relationship for the people who knew him, learned from him, and loved him. Those people were able to hear the quote in his voice and reframe it within the worldview that he taught them. Second, *waiwai*, the Hawaiian word for wealth, literally means 'waterwater'. In a Hawaiian sense wealth and land cannot be separated, for water is what makes a land rich and fruitful. The way Hawaiian water was distributed and cultivated is symbolic of the relationships of Hawaiian people to each other and their Mōʻī. For those who could hear, Ms. Kaniaupio was emphatically stating that she wanted the land valued in a way not measured by money. If one is familiar with a Hawaiian *loʻi*, or taro patch, one knows that it is an oasis for sharing food, sharing stories, and sharing time. These are the things that comprise one's wealth. One cannot say all that succinctly in English, but when Ms. Kaniaupio said it in Hawaiian, she brought all that meaning to the fore and re-placed the wealth of a military nation with the wai that brings wealth to the ʻāina. Thus, even when witnesses testified to the Commission in English, the use of Hawaiian words and Hawaiian worldviews within English-language testimony served to resist the dissociation of the Hawaiian land not only from the metaphors used to connect the land to the people but also from the Hawaiian people themselves.

Today, 33 years after the Kahoʻolawe Nine landed on Kahoʻolawe, the military has spent more than 400 million dollars to clear the island of un-exploded ordnance. The Kahoʻolawe Island Commission, which oversees the cleanup and access to the island, is chaired by Dr. Emmet Aluli, one of the Kahoʻolawe Nine. Ironically, because of the ordnance on the island, it will never be developed, which is how most people would like it to stay.

A Rising Tide: Can Hawaiian Metaphors Take Root in Cultivated Soil?

The Kamehameha Schools were founded in 1887, the same year that sugar interests passed the Bayonet Constitution allowing any Caucasian male to vote in Hawaiian elections, thus eroding native political power (see Osorio 2002 and above).[9] The schools were created by the will of Princess Bernice Pauahi Bishop and funded through the income generated by her vast estates. As the last of Kamehameha's direct line, Pauahi inherited more than 375,000 acres of land from various Hawaiian *aliʻi*. The haole trustees of her estate established a Hawaiian preference policy for the schools, which has meant that with few exceptions only students of Hawaiian ancestry have attended the schools since their inception 120 years ago. In the past ten years, the Hawaiian preference policy has been challenged in court, and in August 2005 the Ninth Circuit Court declared the schools' Hawaiian preference policy unconstitutional (John Doe v. Kamehameha). A successful appeal for an *en banc* review by the 15 Ninth Circuit judges resulted in an 8–7 decision in favor of Kamehameha on 5 December 2006. The plaintiffs appealed to the United States Supreme Court, but all parties arrived at a settlement on 15 May 2007.

Although the point of this essay is not to delve into the history of legal challenges to the schools, it is worth making a brief foray into the atmosphere in which a series of lawsuits could eventually make Kamehameha's unique status as a Hawaiian school obsolete. The Hawaiian preference policy has been challenged in the past and was upheld by the Internal Revenue Service because children of all nationalities and ethnicities were admitted to the schools as long as they were also part Hawaiian. At present, however, there is a trend in the United States to challenge affirmative action laws, including those designed to address Native Hawaiians. Hawaiian entitlements have been the target of a series of lawsuits against the Office of Hawaiian Affairs (Rice v. Cayetano), the Department of Hawaiian Homelands (Arakaki v. Cayetano; Arakaki v. Lingle) and the Kamehameha Schools (Mohica-Cummings v. Kamehameha Schools, settled out of court; John Doe v. Kamehameha Schools). Although local names appear on the lawsuits, the suits are part of a larger movement by groups like the Heritage Foundation and the Society for a Colorblind America which are dedicated to the defeat of affirmative action and opposed to the expansion of native and minority rights in the United States.[10] Both organizations filed amicus briefs in the Rice v. Cayetano case and are believed to help fund the legal effort to destroy Hawaiian entitlement programs.

In addition to the schools' policy being the target of a concerted national effort to rid the United States of affirmative action programs, there were other motives for the Kamehameha suits. Hawai'i is a very expensive place to live; it also has a dismal public education system and a long history of very good private schools. For a long time Kamehameha was a trade school, but in the 1960s it began to put more of its students on a college-bound track and today sends about 90 percent of its students to college. It is a large school with a wealth of resources, and tuition is far less than the nearly $15,000 per year charged by other top private schools in Hawai'i. Those who support the lawsuit feel that all of the children of Hawai'i regardless of race should have access to Kamehameha's heavily subsidized educational programs.

Kamehameha, however, is not merely an educational institution; it is a source of Hawaiian pride and a keeper and perpetuator of some aspects of Hawaiian culture. It is also one of the state's largest landowners. Thus, each of the campuses has the potential to put 'ike and 'ōlelo together again. Over the years Kamehameha has moved toward a more Hawaiian curriculum. The school has installed *Ke Ala Pono*, or the right path, which uses Hawaiian concepts such as *mālama* (to care for) and *lōkahi* (unity or

harmony) as the means to becoming the "virtuous men and women" that
Bernice Pauahi Bishop specifically articulated as a goal in her endowment
of the Kamehameha Schools. More important, in many of the classes, the
students and teachers refer in Hawaiian to Ke Ala Pono concepts as part of
their discussions, leading to a more Hawaiian way of thinking about place.
Thus, a discussion in geography class will not only talk about the location
of the school in terms of longitude and lattitude, but will also include a
discussion of the *ahupuaʻa*, or Hawaiian land division, in which the school
is located. A science class will focus on *laulima*, the importance of working together, and the students use these words as a kind of double language
which functions within the framework of a Western learning environment
but ties them back to their Hawaiian cultural roots. Today, you can hear
Hawaiian spoken on the Kamehameha campuses every day, which is symbolic of the extent to which the language has revived since the schools
were first founded.

Moreover, the institution televises an annual song contest every year
in which the four high school classes compete in singing Hawaiian choral
music. Its Concert Glee Club, Hawaiian Ensemble, and marching band take
Hawaiian music and dance throughout the nation and the world. The
schools have also produced many of today's Hawaiian leaders including
Senator Daniel Akaka, former Maui Mayor James Apana, Olympic Swim-
mer Duke Kahanamoku, and scholars Lilikalā Kameʻeleihiwa and Hau-
nani Kay Trask, as well as a long list of Hawaiian musicians.

In response to the Ninth Circuit Court's initial decision against the
Hawaiian preference policy, a rally was held on 27 August 2005 on the
grounds of the ʻIolani Palace in downtown Honolulu. At that rally several
speakers were invited to talk about the impact of the John Doe v. Kamehameha decision on Hawaiʻi and Hawaiians. Lilikalā Kameʻeleihiwa and
Hina Wong spoke in Hawaiian. Both are graduates of the schools.
Kameʻeleihiwa is the former Chair of the Center for Hawaiian Studies at
the University of Hawaiʻi. Hina Wong is a teacher at Hālau Lōkahi New
Century Charter School. Other speakers included Trustees Diane Plotts,
Douglas Ing, and Nainoa Thompson, who spoke in English. Robbie Alm, a
kamaʻāina non-Hawaiian business leader spoke on how the decision violated his right to have *aloha* for the Hawaiians. Texts of the trustees'
speeches are available on the Kamehameha website (www.ksbe.edu/
lawsuit.php) and the testimony of Mr. Alm was published in the *Honolulu*

Advertiser. However, I have been unable to find the texts of the Hawaiian speakers' speeches in English or Hawaiian.

Why give a speech or testify in Hawaiian, especially at a rally where most of the people are Hawaiian but don't 'ōlelo Hawai'i and where the text might not be translated or even recorded? Because both Hawaiian speakers in fact also translated what they said, speaking in Hawaiian first and English second must send an important message. Osorio asks, "How do we protect our *lāhui*, our kinship with one another? Do we conform our responses within the framework of the American political system, hoping we might bring new benefits to our children thereby, or do we insist on clinging to every tradition that we can recover, insisting on our separateness, our distinctness, from a society that seemingly regards such distinction as anachronistic and dangerous?" (2002:255). Speaking in Hawaiian first, I would argue, is code for keeping traditions, for indicating that one is working on putting 'ike and 'ōlelo together again, even in the face of crowds who do not understand and even on behalf of a powerful mainstream institution that was itself part of the colonization of Hawai'i.[11] Ironically, speaking Hawaiian at a rally for the Kamehameha Schools is an indication that the Hawaiian language has come full circle, because the rally was attended by many mainstream non-Hawaiians, including the governor, who publicly support the school's mission. In this case Hawaiian is not only a language of resistance against anyone who might pass judgment on this special institution; it symbolizes the uniqueness of Hawai'i as opposed to the rest of the United States and puts that difference foremost as one of the reasons for the schools' policies.

Furthermore, the majority of those who did understand the Hawaiian parts of the speech were more than likely of the *'ōpio* generation—teens attending Kamehameha, one of the Hawaiian-based charter schools, or one of the immersion schools, as well as students at the University of Hawai'i. In other words those who understand Hawaiian are tomorrow's leaders and the message being sent was to them. Speaking in Hawaiian is an 'ike Hawai'i moment and helps Hawaiians focus on their kinship and Hawaiian identity, which Osorio (2002:255) says are two of the few things that we have left with which to rebuild a nation. Even though the Kamehameha Schools can rally many people to its cause, speaking in Hawaiian redefines resistance to the legal decisions as not being restricted to the schools. Speaking in Hawaiian suggests that the schools are in part about being Hawaiian, having a Hawaiian place, and being able to define one's own cultural metaphors.

Many non-Hawaiians accept these perspectives because Hawaiians and their relationships to the land make Hawaiʻi unique.

Conclusion: Neʻe Papa I Ke Ō Mau—Moving Forward as One

In a world where most people do not understand the metaphors and worldview of Hawaiians, how can Hawaiians get their meaning across to non-Hawaiian speakers? The choice of whether or not to translate one's language is a tricky one for colonized cultures. I have argued here that Hawaiians often choose not to translate because refusal to translate allows Hawaiian speakers to keep the context of their language intact. For example, as we saw earlier, using the term *waiwai* allows a speaker to maintain the connection between wealth, water, and land, which disappears when only the term *wealth* is used. Maintaining these connections keeps intact an important tie between ʻike, the thought, and ʻōlelo, the word. Saying "the wealth of the land is in the kupuna" is meaningless in English. The terms *waiwai* and *kupuna* emphasize the importance of both water and the knowledge that the kupuna as respected elders have about water in a particular land area. This knowledge of the land is also a kind of wealth. In a real sense, the saying cannot be translated without losing meaning and value.

Choosing to speak in Hawaiian first at a rally makes a similar statement about the importance of the Hawaiian worldview. At the rally for the Kamehameha Schools, speaking in Hawaiian first established Hawaiian rights of primacy in this fight. It asserted that resistance to the lawsuit was not just about equal rights to education but also about the uniqueness of Hawaiians and their right to teach their children about keeping ʻike and ʻōlelo linked in the modern world. At the same time, because it was important for the gist of the argument to be heard and understood by everyone, those who spoke in Hawaiian at the Kamehameha rally also chose to translate their speeches into English.

Resistance to translation can also take the form of choosing not to speak at all if one can't speak in one's own language. Because the United States and Hawaiʻi in particular require translation assistance as part of a person's right to free speech, not allowing native speakers to be heard through translators raises serious constitutional questions about the validity of any public hearing. These factors notwithstanding, Hawaiian speakers are often overlooked and translation is often seen as unnecessary by public officials. The insistence on official translation and the refusal to self-translate in such situations forces public recognition of Hawai'i's autonomous language and culture.

In Hawai'i knowledge of some key Hawaiian words is essential because Hawaiian is the host culture of the state. Therefore the survival of the language at some level is important. A recent *ho'okuleana* (be responsible) campaign initiated by the State Department of Land and Natural Resources taps into Hawaiians' deep-seated sense of responsibility to the land and to the fact that environmentalists in Hawai'i have been touting everyone's kuleana to take care of the land. Although I have reservations about this sort of use of the Hawaiian language because it uses 'ōlelo without 'ike, the appeal of the campaign shows that people are learning to use the language and metaphors of Hawai'i, largely because those metaphors still evoke powerful feelings about the land. Even for non-speakers of Hawaiian, there are certain terms that demonstrate that 'ike and 'ōlelo remain connected.

In relation to translation, resistance can take different forms, depending on one's desired outcome. In the case of the 'Aha Pūnana Leo, the choice not to translate its theme "Ne'e papa i ke ō mau" may have resulted from a sense that translation was unnecessary, as dictionaries are readily available. It may also have been left untranslated because it was seen as a matter of politeness or even an inside joke. Ultimately, however, the choice not to translate strengthens the position of the Hawaiian language. Since you cannot understand Hawaiian without understanding a Hawaiian worldview, perceptions about land and culture are forced to change. When this happens, how we think and speak—'ike and 'ōlelo—also change to accommodate the worldview that goes with the Hawaiian language. While this change is slow, over time there is a definite shift. Like the movement of a tsunami or a phalanx of soldiers, changes in worldview are subtle, patient, and inevitable.

I have used the word "ironic" several times in this essay because Hawaiians' sense of irony is heightened, I think, by having to live in two different gestalts simultaneously. Hawaiian is also a multilayered language, one in which the phrase "Ne'e papa i ke ō mau" is both a call for unity when translated and a rallying cry for a Hawaiian worldview when untranslated. The irony is that in this situation both translation and non-translation work to empower Hawaiians.

Glossary of Hawaiian Terms

'āina: land

ahupua'a: land division, usually running from the mountain to the sea, encompassing all resources necessary for living.

ali'i: person of chiefly rank

aloha: Hawaiian greeting; love

haole: white person, American, Englishman

hapa-haole: half white

hula: Hawaiian dance accompanied by music. There are two forms of hula, the kahiko,or old style hula, and the auana or modern hula. Most people are more familiar with hula auana.

'ike: knowledge or sight

kama'āina: native born. Used to refer to people who are born and raised in Hawai'i.

kapu: taboo, prohibition

kuleana: right, privilege, concern, responsibility

kupuna: elder; grandparent

lāhui: nation

laulima: to work together, as a group

lo'i: irrigated terrace, especially for taro

lōkahi: unity, agreement, accord

maka'āinana: commoner, citizen

mālama: to take care of, tend

mana: supernatural or divine power, spiritual essence

mō'ī: king, sovereign, monarch

'ōlelo: word, language

pono: goodness, uprightness, morality

waiwai: wealth; lit. waterwater

Notes

1. See Tymoczko 1994, 1999, 2000b, 2003b on the effects of colonization on the Irish and its implications for language and translation.

2. The kapu system was a set of religious and sumptuary laws ruling the lives of Hawaiians. The most noted aspect of this law was the *'ai kapu*, which among other things forbade women and men eating together. Ka'ahumanu and Keōpuōlani, high-ranking wives of Kamehameha, signaled the destruction of the kapu by eating with Liholiho (Kamehameha II), Kamehameha's heir, soon after the death of the king. See Sahlins 1981.

3. See Lakoff and Johnson (1980) on the importance of metaphorical gestalts and cognitive metaphors.

4. See Kameʻeleihiwa (1992) for a thorough discussion of the connection between land, culture, and language in Hawaiian society.

5. Hapa-haole music is mostly in English with some Hawaiian words, and the music usually emphasizes romance and the exotic elements of Hawaiʻi. Songs like "Waikiki," "Sweet Leilani," and "I Want to Go Back to My Little Grass Shack" embody the music from this era.

6. For example, Stillman (1999) suggests that "Kaulana na Pua" was also performed as a hula in the days after the counter-revolution mentioned above, but today it is considered a sacred song that should not be accompanied by a hula.

7. See also the essay by Carcelen-Estrada in this volume for a discussion of impact of missionary activity and Bible translation on indigenous language, land use, economics, and sovereignty among the Amazonian tribes in Ecuador.

8. For many years the Hawaiian sovereignty movement was relatively small. Today it is far more organized, although there are still different groups advocating for different aspects of sovereignty. For example, Ka Lāhui Hawaiʻi advocates a nation-within-a-nation, using a model developed by the United Nations. The Nation of Hawaiʻi advocates restoration of the Nation of Hawaiʻi and complete secession from the United States. By contrast, the Kingdom of Hawaiʻi advocates a return of the monarchy. Despite these differences, all the groups remain united over the return of Kahoʻolawe.

9. The institution of the Kamehameha Schools is referred to in the plural for a number of reasons. Originally there was a Kamehameha School for Boys and a Kamehameha School for Girls. When the schools became co-educational, the plural name was retained, in part because there were at that point also a Kamehameha Elementary School, a Kamehameha Middle School, and a Kamehameha High School. All of these were located at the Kapālama Campus in Honolulu, Oʻahu. Today, there are three campuses, each offering K–12 education, one on Maui, one on Hawaiʻi, and one on Oʻahu at the original Kapālama campus.

10. See www.heritage.org/Research/LegalIssues/wmHawaii.cfm.

11. Like other schools, Kamehameha participated in assimilating Hawaiian children into Western culture.

DENISE MERKLE

Secret Literary Societies in Late Victorian England

$\mathbf{D}$URING the second half of Queen Victoria's reign, social fragmentation was being generated by antagonistic social and political forces,
creating what Ernesto Laclau and Chantal Mouffe have referred to as a "fis-
sure" of ideological constructs in need of being "filled up" (1985:7). Not
surprisingly this was also a period of intense translation activity, one response to the sociopolitical context. At least at the outset, the 1880s were a
period of optimism; writers and thinkers believed that the time was ripe for
greater scientific curiosity and literary openness to heretofore taboo subjects after more than a century of predominant puritan values, with duty and
self-control the watchwords of public decorum.[1] Attempts were made to import texts that communicated alternative worldviews and innovative ideas
about sex and sexuality in an effort to renew British literature and culture;
during the period translation appears as a force for cultural (trans)for-
mation (Gentzler 2001:194) or as a reaction to a perceived "intellectual/
cultural lack" (Ellis and Oakley-Brown 2001:5). At the same time, when
texts contested the overarching patriarchal worldview of the British Empire
during this period of (sociological) tensions at home and (colonial) contestations abroad, they were often perceived as threats to the preservation of
the Victorian status quo, and socially sanctioned presses continued to refuse to publish them.

In view of these constraints, it is reasonable to expect that all foreign
texts would have been subjected to close censorial scrutiny. In fact such was
not the case. Untranslated foreign texts circulated freely in Britain (Speirs

2003:85), but the same cannot be said for translated foreign texts. Writers such as André Theuriet and Octave Feuillet, whose novels had won morality prizes in France (Portebois 2003:66), were approved by British moral authorities. But novels that did not serve as innocent entertainment or that were socially disruptive and sexually explicit were condemned. Those who wished to publish the latter did so at the risk of being prosecuted.

One alternative available to translators was clandestine publishing, at times financed completely or in part through the creation of a secret literary society made up of the publication's subscribers. Émile Zola's writings which were censored in translation were published by such a society in the 1890s; similarly, Eastern sex manuals as well as two unexpurgated translations of the *Arabian Nights* were published by such societies in the 1880s. In this essay I explore whether translators who had their translations published in connection with Victorian secret literary societies were resisting the constraints imposed by the cultural hegemony of Victorian England and, if so, to what degree. Two figures are closely tied to these secret societies: the imperialist adventurer and explorer Richard Burton (associated with the Kamashastra Society of London and Benares), and the publisher of pornography Leonard Smithers (associated with the Erotika Biblion Society of Athens and the Lutetian Society). The questions that underpin this study are the following. Were Burton and Smithers "submissive translators," to use the terminology of Theo Hermans (1999:134), simply reinforcing Victorian norms by dominating through translation the imperial rival (France) and the colonized Other (the Orient)? Were they instead "self-conscious resistant" and subversive translators (Hermans 1999:134), actively trying to renew their culture and to fill a gap by freeing the readers of their translations "from the cultural constraints that ordinarily govern their reading and writing" (Venuti 1995:305)? Or were they perhaps both submissive and resistant translators responding to the coexistence of dominant and emergent cultural transformations associated with the complex sociocultural dynamic of which they were products and in which they worked? Before examining their respective translation projects, let us consider the social and discursive constraints facing the translators.

Victorian Control of Discourse and Obscenity

Victorian England permitted the free circulation of a great deal of foreign literature, for example, Zola's so-called pornographic novels and Henrik

Ibsen's revolutionary plays, as well as Greek and Latin erotic—often homoerotic—classics, without the threat of legal prosecution, provided that the works were not translated.[2] Translations, however, were subject to prosecution, for, as Dorothy Speirs explains, "those who were sufficiently cultured to read [foreign books] were less likely to suffer moral damage than were the less well-educated, who could read only a translation" (2003:85). The authorities sought to ensure that pernicious literature was kept out of the hands of women, young readers, and the middle classes, who could not be trusted to read such books "critically"; rather they were to read literature that was morally uplifting with characters (ideally from the upper classes) that gave good examples of moral conduct in keeping with the English "teach and delight" tradition (Decker 1952:31). Generally speaking, literary works that did not provide examples of good moral conduct were considered obscene, which explains the British establishment's condemnation of French naturalist (e.g., Zola's *Assommoir*) and realist (e.g., Flaubert's *Madame Bovary*) literature, as well as of Ibsen's plays (e.g., *Nora*, also called *A Doll's House*).

Obscenity was regulated by means of so-called obscene libel laws which had been passed to control publishers of books for the general public. Whereas books made available to the public could be cause for prosecution, privately printed books could not. The Obscene Publications Act of 1857 gave the courts and the police increased powers primarily to keep the low-end pornography trade out of the hands of the middle classes. The term *pornography* "began to enter the language of international moral campaigners in the early 1880s. . . . In England, however, the first public literary debate about pornography emerged over Burton's translation of the *Arabian Nights*" (Colligan 2002:117–18), largely in response to a section of his "Terminal Essay" bearing the title "Pornography" (Burton 1885–86:10.63–302; see esp. pp. 203–5). Both aristocratic collectors of erotica and supporters of the purity movements agreed that, like objectionable translations, "pornographic literature should be kept out of the hands of the young and ignorant who . . . could only focus on its sexual/immoral content, whereas the educated had the capacity to enjoy its aesthetic and intellectual . . . content as well. Works of a pornographic nature . . . were not an offense before the law so long as they were not available to the young and the uneducated" (Nelson 2000:357n55).

Scientific curiosity about sex and sexuality had grown over the century, ostensibly a natural consequence of puritanical repression, and had

culminated in the emergence of the private printing of uncensored translations of Eastern sex manuals, considered obscene literature, during the latter
decades of the century. The original languages of these manuals were not
mastered by many Britons, even the well educated, so there was a manifest
need for these works in translation, aimed primarily at upper-class men.[3] In
what Colette Colligan (2002) refers to as a flourishing clandestine industry,
obscene works were published for specialized markets. Included in the
grouping "obscene" was literature designed to educate (sex manuals) as well
as literature designed to titillate. "Titillating" literature of primary interest
to male readers included both male/female and male/male pornography.
Reading randy Greek and Latin classics at private school solidified strong
"homosocial bonds" among the sons of privilege, and "the boys' club" was
also a gentleman's reaction against the turbulence created by the New
Woman, a rebellious working class, and middle-class dandies (Middleton
2003:136–37). Much of nineteenth-century pornography was clearly misogynic; women were vilified and objectified, often to an abject degree, particularly later in the century (Kabbani 1986). Moreover, as Byrne Fone has
ably argued, the pornography industry can be at its most "effulgent" when
the official discourse is puritan (1995:117).

During the 1880s the social purity movements gathered momentum
to protect traditional family values by fighting against prostitution; at the
same time various avant-garde ideas pertaining to Victorian feminism,
homosexuality, and sexual libertarianism were also on the rise, supported
by associated social movements. The extremism of the morality leagues,
however, buttressed by the Criminal Law Amendment Act of 1885, severely
curtailed liberty of expression. In fact, any book that "call[ed] the mantling
blush to the maiden cheek" (Decker 1952:9), i.e., any book that was not
listed by the circulating libraries, ran the risk of being attacked by conservative criticism and prosecuted, if it was not relegated to the private domain
of secret literary societies and private presses. Secret literary societies were
ephemeral and composed of relatively few members (usually between 100
and 1,000 subscribers), essentially upper-class men. A number of these
societies—including the Kamashastra, Villon, Athenian, and Lutetian—
published for distribution to their members texts such as unexpurgated
translations of Greek plays, realistic French novels, decadent French poetry, and erotic Latin verse.

Although secret societies are usually considered to be subversive, generally playing a part in revolts against the existing social order by buttressing

openly subversive movements (Webster 1936:3), the status of Victorian secret literary societies is less clear. These societies were perpetuating—perhaps inadvertently so—the existing order by limiting access to unexpurgated books to the upper classes, principally men. A reversal of what are traditionally considered to be the male and female spheres of activity, this situation appears to contradict Pierre Bourdieu's conception of social dominance. In his view, the private, silent, and censured realm is reserved for the dominated: women, workers, children (1980:227). Curiously, in Victorian England it appears that it was the powerful group who was relegated to the private domain. Yet, it must be recalled that censorial mechanisms were at play at the time and, as Bourdieu explains, when censorship imposes recourse to unofficial forms of power (1982:169), alternative strategies for the accumulation of symbolic capital will be found by the socially and politically adept. Richard Burton and Leonard Smithers managed to sell their translations and avoid legal prosecution by creating unofficial (i.e., invisible) literary societies and by printing privately. Thus, the question remains to be answered: were their activities those of self-conscious, resistant translators, or did they also surreptitiously collude with the moral authorities and dominant norms of their society?

The Kamashastra Society of London and Benares and *The Thousand Nights and a Night*

Founded by Richard Francis Burton and Forster Fitzgerald Arbuthnot, the Kamashastra Society is best known for its publication in 1885–86 of Burton's eroticized translation of the *Alf Layla wa Layla*, issued as *A Plain and Literal Translation of the Arabian Nights' Entertainments, now Entituled [sic] The Book of the Thousand Nights and a Night, with Introduction, Explanatory Notes on the Manners and Customs of Moslem Men and a Terminal Essay upon the History of The Nights*. Also called the Kama Shastra Society, the society identified its imprints as being published in Benares, in London and Benares, or occasionally in Cosmopoli. Burton and Arbuthnot are the names associated with the highly secretive society, which was formed in order to print limited editions of various Eastern works, chiefly of an erotic nature, including the *Kama Sutra of Vatsyayana* (1883), the *Ananga-ranga . . . or, The Hindu Art of Love* (1885), and *The Perfumed Garden of the Cheikh Nefzaoui* (1886). The translations are generally attributed to Burton, to Arbuthnot, or to both men, but the translators' names were suppressed, though in some cases inverted initials were used. All but *The*

Thousand Nights and a Night appear to have been relegated in the Library of the British Museum to the depository for morally objectionable publications, the private case, "inaugurated in the tradition of keeping wanton books as a preserve of a small circle of privileged men of letters, rich amateurs, and dilettanti" (Fryer 1966:50). The so-called society existed from 1883 until 1890, the year of Burton's death (Penzer 1967:12). Very little, if any, documentation of its activities has survived. Burton's wife, Isabel, later estimated that it was only the foreign Benares location that had saved the Burtons from prosecution for having published *The Thousand Nights and a Night* in particular (quoted in Nelson 2000:15).

Richard Francis Burton (1821–90) was born into a military family. A freethinking nineteenth-century explorer and wanderer, most notably throughout Arabia, Burton was also a linguist, translator, travel writer, and scholar. Those who sought greater freedom of sexual expression and who rebelled against puritan values could leave the British Isles, thanks to imperialist expansion. The "Orientalist-cum-imperial-agent" (Said 1978:196) looked to the Orient for exotic sexual experiences unobtainable in England and wrote about them. Rana Kabbani has suggested that Burton's obsessive curiosity sought out manifestations of sexual activity that differed significantly from what was considered acceptable at home, sharing an interest in sexual deviancy with his friend Richard Monckton Milnes, who kept the largest known collection of pornography in his day (1986:55) and who nonetheless became a trustee of the British Museum in 1881 (Fryer 1966:50). Burton, however, was also to some degree a sexual reformer, ridiculing what he considered to be the mock modesty of Victorian women. Although he seems to have found himself frequently in conflict with authority figures, he nonetheless reproduced the patriarchal perspective of Victorian attitudes in his writings and translations. In keeping with his apparent proclivity for contradiction, in 1861 Burton married Isabel Arundell (1831–96), a staunch Catholic, who often accompanied him on his travels. Believing her husband to be one of the great men of their age, she did all in her power to present a public image of him as noble and morally upright.

In the 1880s Europe's imperial interest in Africa grew rapidly along with an interest in anthropology, often a euphemism for scientific racism at the time. Egypt and the Suez Canal were under British "protection." Imperialist Britons seeking military careers were motivated to learn Arabic and as much as possible about Islamic culture. Studying a "classic" of Arabic literature in translation was considered an excellent initiation to the linguistic and cultural alterity of the Arabs. Recognized as one of the most knowledgeable Orientalists of his day, Richard Burton had hoped for an appointment in an Arab colony, but coveted posts were withheld from him and official recognition denied (until his wife finally managed to garner him a knighthood in 1886). Burton had been effectively marginalized as a result of his scandalous language and behavior, which kept him in Trieste where he had held a consulship since 1872. From this outpost he collaborated on translation projects from Arabic, as well as other languages.

The traditional Victorian marriage-cum-partnership (in appearance at least) of Richard and Isabel Burton could not be more revealing of the Victorian moral double standard in the publishing industry. Richard Burton published eroticized translations with the collaboration of his wife. While he was a sexual libertarian who sought freedom of expression, writing from Trieste, "I don't live in England and don't care a damn for the Public Opinion" (Wright 1906/1968:2.42–43), she sided with the purity movements that supported censorship. Nonetheless, she sent out 34,000 circulars to potential male subscribers of the *Nights*, though not before having sought legal counsel about the Obscene Publications Act through the criminal lawyer George Lewis, who had worked for the National Vigilance Association (Colligan 2002:119). Burton's *Nights* was published in 1,000 limited edition sets of ten volumes. His seven-volume *Supplemental Nights* was published between 1886 and 1888. The seventeen volumes were fully subscribed and "netted a hefty initial profit of £10,000, followed by royalties from the library edition," for which Isabel later sold the rights (Phillips 1999:249). Burton's unexpurgated verse translation was well on its way to dethroning Edward Lane's (1839–41) expurgated translation aimed at a mass readership.[4]

In July 1885 the flamboyant adventurer distributed the first volume of his limited edition to subscribers who had paid the hefty fee of one guinea per volume. He eroticized his *Arabian Nights* in defiance of Victorian moral norms and of his wife (or so it would appear), discoursing on exotic sexual behavior in his translation, while making a tidy fortune through the enterprise. Isabel by contrast began shortly thereafter to publish a severely bowdlerized version of the book in six volumes dedicated to "the Women of England": *Lady Burton's Edition of her Husband's Arabian Nights: Translated Literally from the Arabic. Prepared for Household Reading by Justin Huntly McCarthy, M.P.* (1886–88). It appears therefore, in keeping with Victorian social roles and their "conventional marriage," that Richard Burton wrote for the "gentleman's club" by publishing "in private" and Isabel Burton for the "angel in the house" by publishing for the public.[5]

In fact, on 15 August 1885 Burton wrote to *The Academy* to emphasize the limited accessibility of his translation: "One of my principal objects in making the work so expensive . . . is to keep it from the general public. For this reason I have no publisher. The translation is printed by myself for the use of select personal friends; and nothing could be more repugnant to my feelings than the idea of a book of the kind being placed in a publisher's hands, and sold over the counter" (quoted in Colligan 2002:199). Yet, despite his "best efforts," it appears that some of his translations did indeed make their way into women's bedrooms. In a letter sent to the newspaper *The Echo* after her husband's death, Isabel Burton wrote that were her husband still alive, "He would have been surrounded by friends to whom he could have explained any objections or controversies, and would have done everything to guard against the incalculable harm of his purchasers lending [his work] to their women friends and to their boyish acquaintances" (quoted in Wright 1906/1968:265).

To better understand what is meant by an "eroticized translation" prepared for "students and scholars" (and printed by a private press) versus a text prepared for "household reading" or for British women (and printed by a socially sanctioned press), two excerpts have been reproduced below from the story of King Shahrayar and his brother, the misogynic frame tale that sets the scene for Shahrazad's storytelling and that opens the *Arabian Nights*. Two versions are given following Richard Burton's text to provide a standard of comparison: the "bowdlerized Burton" edited by Isabel Burton and McCarthy and a modern scholarly translation by Husain Haddawy (1990). Passages excised by Isabel Burton and McCarthy are emphasized in Richard Burton's translation, and words added or changed by Isabel Burton and McCarthy are emphasized in the passage from their edition.

> . . . so he returned privily and entered his apartments, where he found the Queen, his wife, *asleep on his own carpet-bed, embracing with both arms* a black cook of loathsome aspect and foul with kitchen grease and grime. . . . he said, "If such case happen while I am yet within sight of the city what will be the doings of this *damned whore* during my long absence at my brother's court?" So he drew his scymitar and, cutting the two in four pieces with a single blow, left them *on the carpet* . . . (Richard Burton 1885–86:1.4)

> ... so he returned privily and entered his apartments, where he found the
> Queen, his wife, asleep and *gazing at her* a black cook of loathsome aspect
> and foul with kitchen grease and grime. . . . he said, "If such case happen
> while I am yet within sight of the city what will be the doings of this *woman*
> during my long absence at my brother's court?" So he drew his scymitar
> and, cutting the two in four pieces with a single blow, left them . . . (I.
> Burton and McCarthy 1886–88:1.4)

> But when he entered the palace, he found his wife lying in the arms of one
> of the kitchen boys. . . . he said to himself, "I am still here, and this is
> what she had done when I was barely outside the city. How will it be and
> what will happen behind my back when I go to visit my brother in India?
> No. Women are not to be trusted." He got exceedingly angry, adding, "By
> God, I am king and sovereign in Samarkand, yet my wife has betrayed me
> and has inflicted this on me." As his anger boiled, he drew his sword and
> struck both his wife and the cook. Then he dragged them by the heels
> and threw them from the top of the palace to the trench below. (Haddawy
> 1990:3–4)[6]

Richard Burton's version refers to a wife as being asleep in the marriage
bed with her arms wrapped around her lover. The cuckold calls his wife a
"damned whore" and, after killing the illicit couple, leaves the corpses in
the bed where he found them. A number of Victorian taboos have been
broken in this short passage and the rewritten version points them out. In
the rewriting by Isabel Burton and McCarthy, the wife's lover does not
share her bed; she does not touch him, rather she is the object of his gaze.
"Damned whore" has been replaced with "woman" and the final reference
to the "carpet [bed]" has been suppressed. Haddawy's translation indicates
some of Richard Burton's shifts: the wife is more passive than Burton constructs her, and one sees Burton's additions pertaining to prejudices of
race ("black," "loathsome aspect") and class ("foul with kitchen grease and
grime").

A second passage from the frame story is also illustrative of the
translation strategies of the Burtons.

> ... the Queen, who was left alone, presently cried out in a loud voice,
> "Here to me, O my lord Saeed!" and then sprang with a drop-leap from
> one of the trees a big slobbering blackamoor with rolling eyes which
> showed the whites, a truly hideous sight. He walked boldly up to her and
> threw his arms round her neck *while she embraced him as warmly; then he*
> *bussed her and winding his legs round hers, as a button-loop clasps a but-*
> *ton, he threw her and enjoyed her.* On like wise did the other slaves with

the girls till all had satisfied their passions, and they ceased not from *kissing and clipping, coupling* and carousing till day began to wane; when *the Mamelukes rose from the damsels' bosoms and the blackamoor slave dismounted from the Queen's breast*; the men resumed their disguises . . . (Richard Burton 1885–86:1.6)

. . . the Queen, who was left alone, presently cried out in a loud voice, "Here to me, O my lord Saeed!" and there sprang with a drop-leap from one of the trees a . . . blackamoor. . . . He walked boldly up to her and threw his arms round her neck. On like wise did the other slaves with the girls, and they ceased not from *conversing* and carousing till day began to wane; when the men resumed their disguises . . . (I. Burton and McCarthy 1886–88:1.5–6)

. . . the lady called, "Mas'ud, Mas'ud!" and a black slave jumped from the tree to the ground, rushed to her, and, raising her legs, went between her thighs and made love to her. Mas'ud topped the lady, while the ten slaves topped the ten girls, and they carried on till noon. When they were done with their business, they got up and washed themselves. Then the ten slaves put on the same clothes again . . . (Haddawy 1990:5)

The racism of Richard Burton's translation is clear in both passages, especially so in the footnote that he adds to this second episode: "Debauched women prefer negroes on account of the size of their parts. I measured one man in Somali-land who, when quiescent, numbered nearly six inches. This is characteristic of the negro race and of African animals; *e.g.* the horse; whereas the pure Arab, man and beast, is below the average of Europe; one of the best proofs by the by, that the Egyptian is not an Asiatic, but a negro partially white-washed" (Burton 1885–86:1.6n1). This is one of the most severely criticized among a long list of "questionable" footnotes Burton adds to his text. It is clear that certain racist stereotypes are unhesitatingly reproduced by Isabel Burton and McCarthy, provided they are devoid of explicit sexual content. Haddawy's translation illustrates that the *Arabian Nights* is bawdy, but his translation reveals that the eroticism is more controlled than that in Richard Burton's version. An additional significant element is to be noted in the Haddawy text: after the men and women have had sex, they wash themselves. Neither version by the Burtons makes reference to this significant attention to hygiene, which is curious given Victorian England's obsession with cleanliness, a suppression that fits with the racist overtones of the translations.

Clearly Richard Burton did not transcend the racist and class prejudices of his time; rather, he actively participated in constructing them, and this weakness has rightly come under attack (Said 1978; Kabbani 1986; Shamma 2005). Nevertheless, in his time and in the context of his extensively annotated translation, he was considered by many to be a knowledgeable and sound scholar who was importing alterity to his culture with the aim of improving understanding of cultural Others, specifically the understanding of Egyptians and Egypt. Yet, the crudity of his translation and his notes was also criticized even by his contemporaries, and he was labeled a pornographer by some. Tarek Shamma argues that Richard Burton's "proclivity to the sensational and the grotesque . . . damaged the seriousness that could have been accorded his writings" (2005:52).

In response to criticism directed at its sexual content, Burton actively defended his translation and its paratextual materials in "The Biography of the Book and Its Reviewers Reviewed," published in volume 7 of the *Supplemental Nights* (1886–88:6.385–454), an essay that is perhaps as significant as his infamous "Terminal Essay" in volume 10. Writing the same year that the final volume of Isabel Burton's expurgated version appeared, Richard Burton apparently did not feel compelled to defend the racism, classism, or sexism of his version, but indicated that his translation could contribute to freeing his readers from the discursive constraints imposed by Victorian puritanism and reproduced by his wife in her version of *The Nights*.

> The England of our day would fain bring up both sexes and keep all ages in profound ignorance of sexual and intersexual relations. . . . How often do we hear women in Society lamenting that they have absolutely no knowledge of their own physiology . . . [?] Shall we ever understand that ignorance is not innocence? What an absurdum is a veteran officer who has spent a quarter of a century in the East without knowing that all Moslem women are circumcised . . . (1888:6.437–38)[7]

Richard Burton considered himself to be a rebel against the establishment complacency of Victorian puritanism that his wife in many ways represented. In fact, he drew on Arabic culture and Orientalism to criticize English prudery. Ironically, his resistance to the cultural constraints of his society was deeply imbricated in his larger allegiance to British imperialism: they cannot be disentangled (Said 1978, Kabbani 1986). Yet the coexistence of both dominant and emergent sociocultural discourses is not unexpected in a context of social antagonisms and fragmentation (Laclau and Mouffe 1985).

Burton's position on women's access to sexual knowledge may have been unconventional, but he was a rather conventional scholar in terms of the form of his translation, for example his recourse to the copious notes "that he seems to have enjoyed writing most" (Bassnett 1998:33).[8] Edward Lane's annotated and expurgated illustrated edition of *The Thousand and One Nights, Commonly Called, in England, The Arabian Nights' Entertainments* had been published in 1839–41 by Charles Knight and Co. and was aimed at a mass readership, unlike the translations of John Payne (1882–84) and Burton (1885–86). Lane's expurgated translation and reprints had sold in the thousands of copies. The following passages from the translations of Lane, Richard Burton, Isabel Burton and McCarthy, and Haddawy illustrate differences in the erotic quality of the texts. The passage is from "The Story of the Porter and the Three Ladies." Again I have emphasized relevant differences.

> . . . the forms of her *bosom* resembled two pomegranates of equal size . . . (Lane 1839–41:1.137)

> Her throat recalled the antelope's and her *breasts*, like two pomegranates of even size, *stood at bay as it were; her body rose and fell in waves below her dress like the rolls of a piece of brocade, and her navel would hold an ounce of benzoin ointment.* (Richard Burton 1885–86:1.84)

> . . . her throat recalled the antelope's . . . (I. Burton and McCarthy 1886–86:1.76)

> She was all charm . . . with a neck like a cake for a king, bosom like a fountain, breasts like a pair of big pomegranates resembling a rabbit with uplifted ears, and belly with a navel like a cup that holds a pound of benzoin ointment. (Haddawy 1990:68)

Lane's translation is a curious blend of literal and expurgated, omitting the sensuousness of the Arabic original. Burton, by contrast, consistently pushes the boundaries of British propriety even as he asserts his domination over foreign knowledge through his notes. Here Burton adds two characteristic comments: first "The 'high-bosomed' damsel, with breasts firm as a cube, is a favourite with Arab tale-tellers. *Fanno baruffa* is the Italian term for hard breasts pointing outwards"; and second, "A large hollow navel is looked upon not only as a beauty, but in children it is held a promise of good growth." Isabel Burton and McCarthy clearly resist Richard Burton's outspoken bawdiness through expurgation, bowdlerizing the passage so that it is even less erotic than Lane's version.

Richard Burton associated with dissolute aristocrats and may have added his detailed notes for their entertainment, yet the notes also provided new, albeit often questionable, information on cultural and sexual matters to which Victorian readers did not have ready access. A sign of Burton's resistance to the puritanical norms of his time is his "daring" section on homosexuality titled "Pederasty" in the "Terminal Essay" (1885–86:10.203–54).[9] Curiously, although Burton's emphasis on eroticism was designed to appeal to Victorian tastes, he felt that he had compromised scholarship for "marketability," writing, "I translate a doubtful book in my old age, and I immediately make sixteen thousand guineas. Now that I know the tastes of England we [Richard and Isabel Burton] need never be without money" (qtd. in Kabbani 1986:95).

Because Isabel burned her husband's diaries and many of his letters, it is virtually impossible to ascertain whether or not Burton's misgivings were sincere and it is equally difficult to know how much Isabel was complicit in his project of challenging Victorian mores. The books published by Isabel Burton about her husband all portray him in the most socially acceptable light possible; they are not objective accounts. It is, nevertheless, certain that books dealing with sexuality were much in demand. In fact Burton's translation of the *Arabian Nights* is known less for the originality of the translation or the quality of its scholarship "than for the eroticism of its footnotes and its 'Terminal Essay'" (Phillips 1999:243, Colligan 2002). Burton attempted to bring a version of Cairo to England, writing in the introduction that his purpose was to produce a "full, complete, unvarnished, uncastrated copy of the great original" (Burton 1885–86:1.ix), yet he appended copious notes that were meant to appeal to Victorian prurience or to shock prudish sensibility (Colligan 2002). *Allen's Indian Mail* of 17 January 1887 notes that Sir Richard Burton's translation, "valuable and sound as it was, possessed the demerit that the indelicacy of the original text appeared in all their [*sic*] glaring hideousness" (qtd. in I. Burton and McCarthy 1886–88:6.466).

Nonetheless, the critical reception of Burton's poetic translation of the *Arabian Nights* was generally positive. In a letter to the editor of the *Pall Mall Gazette* of 12 September 1885, an Anglo-Egyptian writes, "'students' ... will buy Captain Burton's translation as the only literal one, needing it to help them in what has become necessary to many—a masterly knowledge of Egyptian Arabic. ... [The translation] is not coarser than the classics in which we soak all our boys' minds at school" (quoted in I.

Burton and McCarthy 1886–88:6.430). Repeatedly critics wrote to the effect that Sir Richard Burton's "literal" *Arabian Nights* (as well as his wife's rewriting for household reading) was a valuable educational document. A letter published in the *Gazette* of 18 December 1886 claims:

> under the guidance of this omniscient Professor [readers] may know the East . . . much better, than if they journeyed thither and trusted to their own eyes . . . the time has come for dethronement, and Lane must yield to a scholar of wide research, to an Orientalist who, during one part of his career, lived as a veritable Moslem . . . Lane's idea was to give but a portion of the "Nights," to please himself and his printer and publisher as to what should be selected, what omitted. If a story resembled another story, he rejected it on the score that it might prove wearisome. . . . These are but indications of Lane's arbitrary method, and people have submitted because quite unconscious they have been defrauded, and that treasures have been withheld. . . . Sir Richard Burton does not pick and choose. (quoted in I. Burton and McCarthy 1886–88:6.462)

The British reader who needed to learn quickly as much as possible about Arabic and the Arab world, specifically Egypt, for the reasons outlined above, trusted Burton's scholarship and appreciated having access to the "integral" *Arabian Nights.* This segment of the population did not condone preventive censorship on the part of the translator or the official publishing industry.

Translation and Secret Literary Societies

In an essay of this length, it is not possible to do a full survey of the use of translations by secret literary societies to promote domestic ideological agendas in Britain. On a partial list of societies involved in such enterprises, one would have to include the following: Richard Burton's Kamashastra Society of London and Benares, as we have seen; John Payne's Villon Society; Charles Carrington's Athenian Society; and Leonard Smithers's Erotika Biblion Society of Athens, as well as his Lutetian Society.[10]

In this list the Erotika Biblion Society of Athens and the Lutetian Society stand out because they were created by Smithers, a young solicitor working in Sheffield, who had subscribed to Burton's *The Book of a Thousand Nights and a Night.* Smithers began a correspondence with Burton while the latter was the somewhat despondent British consul in drab Trieste, building a friendship that would culminate in the collaborative erudite translation of the famous collection of erotic Latin verses to Priapus, *Priapeia sive diverso-rum poetarum in Priapum lusus*, an anonymous collection of bawdy epigrams to the phallic garden god Priapus. The translation was published by Smithers as *Priapeia or the Sportive Epigrams of Divers Poets on Priapus: The Latin Text now for the First Time Englished in Verse and Prose (the Metrical Version by "Outidanos") [Good for Nothing] with Introduction, Notes Explanatory and Illustrative, and Excursus, by "Neaniskos" [A Young Man].* Outidanos was Burton and Neaniskos, Smithers. Smithers also published Burton's translation of the poetry of Catullus, infamous for its erotic and homoerotic themes, which appeared posthumously in 1894 as *The Carmina of Caius Valerius Catullus, Now First Completely Englished into Verse and Prose; the Metrical Part by Capt. Sir Richard F. Burton, R.C.M.G., F.R.G.S., etc., etc., etc., and the Prose Portion, Introduction, and Notes Explanatory and Illustrative by Leonard C. Smithers.*[11]

Smithers and Harry S. Nichols, a printer and rare-book dealer, modeled the Erotika Biblion Society of Athens, their venture into high-class pornography, on Burton's Kamashastra Society of London and Benares, the so-called publisher of the infamous *Arabian Nights*. Smithers was much impressed with the considerable financial success of the private edition of Burton's *Thousand Nights and a Night* and subsequently decided to follow in Burton's footsteps, printing books that the socially sanctioned presses refused to print and dedicating his career to publishing works that contested Victorian public values. His law studies had led to a solid reading ability in Latin and the education to circumvent legal problems with astute agility.

Smithers's predilections set him apart from the conformist mainstream publishers who produced bowdlerized three-deckers for the reading classes that borrowed books from the circulating libraries. Much more so than Mudie's Select Library, Smithers's interests were directed to a very select market: people who were well educated, moneyed, and male. His limited runs (usually fewer than 500 copies) were printed privately and meant to become scarce relatively quickly, which made them attractive collectors' items. Many of these books were translations of upscale erotica that circulated freely in the original, whereas the translations, if they existed at all, remained underground (Manton 1984:7).[12]

In 1891 Smithers and Nichols moved from Sheffield to London to open a rare book shop and a printing business, Nichols and Co., just within Soho's boundaries, Soho being the center of London's pornography trade (Colligan 2002:15). The pinnacle of the Smithers-Nichols partnership was the production of a "handsome, well annotated new edition of Burton's *Nights*" in 1894 (Nelson 2000:3–4), edited in collaboration with Isabel Burton. Smithers and Nichols issued four editions of Burton's *Nights*, ultimately restoring more than four-fifths of the passages that had been bowdlerized by Isabel Burton for her family edition (Nelson 2000:40). Smithers went on to open his own bookshop and then to become the most celebrated publisher in London: "his audacious and keen instinct" made him "willing and eager to publish the new, the dubious and even the outrageous," and after 1895 he was the only publisher who would touch the works of Oscar Wilde (Flower and Maas 1967:264). For his part, Wilde considered Smithers "the most learned erotomaniac in Europe" (qtd. in Flower and Maas 1967:264).

Through his secret literary societies, Smithers published retranslations of six novels by Zola (1894–95), Samuel Smith's translation of Aristophanes' *Lysistrata* (1896) lavishly illustrated by Aubrey Beardsley, and Ernest Dowson's translation of Choderlos de Laclos's *Les Liaisons dangereuses* (1898), Voltaire's *La Pucelle d'Orléans* as *The Maid of Orleans* (1899), and Balzac's *La Fille aux yeux d'or* as *The Girl with the Golden Eyes* (1896).[13] Desmond Flower and Henry Maas indicate that the most original younger writers and artists of the 1890s joined Smithers's circle, including Arthur Symons, Aubrey Beardsley, Ernest Dowson, Charles Conder, and W. B. Yeats, as well as Havelock Ellis, whose writings on sexuality had been banned (1967:265). In various ways Smithers struggled against Victorian puritanical norms, making common cause with early feminists, the Aesthetes, the Decadents, and the emergent gay community. The trajectory of Smithers's career demonstrates the connection between the translation projects of the secret literary societies and the resistant ideologies of the avant-garde literary movements in late nineteenth-century Britain.

Secret Societies: Submission and Resistance

The complexity of the translation situations and the ambivalence of the translators, demonstrable in the case of Richard Burton, indicate that the either/or opposition of submission or resistance falls into the trap of what Hugh Osborne calls Venuti's "simplistic" binary opposition of foreignizing versus domesticating translation that "cannot accommodate other modes of translation" in the nineteenth-century British context (2001:154). Human beings are complex creatures and translators are human beings. Although the translations considered here did clearly challenge some presuppositions and norms of English culture, they also served to rationalize certain imperialist attitudes, as well as other racial, class, and gender biases. In other words the translation products both conformed to and contested Victorian cultural norms. Their translators were resistant to some aspects of British imperial and cultural ideology and submitted to other aspects seemingly without question.

Burton's text on pederasty included in the "Terminal Essay" appended to volume 10 of his *Arabian Nights* is an interesting example of such ambivalence. When Burton published the essay, writing about homosexuality was dangerous business, and Burton's was the first history of the subject published in English, as we have seen. Nonetheless, his use of the theory of the "Sotadic Zone," namely that homosexuality was "geographical and climatic," though not widely adopted, "may have confirmed the opinion of many British readers that homosexuality was essentially a foreign vice" (Hunnicutt 2004). Thus, although Burton dared to broach a taboo topic in one of his paratexts accompanying his translation (an example of resistance in translation), his work did not serve to free his countrymen from Orientalist and imperialist preconceptions about homosexuality (a case of submission to or collusion with dominant norms).

In "The Exotic Dimension of Foreignizing Strategies," Shamma argues that translation "must be seen as the outcome of a complexity of circumstances that comprise the intervention of the translator and the choices that he or she makes, the larger context of reception, and the relation of the translation text to other texts in its cultural environment" (2005:66). The present case study goes a step further by examining the translating subject's often intricate negotiations involving both resistance and submission with a complex publishing system and sometimes contradictory target culture norms. To begin to appreciate the translation products considered here, at the very least the following factors must be considered: the two-tier publishing industry, Burton's penchant for scandalous behavior, his exile, his personal ambitions, the lack of official recognition for his achievements, his curious relationship with his apparently ultra-conventional wife, his homosocial bonds with the sexually curious and even with the sexually deviant, Smithers's legal training, and the Smithers-Nichols partnership. And this list is far from the complete inventory required to comprehend fully the translation strategies deployed. The question of resistance in translation relates to all of these factors. What is also interesting in the study of translations issuing from nineteenth-century secret literary societies in Britain is to see how resistance to the highly rigid and restrictive sexual norms of the dominant culture is at the same time inscribed within larger pre-existing regressive frameworks of class, race, and empire that the translators consciously support.

On the surface, late-Victorian morality was puritanical. There were attempts (ranging from social movements to laws) to ensure that the general public read only what would make them into "better" British citizens. The general public was not "erudite" and thereby was seen as unable, from the establishment's point of view, to integrate positively into the desired British worldview "principles and doctrines" that differed from what they had been taught. To protect the public, French naturalist novels had been banned and writings dealing with homosexual and sexual libertarian themes were rejected by the socially sanctioned presses. Indeed in 1888 and 1889 the two trials of Henry Vizetelly made a public example of a small publisher of unexpurgated naturalist novels in translation, for Vizetelly had made available to the general public novels that dealt with three themes that in the minds of British authorities warranted burying: subversion of the throne, subversion of religion, and obscenity (Fryer 1966:52, Merkle 2009).

Beneath the surface, however, under cover of secret literary societies and private presses, naturalist novels (such as those by Zola), homoerotic poetry (including the work of Catullus), and sexually explicit texts (such as Burton's *Arabian Nights* and his *Priapeia*) were all published in unexpurgated English translations. Many of the translations were designed to fill gaps that existed in the British literary and cultural systems, in terms both of controlled or suppressed texts and of forbidden content. They were published for "homosocial" gentlemen who had gone to the right schools, having learned there how to read "viril" texts critically. While socially censured and considered "scandalous outspokenness" (Bourdieu 1982:169, my translation), the publications of the Kamashastra Society of London and Benares, the Erotika Biblion Society, and the Lutetian Society were not censored. In fact, it can be argued that the translators were playing into the hands of an institutionalized two-tier publishing system, thereby reinforcing norms having to do with gender and class.

This case study presents an interesting paradox relating to the translator's visibility and invisibility (Venuti 1995). Public publishing was above the surface and private presses beneath the surface. The only translation published by the Kamashastra Society that was not anonymous was Burton's *Nights*, although the identity of the translators was an open secret among the society's friends and subscribers. The two-tier publishing field ensured that printing privately for members of a secret—or learned—literary society made the translators and their translations untouchable from a legal standpoint, much to the consternation of the moralists. Paradoxically, thanks to their invisibility, these translators and their translations were protected from prosecution while they were being read in secret by socially powerful readers who often exerted visible, political, and official influence. Within this elite circle the identity of the translators was known.

Finally, this study of nineteenth-century secret literary societies is also an example of how resistance in translation is often associated with a larger matrix of resistance in society, through loose affiliation with people involved in progressive social movements (Tymoczko 2000a). Burton wished to publish texts on foreign mores and customs, especially regarding sexual matters, that no publisher, not even the Anthropological Society, would accept to print. From the perspective of the twenty-first century, his works clearly reproduce the class, gender, and racist stereotypes of his day, yet they were considered scandalously outspoken by many of his contemporaries. For his part Smithers wished to publish avant-garde writers and to collaborate with Burton on integral translations of Greek and Latin erotic classics. Conscious of the constraints imposed by the British publishing system, Burton and Smithers manipulated the rules in place in order to achieve a degree of symbolic domination. Through collusion with the publishing and legal systems, they achieved visibility among the members of society to whom their translations were directed. In doing so they were players in a broader social movement of resistance against the confines of Victorian morality.

Notes

1. Free-thinkers (e.g., secularists) and the "morally loose" (e.g., libertarians from all social classes) added to the complexity of Victorian culture.

2. Although Zola was labeled a pornographer by moralists in France and England, he did not meet the definition: "The writer of real pornography is aiming . . . to make the reader as randy as possible as often as possible. The reader is seeking a substitute for sexual experience, or for sexual experience of a certain kind which he may be unable, or unwilling, to secure" (Fryer 1966:95).

3. "Respectable" women—in fact, "the majority of British women"—had little if any "sexual feeling," it was assumed, so there was no need to make information on sexuality available to them. This was not only in their best interest, but also in the best interest of society (William Acton, quoted in Fryer 1966:17). Yet, the New Woman,

who was the antithesis of the Victorian ideal of the "angel in the house," was eager to challenge the cult of female domesticity and to read about foreign ideas, especially those regarding sex and sexuality.

4. According to Haddawy (1990:xv–xvi), "Lane based his translation on the Bulaq, the first Calcutta, and the Breslau editions; [John] Payne on the second Calcutta and the Breslau; and Burton on the Bulaq, the second Calcutta, and the Breslau. These translators did not . . . compare the various editions to establish an accurate text for their translations . . . ; instead they deleted and added at random . . . to piece together a text that suited their individual purposes: in the case of Lane, a detailed but expurgated version; in the case of Payne and Burton, versions that are as full and complete as possible." Wright analyzes Payne as having combined the Calcutta, Macnaghten, Bulaq, and Breslau texts, and Burton as having paraphrased Payne's translation (Wright 1906/1968:2.37 and 2:105–20 for a full discussion). In fact Burton wrote to Payne on 9 September 1884, "As you have been chary of notes my version must by way of raison d'etre (amongst others) abound in esoteric lore" (Wright 1906/1968:2.54).

5. Nelson (2000:37) notes that Burton severely criticized his wife's six-volume bowdlerized edition of the *Nights*, threatening to publish everything his wife had cut in his "Black Book of the Arabian Nights." Burton's translations were ostensibly aimed at a male readership, especially scholars, but "he once sarcastically said that he knew that his *Nights* once published would quickly find its way into every woman's bedroom" (Nelson 2000:355n30).

6. Haddawy (1990) explains in his introduction that the textual history of *The Nights* is very complex. He based his translation on a fourteenth-century Syrian manuscript, a different source from those used by Lane, Payne, and Burton. Thus, the translations cannot necessarily be compared word for word; nonetheless, Haddawy gives us a modern scholarly baseline for our assessments of the Victorian translations. Haddawy credits Burton with "an admirable command of Arabic diction, grammar, and syntax" (1990:xvi).

7. Ironically, according to Rana Kabbani, "Clitoridictimies [*sic*] and ovary-removals were two operations carried out with disturbing frequency in Victorian England, in an attempt to render women 'tractable, orderly, industrious and cleanly'. The medical profession supported the values of patriarchy, and sought to aid in the enforcement of the acceptable image of woman, a creature who was pious, passive and passionless, an image for which Victorian women were forced to pay very dearly" (1986:61–62; see also sources cited).

8. Jorge Luis Borges has written that one of the secret aims of Burton's work was the annihilation of the work of Edward Lane, for Lane's translation had supplanted that of Antoine Galland (Borges 2000:34). Borges goes on to observe that Burton's conventional and "inconvenient precursor" had already provided copious notes on "the manners and customs of Moslem men," but had scrupulously avoided the erotic; Burton would fill the gap (Borges 2000:40).

9. Burton provides a short history of the subject and promotes a geographical theory of homosexuality. He concludes with a condemnation of bowdlerizing (homo) eroticism and chastises literary critics who attack his work.

10. On these societies see Ó Cuilleanáin (2004), Nelson (2000), Merkle (2003), and Manton (1984).

11. This translation was published only after it had been expurgated by Lady Isabel Burton and Burton's manuscript destroyed, much to Smithers's consternation (Nelson 2000:26).

12. According to Colligan, compiling a history of English obscenity, though difficult, is possible thanks to the scholars, collectors, and librarians who consigned books to the private case housed in the Library of the British Museum (2002:25). Colligan adds that "the study of literary obscenity has largely been limited to upper-class publications because the prints and magazines sold in the streets have not survived the test of time" (2002:26).

13. See Nelson (2000:311–52) for more information about the books Smithers published under the Erotika Biblion Society and the Lutetian Society imprints.

NITSA BEN-ARI

Reclaiming the Erotic: Hebrew Translations from 1930 to 1980

In January 2004 a new publishing house called Katom (Orange) was launched in Tel Aviv, announcing the publication of a new series of pornographic novels, all written by women. The news was acclaimed in the electronic media with exclamations such as: "Well done," "High time," "Pornography and in Hebrew!" As though finally retrieving what had been for men only, young women reacted enthusiastically to the exclusive female-writers aspect; only one female reader, obviously unaware of the historic prominence of male writers in the genre, protested: "What about men-writers!"[1] Somewhat earlier, in February 2003, a high-court decision overruled the 2002 prohibition of the Playboy channel on Israeli cable TV. The prohibition was a direct result of the strengthening of the right-wing coalition between the national Likud party and the Orthodox parties which had issued in a 2002 parliamentary law canceling pornographic channels on Israeli TV. Presiding over a panel of eleven judges, Chief Justice Michael Heshin justified the decision by evoking the principle of freedom of speech, concluding with the remark that the historic decision to ban D. H. Lawrence's *Lady Chatterley's Lover* would nowadays be shrugged off with a smile. Welcome as they may be, these two incidents stand out in twenty-first-century so-called liberal Israeli society and should be viewed in their historical and cultural contexts; they are minor illustrations of the ongoing discourses concerning erotic literary material and the freedom of speech.

This essay indicates how ideological mobilization can explain the puritanical tendencies in modern Hebrew literature and in literary translations into Hebrew in one of its most critical formative periods, 1930–80, but it indicates as well the subversion of and resistance to that ideology. The essay covers a long stretch of time, allowing for synchronic and diachronic analysis, through risking generalizations. Two milestones in this period are the 1936 adoption in pre-state Israel of the Mandatory British Obscenity Law and the 1977 political upheaval that ended the long rule of the Israeli Labor party. The tendencies exposed in the half century covered by this essay lie behind current discourses about pornography in Israel illustrated above.

Research in semiotics and translation studies has provided insight into the mechanisms of ideological manipulation, making it possible to understand what an influential and effective vehicle of ideological manipulation translated literature can be within a national literature (Even-Zohar 1990, Tymoczko 1999, Gentzler 2002). My research on issues pertaining to the formation of national identity in what I call "mobilized" translations of historical novels (Ben-Ari 1997, 2006b) and on the censorious manipulation of religious, particularly Christian, elements related to the formation of Self and Other in Hebrew translation (Ben-Ari 2002) has motivated me to look further into moral censorship. Puritanical trends in Hebrew literature offer insights into the processes that helped construct the valorized representation of the puritanical native-born Israeli, called the *sabra*. Within this large context the role of translation is doubly interesting. Mobilized within canonical culture, it led to censorship of the most effective type, that is, self-censorship. Mobilized within the margins, it had a completely different role, that of initiating and canonizing erotic models.

Two remarks before I proceed. In this essay I use terms like *obscenity* or *pornography* as descriptive terms rather than evaluative ones. I do not attempt to define *pornography* or to supply a historical overview of the various definitions the word has been given. The only (non) definition I adopt is a semiotic view of obscenity as writing about sex or eliminative functions that past or present officials or influential groups have suppressed or tried to suppress on the grounds that they were morally corrupting or degrading (Loth 1961:8). It seems impossible in a post-Foucauldian era to view sexuality in any cultural context without considering power relations and their role in the shaping of personal as well as national identity.[2]

Moreover, terms like *puritanism* and *Zionism* are obviously much more complex and diverse than can be discussed adequately in a short study. Like many other broad terms, they are place- and time-dependent. Modern studies of Victorian puritanism (Marcus 1966, Morgan 1966, Gay

1998) have undermined customary notions about Victorian prudery. Research has demonstrated the many faces of puritanism within different social classes, as well as how different New England puritanism was from its English counterpart. What I term *sabra* puritanism is shorthand for a complex set of values that constitute the pure moral image attributed to the sabra or required of him. The term *puritanism* is not used accidentally because, as will be shown below, the ethos in fact began to pervade Hebrew culture during the period of the British rule of Palestine.[3] Studies of Zionism have likewise refuted notions of ideological homogeneity at any given time related to moral orientations among others.[4] Indeed research on hegemony has stressed the necessity of expecting and accepting the coexistence of both dominant and emergent cultural formations, particularly during periods of change and crises of identity.[5]

In the very early stages of its revival, especially with a new cultural center established in Israel, modern Hebrew literature acknowledged the importance of translation as the basis for any new cultural infrastructure. As is to be expected, the selection of what to translate, which prestigious source cultures to draw from, and what ideological lines to follow were in the hands of culture shapers. In the 1930s and 1940s, respectable publishers pre-selected texts, genres, writers, and possible source cultures, favoring either classical or social realist material for translation (Shavit 1998, Toury 1977:123). Before the establishment of the state of Israel, love and sex were considered irrelevant to the pioneering nationalist agenda, if not altogether depraved. This tendency was intensified when socialist publishers became predominant in the 1940s and 1950s, helping to maintain a puritanical approach to literature well into the 1980s.

Judaism has historically not preached abstinence or asceticism; in fact its basic attitude regarding sexual matters has always been positive and pragmatic, as can be illustrated by the detailed rabbinical literature on everyday sexual issues. Yet at the same time some puritanical attitudes have deep roots in Jewish culture; there is a long tradition in rabbinical literature of using euphemisms rather than calling sexual acts or body parts by name. In addition there have always been sects or individuals who promoted partial or total sexual abstinence for the sake of "higher" goals, such as absolute dedication to the study of the Torah. Moreover, in certain communities in Eastern Europe, child marriages associated with early and traumatic sexual encounters may have driven many young men to join the strictly male entourage around a rabbi or a Chassidic leader (see Biale 1997/1992:127–29).

The Enlightenment brought new dilemmas: the old image of the ghetto Jew had to be replaced with that of the new masculine and muscular Hebrew (Shapira 1997).[6] The new emancipated woman, evoking admiration in some, also provoked unease and fear of an as yet unknown being, the sexually liberated woman (Feiner 1998:253–303).

Victorian puritanism, which had invaded Europe and America in the nineteenth century, could thus find an echo in Jewish culture, if not in the fear of the new erotic liberation then in ancient strands of asceticism. Nicknamed "the Golden Age of Puritanism and the Golden Age of Pornography," the nineteenth century in England was heralded by the establishment of the "Society for the Suppression of Vice" in 1802, and it culminated in Chief Justice Alexander Cockburn's notorious obscenity law in 1868.[7] Judge Cockburn's definition of pornography resulted in the banning of erotic books for a century until the ban was lifted as a result of a series of book trials in England beginning in the 1930s and culminating in the 1960s, trials that reverberated throughout the Western world. Cockburn's definition of pornography was so broad that it encompassed all material written with the intention of corrupting the minds of those open to such influences and into whose hands such material might fall (see Greenawalt 1995:99). The result was the banning of countless books, many of which later came to be considered masterpieces of modernism.[8]

In various manifestations puritanism swept through most of Europe and the United States during the nineteenth century. It was acclaimed in Boston, where the first trial of a book took place as early as 1821; the book was John Cleland's *Fanny Hill: Memoirs of a Woman of Pleasure*, and, under the reign of terror of Anthony Comstock, who initiated the Society for the Suppression of Vice and began a crusade to abolish pornography, puritanical norms were imposed on all aspects of life. One of Comstock's early achievements was persuading the United States Congress to adopt Lord Cockburn's obscenity law, not merely as part of Anglo-American common law but in the form of federal statutes, thereby granting the postal and customs authorities the power to implement the standards.[9]

Puritanism infiltrated Israel, then part of the Ottoman Empire, at the turn of the twentieth century, with the first waves of Jewish immigration from Eastern and Central Europe. When the League of Nations invested the British Empire with the mandate to rule Palestine, however, puritan thought and law made its official and formal entrance into Hebrew culture. Before the 1948 establishment of the state of Israel, the thirty years of the

British Mandate enhanced the spread of puritanism, especially in consequence of the insertion of the British obscenity laws into Israeli Mandatory Law in 1936. Simultaneously in pre-state Israel, puritanism encountered a second seemingly different ideology, namely the ideal of sexual freedom and the equality of the sexes borrowed from the Bolshevik revolution. On the face of it, the promise of freedom and equality was anti-puritanical, but Bolshevik ideology soon undermined the erotic, ultimately regarding sex and marriage as capitalist, bourgeois notions that had to be abolished (Kon 1995:51–66). This Bolshevik ideology permeated the early Jewish settlements and became a major factor in the shaping of Israeli culture.

Thus, Zionism started with the promise of being, among other things, an erotic revolution, preaching equality and sexual freedom (Biale 1997/1992:176). In fact it succeeded in maintaining this myth for decades, and the "woman question" was one of the key ideological issues discussed in the first stages of this Jewish cultural revolution. In 1897, for example, the first Zionist Congress assembled in Basel, formally laying the foundation of Zionism; it granted women the right to vote, but because of opposition from Orthodox sectors, this right was not implemented in Israel until 1926. Even after the establishment of the state of Israel, however, marital rights were kept in the hands of the Orthodox rabbinate. Women who had joined the radical movement with the hope of virtual and real gain found they had been pushed aside (see Safir 1991).

The Jewish cultural revolution assumed a more "virile" character as it grew more nationalistic. As George Mosse (1985) points out, the nationalist movements of the nineteenth and twentieth centuries tended to be predominantly "virile"; they had to confront accusations of Jews being effeminate and neurotic, including those of Sigmund Freud and his followers, such as Otto Weininger (Gilman 1993).[10] Growing violence and tension in the late 1930s and impending war with the Arab population in the 1940s intensified the need for a more virile image of the New Jew, now called the *sabra*, a term including youths born in Israel or raised there, as we have seen (see Almog 1997:341). Utopian communes advocating free love, no couples, and no marriage created much controversy, but they soon died away, faced with the small number of (reluctant) women and material difficulties. Communal education, such as that undertaken in the kibbutzim, mobilized all its efforts to create what Melford Spiro (1965) calls "the puritan sabra": it stripped sex of its mystery with methods of coeducation and cohabitation, only tolerating couples as long as they did not interfere with community life. The Freudian slogan "sublimation without repression" was heralded with enthusiasm by youth movements, psychologists, and educators.[11] The new principles of "sabra purity" were formed, and they were all-encompassing: purity of thought, word, and deed. The tenth commandment of the popular youth movement called Ha'shomer-Ha'tzair (The Young Guard) required the sabra not to smoke, not to drink, and to maintain sexual purity (Biale 1997/1992:195).[12]

Growing violence and wars (both actual and impending) functioned to remove the "woman question" from the national agenda. The Israeli war of independence, closely following the establishment of the state of Israel, is a prime example. War was a man's affair and woman was a distant image back home to long for and dream about (Rattok 2002:287–88). The *palmach*, the young volunteer fighters who preceded the establishment of the regular Israeli army, were said to be so puritanical that it is estimated that 99 percent of the soldiers who died in battle were virgins (Ben-Yehuda 1981:266).[13]

In the 1950s, when violence ceased to be the dominant issue in Israel, the country turned to the unequivocal demands of a melting-pot ideology. With the 1948–53 waves of massive immigration (especially from Arab countries), the image of the sabra was firmly established in opposition to the Other: the new immigrant, the speaker of Yiddish who refused to promptly sever his ties with the diaspora, the "Oriental" Jew who would not give up his past traditions to be remodeled in this radical secular mold. The latter retained an overtly erotic association, negatively connected with a Levantine culture of cards, cafés, and brothels. Much like the image of the Arab, the Levantine male immigrant was suspected and feared for his sexuality; unlike the Arab, however, he had a rightful claim on whatever female the sabra considered his own, which made him a bigger menace (Laor 1995:88–93). Despite the end of massive immigration and the prospect of relative normalization, in 1973 the Yom Kippur War threw the country and its culture into yet another traumatic period of reassessment of national values.[14] Original Israeli literature promulgated this strain of ideological indoctrination, maintaining until the 1970s a Zionist, "male," ascetic narrative, reflecting an almost Oedipal break with the fathers' generation. After the first settlers had turned their backs on the Old World in the 1880s, generations of male Israeli writers pursued this Oedipal revolt, and it is significant, even symbolic, that women writers should have eventually put an end to this streak in Israeli culture in the 1980s.

Translated literature could well have introduced changes in this atmosphere of erotic suppression, because translation can import other models of writing without necessarily being attacked for violation of the laws or norms. Yet in Israel translation also adhered to the general puritanical norms and was used to further the national mobilization, through careful selection of texts and the manipulation of texts and genres to screen out erotica. Self-censorship more than fear of legal action motivated cultural agents to forfeit the innovative and possibly subversive function of translation in favor of mainstream doctrines. True, publishers had to contend with the 1936 obscenity law, an adaptation of the 1868 Cockburn law adopted as common law during the Mandatory British rule of Palestine (1922–48). It was, in fact, made even stricter in 1960, when an Israeli law decreed that the penalty for obscenity would be increased to three years imprisonment, which was more than the three months in the Mandatory law and the two-year maximal penalty in British law (Cohen 1973:82–86).

Only one member of parliament, Uri Avneri of the extreme left, protested against this increased measure (Gluska 1979:63). In 1968 the Vitkon Committee recommended that Israeli obscenity law be reviewed or canceled, but these recommendations never had any legislative follow-up. The obscenity law was strictly enforced in the theater and the cinema, where a precensorship committee determined the fate of every single play or film. Literature was spared, because there was no formal precensorship for literature, and very few cases of obscene literature were brought to court.

Yet, although literature was spared, it functioned as if it had been subjected to censorship. No attempt was made by a respectable publishing house to publish notorious modernist banned books; no public outcry was raised against this suppression. Furthermore, in 1963 an initiative of the Ministry of Education, by Dr. Yossef Michman-Melkmann, established a voluntary precensorship committee, calling for the "gentlemanly" participation of all respectable publishers, with the aim of cleansing obscene literary works. Submission of material to the committee was voluntary, and the committee had neither legal nor effective power, so its sanctions were more symbolic than anything else. But nothing further was needed: self-censorship was more effective than any formal measures. A small, single voice of protest against the obscenity law was raised in 1966, when the leftist Hebrew writer and journalist Dan Omer published his scandalously pornographic *Ba'derech* (*On the Way*) and went through all appeal procedures to attempt to overturn a ban on the book. From the judge's final verdict, it is obvious that Omer's virulent attacks on sacred national images and on Orthodox religion were the underlying reasons for the enforcement of the obscenity law in this case, not the "pornography" in his text.[15] Even when the ban on "obscene" books had been lifted in most of the Western world, such books were slow to penetrate the self-inflicted Hebrew puritanism. Some, such as the notorious masterpieces of D. H. Lawrence, Henry Miller, and Vladimir Nabokov, were translated or retranslated in full by prestigious publishers in the 1970s and 1980s; some, such as the sadomasochistic, eighteenth-century French libertine novels or risqué twentieth-century works by Guillaume Apollinaire and Georges Bataille, have had to wait until the twenty-first century; still others were doomed to oblivion.

A literary system, like any other cultural system, must be stratified lest it stagnate. Thus, erotic literature also found its own outlet in Israeli culture. Typical of puritanical cultures, erotica flourished on the periphery, taking three main channels: (1) erotica read in the original source language or in non-Hebrew translations, (2) erotic pulp fiction, and (3) pseudo-medical sexual handbooks. The periphery was the "natural" outlet for these subversive genres to escape to, but it was also the right place for them to be channeled to. There they could be supervised and, if necessary, controlled; there they could also be labeled "obscene," "perverted," and "dirty," a matter no less vital for the culture shapers. The rare surveys of reading habits in Israel after 1948 that did inquire about the habits of the "pulp" readership found almost no readers of erotica: people were reluctant to admit to such non-normative behavior.

Some form of passive resistance to the puritanical sabra norms could be observed in the habits of the majority of newcomers who formed their own native-language libraries and newspapers, and who could read erotica in languages other than Hebrew. Yet the option of reading literature in the original, though quite widespread in reality, remained ideologically marginal and was relatively short-lived, for it undermined the melting-pot ethos of Israeli culture. It was also rejected by the chauvinistic Israeli-born offspring of immigrants, as were newspapers and theaters in languages other than Hebrew.

Hebrew literature that developed outside the canon defied censorship and, on the face of it, self-censorship also. In spite of its tremendous commercial success, this second option for accessing erotica, namely pulp fiction, was considered "shameful" and "depraved" by culture shapers and eventually by the general public. Culture shapers, aware of the need for popular culture, were adamant in their attempts to impose a "proper" popular culture on the masses and, in fact, succeeded in creating so-called folk music, folk songs, folk dances, theaters, and libraries for the working classes. Side by side with this mobilized effort, a spontaneous popular culture evolved in apparent protest against institutionalized sanitized culture. Pulp literature was a form of protest and resistance insofar as it followed the much despised Yiddish tradition of *Schund* (trash) chapbooks at the very period when the sabra were breaking with Yiddish as the epitome of the diaspora and "the Old Jew." This is not surprising in a period of multiplicity and change, when identities were threatened, to use the terms of the hegemony theory of Ernesto Laclau and Chantal Mouffe (1985), or when minorities do not see a potential gain in assuming the dominant culture, to use the terms of the theory of maintaining cultural entities developed by Itamar Even-Zohar (2005). At the same time pulp fiction included translations of some of the prestigious banned books, that is, "higher" forms of literature. Together with "cheap" pulp fiction, banned books were driven under the counter. They were brought out in inexpensive editions, published by ephemeral printing establishments with a minimal investment in production, and sold in kiosks or newspaper stands. Kiosks had cheap pulp stacked in piles, with porn underneath the counter. Distribution to kiosks was in different hands, and prices were significantly lower than in conventional bookstores, thus ensuring broad circulation of the erotica. Serialization, typical of kiosk publications, also increased circulation. Books and booklets sold in this way included both "high" and "low" literature indiscriminately: D. H. Lawrence and Henry Miller, Agatha Christie and John Cleland all figured together as pulp.

No precise data exist regarding the scope of this subversive production, but it was obviously quite large. The 1950s and 1960s were the peak of this production, motivated by the proliferation of the double standard. Pornographic literature anywhere is hard to trace and this case is no exception. The translated banned books were printed in pirated editions which reveal considerable effort to erase any traces that could lead to the printers. Names of the translators, as of the authors of originals of pulp erotica, were usually fictitious. Printing firms appeared and closed overnight. Even if a few publishers could retrospectively quote sales numbers, their data were based on memory and concerned principally their bestsellers. According to one of the publishers, for example, five thousand copies of the serial *Captive from Tel Aviv* were sold in the late 1930s (Eshed 2002:234). These numbers, however big for their time, do not represent the vast scope of hand-to-hand distribution that is typical of underground material of this sort.

Yet this form of resistance, as brazen as it may seem, was less daring than could have been expected. As is often the case in a clash with mainstream ideology, the minor erotic genres looked to the canon for legitimation. The names of the translators and editors involved in the production of these books recur, and investigation of the persons behind the many pseudonyms confirms that a relatively small group of people was engaged in this activity.[16] This group consisted of young writers, journalists, soldiers, and students who had higher literary aspirations but who wrote or translated erotica as their secondary jobs. Years later, when they became prominent as writers, translators, or journalists, they openly admitted to and even boasted of writing this "trash"—now considered collectors' items—for money.

The seemingly paradoxical efforts to gain legitimation for the banned books in translation consisted of (1) quoting positive recommendations from critics in the source culture, (2) "cleansing" the book of excessive eroticism, and (3) embellishing the language so as to emphasize that the book was high art. Language was often of high and pompous register; style had to be elevated and "literary," using old turns of phrases, binomial nouns, and rare vocabulary. It was an old-fashioned Enlightenment norm, and the result was what Rachel Weissbrod calls the mock-epic style (1999:245–49). In the process of legitimating the texts, specific terms for sexual body parts and acts were euphemized, and older biblical and Talmudic terms were employed instead of slang Hebrew terms in general use in the spoken vernacular. Slang expressions (such as those in Henry Miller's books, for instance) would occasionally but boldly be replaced with Hebrew equivalents, only to be embedded in a highly correct and normative prose style. One must remember that because the Hebrew language developed anormally over the centuries, it was conservative in adapting to modern demands regarding the use of colloquial and slang lexemes in written texts, even when representing dialogue. Modern Hebrew maintained didactic as well as linguistic inhibitions against introducing spoken dialogue into literary texts; only in the late 1970s did a normalization of sorts take place. At the same time, over-literariness in the translated banned books was not encouraged either; even in the noncanonical production of erotica, excessive literary modernisms were not tolerated and were replaced with worn-out "safe" clichés.

Rather naive by today's standards, pulp pornography was even less specific in terminology than the banned books from other languages, for pornography tends to prefer the lewd allusion to the outspoken. Surprisingly or not, it too looked to "higher" genres for valorization, disdained slang, and adopted literary (though epigonic) models of style. What was deemed "literary" style was strewn with clichés, similes, and binomial collocations; the result was almost a chapbook formula. For example, pomegranates figuring in lieu of breasts would always be hard and bulging, at risk of bursting from a tight blouse. Masquerading as translations granted some of these pulp erotic books some small prestige, and publishers did not hesitate to adorn the covers with profuse words of praise from authoritative figures in the "source" culture.[17] Because these pornographic pseudotranslations of the 1940s and later were an entirely new production, their models had to be adopted from abroad, yet even the most daring were relatively subdued.

The magazine *Gamad* (Dwarf), a cheap imitation of the 1937 British (later American) *Lilliput*, was a collection of jokes, most of them not even "dirty," strewn with lewd illustrations; *La-Gever* (For the Man) was somewhat more risqué in content but it, too, stressed visuals, which were mostly photographs of half-nude women. Models for Yiddish pulp novels, the damsels-in-distress type such as *Regine* or *Sabine*, themselves translated or adapted from French and German chapbooks, enjoyed much popularity; they used equivalent Hebrew girl-names for titles, such as *Tamar* and *Smadar*, or *Hashvuya mi'tel aviv* (The Captive from Tel Aviv). The 1964 pulp translation of *Fanny Hill*[18] inspired dozens of "sequels" in Hebrew, such as *Hadar ha'mitot shel Fanny Hill* (Fanny Hill's Bedroom) and *Bita ha'tzeira shel Fanny Hill* (Fanny Hill's Youngest Daughter), both published in 1964 and both among the most blatant pseudotranslations.[19] A controversial daring variation, the so-called *Stalag* series, using Nazi concentration camps as the background and pretense for sadomasochistic elements, was the acme of explicitness in its sexual repertory, yet it remained just as allusive in its lexical repertory and specific elements. It also was the most popular of the pulp publications; the prototype *Stalag 13* (modeled on Billy Wilder's *Stalag 17* and written by "Mike Baden," alias Eli Kedar) sold over 25,000 copies when it appeared in the early 1960s, an enormous commercial success in terms of both past and present standards.

The third option for obtaining erotica took the form of reading literature about sex that was legitimate, though just as marginal. It consisted of a variety of pseudoscientific sex handbooks. The translation into Hebrew in the 1930s of Auguste Forel's famous turn-of-the-century handbook titled *The Sexual Question* launched a vogue for translating Central European textbooks, mostly with a Freudian bent. British and American texts, including Havelock Ellis's *Studies in the Psychology of Sex* (in seven volumes, 1897–1910) and, later, the Kinsey reports, *Sexual Behavior in the Human Male* (1948) and *Sexual Behavior in the Human Female* (1953), were either not translated into Hebrew (the case with Ellis's work) or only partially translated (the case of *Sexual Behavior in the Human Female*, in 1954).[20]

It is true that many translators came from Central Europe and were familiar with Freud's theories, but the disparity in the works chosen for translation probably reflects mainly a preoccupation with sublimation. Otherwise it is hard to explain why the study of the individual would carry such weight in a society preaching sacrifice of the individual for the sake of the community. Sublimation became an integral part of Zionist ideology, both reinforcing the puritanical character of the movement and reverberating with echoes of the past. Although it professed to aim at severing all connections with the past, in fact Zionism continued to subscribe to the suppression of the erotic for the sake of "higher goals." Sex was channeled to "safe" and "free" clinical discourse, where it could be verbalized, regulated, and surveyed. And where, most important, it could be explained and "taught" as seen fit by the shapers of culture (Foucault 1976:1.26; Dworkin 1981/1979:xxxiii).

Together with translated literature of a Freudian nature, a Hebrew equivalent evolved. A prominent figure in sex education was Shmuel Golan, coauthor of the pedagogically oriented *Sexual Education* (1941) mentioned above, a leader in kibbutz education, a prolific writer of sex education guides, and a man who exerted much influence over the general public as well. He represents a line of kibbutz educators who advocated the then-popular "Marx and Freud" ideological combination favored by philosophers such as Herbert Marcuse.[21]

It is not surprising, therefore, that although the numerous translated texts and Hebrew textbooks differ in detail, they share several basic features. First, their approach to sex was ambivalent: they all waged war against prejudice and ignorance, yet underlying a discourse of modern tolerance, there still lurked a preoccupation with moral questions, with hygiene and, as mentioned, with sublimation. All the publications continued to instill a fear of prostitution and disease. The 1962 Hebrew translation of Dr. Fritz Kahn's *Unser Geschlechtsleben* (*Our Sex Life*, 1937) begins with the phrase, "Sefer ze nichtav mitoch shnei gormim: nisayon ve'shutfut le'sevel" (This book was written with two motives: experience of and sympathy for suffering).[22] Not only was the research of Havelock Ellis missing in Hebrew translation, his spirit of "enthusiasm" for sex was also absent.[23]

Second, the style of these sex manuals is a rather confusing combination of German terminology, Hebrew innovations, and biblical and Talmudic archaisms. The founding fathers of the Hebrew-language revival had avoided erotic terminology, thus leaving amateurs to deal with the lacunae in the lexical repertory; this gap is immediately obvious in the language of the books we are considering. Shunning the spoken vernacular, the translators choose a register that is overall high in stylistic and linguistic markers, as we have seen. Moreover, because authors and translators alike lavishly quote classic poetic sources, the style is, to a certain degree, "literary." This odd combination characterized sexual textbooks until the 1970s, when the Hebrew translation of Dr. David Reuben's *Everything You Always Wanted to Know about Sex* (*Kol ma sh'etamid ratzita la'daat al ha'min*) broke with this tradition, a fact that may have accounted for its immense popularity. Part of the growing Americanization of Hebrew culture as a whole, the book also announced a transition to American sources, showing a marked leaning toward "the joy of sex" and the influence of the sexual revolution sweeping Western countries.

Except for the use of elements such as statistics or diagrams, in many ways the production of pseudoscientific sex handbooks did not differ categorically in style from the erotica that took the form of pulp fiction or translations of banned books, and in fact sex guides, encyclopedias, and pamphlets also must have served as a source of erotic excitement. Some of these handbooks even went to the trouble of warning readers not to use them as such. In the introduction to his handbook called *Chayey ha'min shel ha'adam* (Human Sexual Life, 1938), written originally in Hebrew, Dr. A. B. Talmon warns somewhat disingenuously, "This book is absolutely scientific and it is written on a purely scientific basis. Seekers of sexual stimulation will kindly not search it for piquanteria to stimulate their sick urges" (1983:1). Erica Jong describes a similar experience in the puritanical America of her youth: "It was impossible to obtain a copy of John Cleland's *Memoirs of a Woman of Pleasure* outside the rare-book room of a college library or a private erotica dealer. (I tried.) Henry Miller's *Tropics* and D. H. Lawrence's *Lady Chatterley's Lover* could not be purchased at your local bookstore. The raciest sex manual available to the panting adolescent was *Love Without Fear* by Eustace Chesser, MD" (quoted in De St Jorre 1994:125).

This basically self-inflicted restraint even in marginal literature over such an extended period of time had far-reaching consequences for Israeli culture. A principal effect was the continual dwindling of the erotic repertory. A spoken slang vernacular in Hebrew developed independently, mostly borrowing lexical items from foreign languages, usually words with negative connotations. This lexicon had hardly any impact on the literary repertory, which developed with marked disdain for spoken Hebrew until well into the 1970s. While great translators, authors, linguists, and innovators used translation as laboratories for reviving the Hebrew language, they did not see fit to deal with "obscene" material, and a whole stratum of the language remained neglected. The petrified literary repertory did not offer any creative Hebrew alternatives either. Solutions to terminological problems were left in the hands of writers and translators of marginal literature, rather than professional lexicographers.

When prominent Hebrew writers finally attempted to find a private, intimate tone for their works in the 1970s and 1980s, they had hardly any modern erotic repertory to fall back on, and their love scenes always were at risk of becoming farce. Faced with the choice of old-fashioned petrified Hebrew terms, scientific German-sounding ones, or the slang street vernacular (mostly foreign), writers usually chose to avoid explicit descriptions of sexual or erotic aspects of life, which in turn was not productive for the development of the culture. S. Yizhar, one of Israel's most important writers, has refrained from overt descriptions of sex scenes, and his most intimate and passionate erotic moment is that between a common flower and a bumblebee pollinating it (1998:110–11). Novelist Amos Oz, renowned and respected, almost became a laughingstock when he attempted an explicit love scene in *Menucha nechona* (*A Perfect Peace*, 1982), where the vocabulary of "thrashing" and "plowing" echoes past traditions of sublimating sexual acts into metaphors associated with the conquest and fertilization of the land (1982:282–84).[24] By contrast, David Shahar, a subversive in his revisionist, right-wing political affiliation, provides rather conscious, tongue-in-cheek, and amusing literary renditions of pulp pornography, particularly in his 1979 novel titled *Sochen hod malchuto* (*His Majesty's Agent*). Retrospectively this seemingly playful "high porn" must be read as a form of resistance to the puritan mainstream.

The dwindling and eventual stagnation of erotic repertories are not restricted to Hebrew alone. Similar cases have been described in formerly communist regimes, which had for prolonged periods banned love and sexuality as "capitalistic," or in countries like Japan, where contacts with the West necessitated first euphemizing, then reevaluating erotic vocabulary. In these cases new vocabulary also had to be coined when old-fashioned terminology was found lacking or was judged to be implicitly "negative." This was the case, for example, in the new Japanese translation of *Our Bodies Ourselves: A Book by and for Women*. When a group of 23 translators and 25 editors set out to prepare a full translation of the book in 1988, they found that the old terms for women's body parts used in the 1974 Japanese translation had been negatively marked and would have to be replaced (Buckley 1997:202; Wakabayashi 2000:72). As opposed to Japan, however, where prior to its Westernization, the culture had known rich and stratified forms of erotica, in Hebrew culture there was no previous repertory of the erotic to fall back on.

Israeli authors Yonat and Alexander Sened represent this frustrating lacuna in terminology in their 1974 novel *Tandem*. When attempting to imagine and depict what the neighbors are doing on the other side of the wall, the narrators lack words, sentences, models (1974:73–74):

"He entered her." "I would appreciate a description of the whole act." Bless D. H. Lawrence. Well, he entered her. But if you want to be consistent, this too is a romantic roundabout way to say it. So, one more moment of courage, one more step forward: he put his sex organ into her sex organ and his body . . . his body . . . Just a minute. Don't we have a name for this simple body part in our Hebrew language? We have a hand, an eye, a forehead, even a belly, and we have a sex organ. No one would ever imagine calling the hand a work organ or a writing organ. This is a trick of original sin. But that idea doesn't even belong to us. Ten-year-olds jump on every new dictionary to see if the words they hear appear in them. . . . Our neighbor the flute player is again immersed in a passionate storm. End of chapter or double space or a series of hyphens open to the imagination. The movie camera shifting from the bodies that are— making love? Sleeping with each other? Immersed in . . . why immersed? Having intercourse, procreation, insemination. . . . So, the penis is going into the vulva, nearly Latin, *pin* and *pot*, very charming, like names you give your two doggies.[25]

Only in the 1980s and 1990s did Israeli literature emerge from this self-inflicted puritanism. Translation introduced belated innovations such as feminist writing, gender studies, and queer literature, as well as modernist and postmodernist literary works and criticism. Translation of such works necessitated a reevaluation of the existing literary repertory and in due course supplied material for the renewal of literature composed in Hebrew. For historical reasons mentioned above, Israel seems to have missed feminism, in part because the myth of the Israeli "liberated woman" must have made feminism appear irrelevant. Many of the basic feminist texts have still not been translated and others were translated quite late. For example, only the first part of Simone de Beauvoir's *The Second Sex* (1949) has been translated into Hebrew, and that translation appeared as late as 2001.

Nonetheless feminist trends, if not directly responsible for the revival of literature written by Israeli women, certainly helped young women writers develop a modern erotic voice of their own. The last two decades have witnessed both the vigorous growth of women's writing and a refreshing change of norms altogether. But the gap, a whole stratum of language and literature, has not been closed, so that the mere mention of a pornographic series for and by women provokes exclamatory reactions, as we saw at the beginning of this essay in the enthusiastic voices supporting the launching of the pornographic publishing house Katom. The belated establishment of an erotic series written entirely by women, its provocative promotion strategies, and the enthusiasm it evoked all indicate that real normalization is still to come. Ironically because Katom was a subsidiary of a more mainstream publishing house, the first three books issued by Katom Publishing were also the last.

In mainstream Israeli culture (non) translation of erotica helped establish a new identity for the sabra: youthful, pure, shunning obscenity of any kind, and sublimating personal passion for the communal good. At the same time translation helped define the non-sabra, the new immigrant, the speaker of Yiddish, the consumer of foreign pornographic chapbooks, and especially the Oriental Jew as the significant Other who was obscurely menacing in his sexuality. Adopting the sabra values led to a well-traveled route: agricultural school, the youth movement, the palmach, service in the Israeli army, and party affiliation that guaranteed promotion to the right jobs and the right sociocultural positions. Being different did not grant any advantage, not even membership in the avant-garde.

In the light of post-Foucauldian and postcolonial theory, censorship has come to be understood as one of the most influential elements in the formation of cultural and national identity (Greenblatt 1992, Malena 2002, Wolf 2002, Sturge 2002, Ben-Ari 2000, Wakabayashi 2000). Moral censorship in particular involves crucial elements pertaining to the definition of the sexual self. At the same time sexual issues are at the core of national and cultural identity, just as they are at the core of modern subjectivity.[26] Overt censorship may create antagonism and lead to resistance. By contrast, self-censorship of the kind practiced by Hebrew culture shapers results in an inventory of much subtler manipulations—and much better results—than any formal, imposed dictates. In Israel people bought into the censorship in part because they shared the need to belong to the new representative Israeli self; they were therefore ready to adhere to the norms dictated by a very small minority as to what was proper and what was not, and literature supplied them with "proper" representations of behavior. The marginalization of the erotic gave it negative associations that took generations to erase and that produced long-lasting effects on language and culture alike. The process in Israel was similar to the fervent censorious puritanical forces operating in New England when the New Jerusalem was being built and a new identity was being shaped in North America. The virginal land, referred to in female terms, absorbed all passion. A new cultural identity had to be imposed on all newcomers, excluding Others, establishing a hierarchy of old-comers versus new arrivals, and pioneers versus immigrants.[27]

Nonetheless, the extent of the productivity in the margins of the Hebrew literary system indicates a subversive vitality of great force. The small contributions of divergent models—intimate, sexual, erotic, and overtly pornographic—had an indirect but invigorating effect on canonical literature, however much it went without acknowledgment. This resistance prevented total stagnation of the literary system. Actual underground translations ranging from pornography and modernist classics to medical manuals played their part. Masquerading as translations, erotic novels found a large albeit peripheral market. Unknown amateur translators and authors working with ephemeral racy printing houses could experiment with colloquial terminology and offer more daring solutions to the gaps in Modern Hebrew simply because they did not count. In the face of the large market for these varied types of publications, even prominent publishers, moved principally by commercial considerations, gradually began to relax their norms. Mainline news-papers began to mention erotic novels in their literary reviews, and even if the tendency was to cut them to pieces, mere reference in a central news organ meant institutional recognition. Meanwhile, literary journals and academic publications established in the 1970s began to take an interest in marginal literature as well, changing translation norms and introduc-ing greater claims for adequacy in the representation of the source texts. In a culture that was somewhat more sure of itself, a normative puritani-cal Israeli identity began to give way to pluralism. Resistant translations of erotic texts had a significant role in all these changes that allowed the erotic to be reclaimed in Israel.

Notes

1. "Sichot Maariv" [Maariv Conversations], *Maariv*. Accessed 2 February 2004. All translations are my own, unless otherwise noted.

2. See Foucault (1976), particularly volume 1.

3. The term "puritan sabra" has been borrowed from Melford Spiro's (1965) re-search on the behavior of kibbutz children.

4. Ben-Ari, *Suppression of the Erotic in Modern Hebrew Literature* (2006c), pro-vides a more diversified overview and analysis. A Hebrew version of the book (Ben-Ari 2006a) is also available. An abbreviated version of this essay was presented at the meetings of the American Translation Studies Association in March 2004 in Am-herst, MA.

5. See, for example, Laclau and Mouffe (1985).

6. See also Ben-Ari (1997:234–41 and 2006b) for the image of the New Jew/ess in the very first Jewish novels, namely nineteenth-century German-Jewish historical novels.

7. For a historical overview of puritanism in literature see Loth (1961:47–116). The history of the "banned books" is discussed in Greenawalt (1995). D. H. Lawrence's view of puritanism as a product of the Victorian age is interesting; see Lawrence (1961 [1929]:60–85).

8. The Delvin-Hart controversy in London in the 1960s (Rubinstein 1975:43–53, Nattrass 1993) aroused a great deal of interest in Israel: it demonstrated that the old di-lemma of whether governments should be responsible for the enforcement of morality was still unsolved. First, it suggested that it is problematic to determine any moral stan-dard, let alone one that is shared by all. Establishing a moral standard on the judgment of the "reasonable man," as suggested by Lord Delvin, is even more problematic, for many of these norms have no "reasonable" basis and are a residue of age-old religious intolerance and deeply rooted taboos. In the final analysis the so-called reasonable man may have to lean on his feelings, that is, on emotional considerations. At the same time Lord Delvin's perception of norms is much too static; society's tolerance of deviations from moral standards varies from generation to generation, and the standards usually

change faster than the laws, a fact that legislative authorities must take into consideration as well.

9. For the Comstock Crusade and the Comstock Law, see Lefkowitz Horowitz (2002:358–403).

10. Weininger published his (self) deprecating work *Geschlecht und Charakter* (Sex and Character) in 1903, accusing Jews of lacking intellectual or cultural characteristics, thus being like women (i.e., animals).

11. See, for example, the textbook by Zohar and Golan, *Ha'chinuch ha'mini* (Sexual Education; 1941:24, 61).

12. Spiro (1965:331) discusses the aversion of the puritanical sabra to "dirty jokes."

13. Netiva Ben-Yehuda (1981), a member of the palmach youth, supplies invaluable information concerning the puritanical codes of the movement, including shying away from sex, foul language, and dirty jokes, all of which are unusual for armed forces. Her memoirs also expose the way the palmach appropriated a male image, underplaying the role of women soldiers.

14. For this periodization, see Miron (1993) and Schwartz (1995).

15. Omer initiated a translation of a then-revolutionary collection of poetry of the "Beat generation" into Hebrew, which was published in *Nahama* (Howl) in 1967, and his choice of title for his own book may have been an echo of Kerouac's famous *On the Road*. Both proved to be too radical for Hebrew culture to digest. For the trial's proceedings, one of the few precedents in Hebrew law, see Gluska (1979:21–22).

16. Eshed (2000:227) offers interesting data on pseudonyms in Hebrew pulp fiction; I am also indebted to personal communication with various authors.

17. Toury (1995:40–52) discusses pseudotranslations.

18. Translated by "G. Kasim," a pseudonym of the poet Maxim Gilan.

19. See Clay (1964), Clealand (1964). The "variations" in the spelling of Cleland's name may have been a way of avoiding copyright claims, but at the same time characterize a genre where typing errors were almost a trademark. Both *Fanny Hill* sequels were probably the work of Miron Uriel, a tireless writer of pulp fiction.

20. For some reason Kinsey's volume on the human male was not translated, the gender choice reflecting perhaps the tastes of heterosexual male consumers.

21. Marcuse's *Eros and Civilization* (1955) is a good example of the school.

22. Kahn (1962:25). Kahn was a prolific writer of such guides. His volumes on the sexual hygiene of the boy and the sexual hygiene of the girl were translated in the 1930s into Hebrew. His books were highly recommended by Shmuel Golan mentioned above (Zohar and Golan 1941:259).

23. Robinson (1989/1976:2–3) applies the epithet "sexual enthusiast" to Ellis; following Ellis (1890:129), Robinson (27) sums up Ellis's view of sex as "the chief and central function of life . . . ever wonderful, ever lovely."

24. Compare the Hebrew vocabulary with Kibbey's (1986:3–7, 119) analysis of early New England Puritan discourses.

25. In her novel *Wild Ginger* (2002:150–51), the Chinese American writer Anchee Min gives a similar humorous description of a young couple who are products of the Cultural Revolution. They make love using quotations from Mao's Red Book, for lack of basic intimate sexual or romantic vocabulary.

26. Related discussions of puritanism and modern attitudes to cultural issues of sex and sexuality are found in Fessenden, Radel, and Zaborowska (2001); Lefkowitz Horowitz (2002); and Allison (2000/1996).

27. Fessenden, Radel, and Zaborowska (2001:1–15) offer an enlightening analysis of the formation of American identity via its literary Puritan origins.

BRIAN JAMES BAER

Literary Translation and the Construction of a Soviet Intelligentsia

Iɴ the preface to his monumental two-volume collection of poetry in translation published in 1968, *Mastera russkogo stikhotvornogo perevoda* (Masters of Russian Verse Translation), Efim Gregorievich Etkind made the following claim: "Deprived of the possibility of expressing themselves to the full in original writing, Russian poets—especially between the nineteenth and twentieth Party Congresses, used the language of Goethe, Shakespeare, Orbeliani, or Hugo to talk to the reader" (Etkind 1978:32).[1] This rather innocuous statement set off a political firestorm in the reactionary 1970s, and Etkind, a professor of French literature at the Herzen Pedagogical Institute, was subjected to a humiliating *prorabotka*, or public scolding. As a result the offending sentence was removed from the preface and the surrounding paragraph rewritten, despite enormous costs to the publisher: the book was already in print, awaiting distribution.

This incident, which came to be known as the "affair of the sentence" (*delo predlozheniia*, Etkind 1978:111), suggests how translation—not only the practice of translation but also commentary on translation—became a site of resistance to official Soviet culture and values. Through the selection of texts for translation, the various choices made in the course of translation, and commentary on translation in the form of footnotes, prefaces, and reviews, literary translators in the Soviet period became adept at encoding resistance for a select intelligentsia audience. Moreover, the successful decoding of subversive content automatically constructed the reader as more insightful, if not more intelligent, than the censor, who functioned as

149

a metonym for the entire Soviet bureaucracy. In those situations where knowledge of a foreign language was necessary to fully decode the oppositional message, even more cultural capital accrued to the reader, all of which lent support to the intelligentsia's claims to cultural leadership.

The use of translated literature as a vehicle to comment critically on contemporary society formed part of what Vladimir Shlapentokh referred to as a "second culture," or an intelligentsia subculture within Soviet society. This second culture, Shlapentokh explains, "to some degree parallels the 'second economy' created by people far from the intellectual stratum. Both the second culture and second economy serve to undermine the state's monopoly in several vital spheres" (1990:75). This second culture, which has parallels with the Renaissance topos of literature as an idealized "second government," functioned to create and to socially reproduce Russia's creative or "moral" intelligentsia. The concept of the intelligentsia that I am using here has deep roots in Russian society and goes far beyond one's level of education, although that is an essential attribute of members of the Russian intelligentsia. It supposes, in Shlapentokh's formulation, "that a member of the intelligentsia or an intellectual is one who possesses a cluster of intellectual, cultural, and, most importantly, moral virtues such as kindness and altruism, and who serves as a model for the rest of society" (1990:ix). Also crucial in the Soviet period was an oppositional mood. As Masha Gessen points out, "the intelligentsia drew its identity in part from its relationship to and its distance from the regime" (1997:7). The successful decoding of oppositional content (re)produced the individual reader as a member of an alternative "reading public," situated within official Soviet literary culture.

This oppositional stance may in fact be the most significant aspect of the intelligentsia's resistance, for, as Lev Loseff points out, the messages encoded in these texts did not contain any new or vital information: they "tell the reader nothing which the reader would not have known beforehand without [the author's] help" (1984:219). Loseff argues that "again and again in a society where ideological censorship prevails, the reader will animatedly follow this dangerous game in which intellect bests authority; again and again the reader will participate, albeit passively, in the game, not analyzing or responding emotionally to the text, so much as celebrating it as he would a mythical ritual" (1984:222–23). To the extent that this mythical ritual was shared by many readers, it served, as rituals often do, to create a common group identity, an ersatz community, that was defined by its intellect and its "oppositional mood," among other things (Shlapentokh 1990:83).

"The coding and decoding of artistic works," Shlapentokh noted in 1990, "has become an important element of intellectual activity in the U.S.S.R. and is a common topic for conversation at social gatherings" (66).

On a symbolic level in this context, literary translators came to embody resistance, especially during the worst periods of repression. In part through that resistance, the Soviet-era intelligentsia bolstered its "claim on the spiritual leadership of society" (Shlapentokh 1990:122). What was perceived and celebrated in intelligentsia circles as translators' selfless devotion to the "word" and to the genius of individual artists was put forward as an alternative to the active, collective heroism of socialist realism. By devoting themselves to the preservation of the "classics of world literature" for a Russian reading public, literary translators perpetuated the concepts of timeless "universal values" and "world culture" that were in opposition to what they saw as the tendentious, politicized, and class-based official culture of the Soviet Union. In fact studies of the tastes of Soviet readers reveal that the nineteenth-century "classics" of Russian literature and translated foreign literature were always significantly more popular than original Soviet literature, largely because they were perceived to be "nonpolitical" (Friedberg 1962:168). The intelligentsia sought to create a subculture that was distant and distinct from "everything official, officially approved, officially ideological" (Gudkov 1995:171).

The intelligentsia's resistance to Soviet culture, which Etkind insists was "not clearly dissident in character (1978:1), was an attempt to "protect" literature from politicization and to preserve an appreciation of the formal innovation and moral complexity of literary works at a time when literary scholars in the West were insisting on the impossibility of separating ideology from the study of literary forms and themes. In other words, when poststructuralism was leading literary scholars in Europe and North America to "deconstruct" literature's pretensions to eternal esthetic and moral values, members of the Russian literary intelligentsia were struggling to support those very pretensions. For this reason the resistance of the Russian intelligentsia appears to the Western observer to be culturally conservative, while it was nonetheless politically daring. Such resistance was seen by the intelligentsia not so much as political but as moral or even spiritual in nature. As Joseph Brodsky put it, "Art is a form of resistance to the imperfection of reality as well as an attempt to create an alternative reality, an alternative that one hopes will possess all the hallmarks of a conceivable, if not achievable, perfection" (1992:221).

The Context of Resistance

To understand how literary translation became a site of resistance during the Soviet period, it should be acknowledged that literature in general had, at least since the early nineteenth century in Russia, been a privileged site of opposition to the government, a site of what Dina Spechler refers to as "permitted dissent" (1982:xvi). Spechler notes that "in Russia the boldest most incisive criticism of social and political phenomena in the legal press has, since prerevolutionary days, most often appeared in the form of novels, poetry, and memoirs" (1982:xix). In the 1960s poetry readings were political events (Shlapentokh 1990:112). Within that cultural milieu, literary translation, although certainly subjected to censorship, was nonetheless considered to be a relatively "safe art" (Etkind 1978:146). As is well known, writers such as Anna Akhmatova, when they were not allowed to publish their own original work, were given work as translators. Lauren Leighton observes, "The same political leaders who consider translation a key to their nationalities policy and a door to the world, and are thus presumably appreciative of the ideological perils of literary translations, have been indifferent to and at times even oblivious to works in translation that would have enraged them had they been written by a Soviet author" (1991:38).

Moreover, translated literature acquired special significance in the context of Soviet restrictions on travel to non-socialist countries and restrictions on interaction with foreign visitors from the West. For many Soviet readers works of foreign literature served as a window onto a semi-forbidden world and were integral to the intelligentsia's concept of "world culture" (Leighton 1991:18). This concept was markedly different from that of the official Soviet literary establishment, for which world culture was restricted to works considered to be ideologically correct.

Leighton separates literary translation in the Soviet period into two major categories: academic translation and propagandistic translation, both made possible by the support given by the Soviet regime to Maxim Gorky's World Literature project (1991:6). In the years immediately following the October Revolution, literary translation was celebrated as a political vehicle in the service of Soviet policies of internationalism and the "friendship of peoples." The translation of literary works both into and out of the languages of the various peoples of the Soviet Union was relatively well paid and was seen in a patriotic light as contributing to mutual understanding and friendship among Soviet peoples. Etkind remarks that "in order to support the unity of a multiethnic Soviet Union, it was necessary to constantly recreate the illusion of brotherhood among the various republics and peoples; poetic translations played no small role in that performance" (1997:39). The establishment of a Soviet sphere of influence in Eastern Europe after World War II, not to mention special relations with other socialist countries throughout the world, also produced a translation boom.

The translation of works among the various peoples of the Soviet Union provided a good deal of work for translators. There were at least 100 different linguistic groups within the U.S.S.R., some of whom, such as the indigenous peoples of north Siberia and the Soviet Far East, were given an alphabet and, as a consequence, access to the literatures of the world through translation as part of a government initiative to spread literacy. As Werner Winter indicates, however, "the use of translation as a tool in political strategy" left a dubious legacy (1964:295). Although the gift of literacy allowed many younger people to study and work within the party and the state administration, it also led to "the forcible destruction of religion"; in addition "the 'modernization' of 'backward areas' meant the loss of enormous literary wealth" (Ginsburg 1970:358). Rather than commission the translation of works of oral literature that reflect a traditional religious worldview, the Soviet literary establishment sought out new works that exhibited class consciousness and modern, secular values. To the extent that these literary works were "political" in nature and subordinated form to content, intelligentsia readers considered them to be in collusion with Soviet literary policy.

Such translation "on command" eventually became the butt of jokes among the intelligentsia. Felix Roziner offered a hilarious send-up of the policy of translation among the ethnic peoples of the Soviet Union in his novel *A Certain Finkelmeyer* (1981). The eponymous hero of the novel is a Jewish poet of rare talent—clearly fashioned after the actual poet-translator Joseph Brodsky—who, in order to publish his poems, passes them off as translations of the "first poet of the Tangor people," a tiny ethnic group in Siberia (Roziner 1991:86). The premise of the novel is not entirely absurd, if one considers the experience of the prose writer Sergei Dovlatov while on a trip to the Kalmyk city of Elista. There a local poet greeted Dovlatov and presented the Russian writer with what he said was an interlinear translation of one of his poems and asked Dovlatov to provide a poetic Russian translation. It turned out, however, that there was no original (Freidberg 1997:179). The poet Arsenii Tarkovskii, father of the filmmaker, penned a damning portrayal of such translation "on command" in the poem

"Perevodchik" (The Translator), which contains the refrain, "Akh, vostoch-nye perevody, kak bolit ot vas golova" (O, those eastern translations! How they make my head hurt; 1982:69).

In intelligentsia circles these translations were often unfavorably com-pared to "artistic translation," that is, the translation of the great works of world—often Western—literature, which were done at times "for the drawer," as the Russians say, with no expectation of publication. The distinction between artistic and propagandistic translation reflects the split between Russia's "two cultures": the official one supporting the political and eco-nomic goals of the regime, and the other resisting not so much the regime's specific political goals as the general politicization of literature, epitomized by the Zhdanovite criteria for the production of art and literature. The great practitioners of artistic translation during the Soviet era rejected the basic tenet of socialist realism, according to which "the aesthetic value of a work was virtually equated with its ideological and political effectiveness" (Ermo-laev 1985:430).[2]

Encoding Resistance

In order for translated literature to function as a site of resistance, its sub-versive or oppositional content had to be accessible to its intended audi-ence while remaining inaccessible to the censor. To achieve this double voicing, translated literature participated—albeit somewhat uniquely—in the elaborate system of Aesopian language that lay at the very heart of Russia's "second culture" during much of the Soviet period. The term "Aesopian language" was developed in the nineteenth century to describe "indirect" social criticism embedded in literary texts, based on the classic example of Aesop's use of animal characters for the purpose of social satire. In *On the Beneficence of Censorship: Aesopian Language in Modern Russian Literature* (1984), Loseff explains how Aesopian language func-tioned by means of textual screens that diverted the attention of the censor from any parallels between the content of the literary work and the reali-ties of contemporary society, as well as textual markers that cued the "ideal" reader to make precisely those parallels (1984:50–52).

Loseff includes translation in his discussion of Aesopian language, although the section dedicated to the subject is arguably the weakest in the book. He classifies translated literature as a "genre" and dedicates most of his discussion to pseudotranslations, in which the bogus claim that a text is a translation functions as the screen. Loseff gives much less attention to actual translations, which have a somewhat unique set of screens and markers at their disposal. For example, although the status of a text as a translation may serve in and of itself as a screen, the choice of texts for translation and the approach to translation can be very effective markers as well.

The encoding of resistance in literary translations was not unique to the Soviet Union; it had in fact a long history in Russia. In the latter half of the nineteenth century, for example, after the death of the repressive Czar Nicolas I, censorship restrictions loosened. Translators took advantage of this situation to introduce to Russian readers a number of politically charged translations of poems. The finest practitioner of such engaged translation was undoubtedly Vasilii Kurochkin, whose translations of Pierre Jean de Béranger in the 1850s and 1860s were responsible for the broad popularity of the French poet in Russia. Kurochkin's translations invited his readers to make associations between the events and ideas expressed in the poems and the political situation in contemporary Russia. The critic Count Petr Ivanovich Kapnist describes Kurochkin's translations in the following way: "With his light, flexible, and sonorous verse, Kurochkin has dedicated himself primarily not to translation but to the adaptation in the Russian manner of the songs of Béranger. Often preserving the spirit of the original, he is able most adroitly to apply various couplets by Béranger to our contemporary circumstances, so that in essence Béranger is just a powerful weapon and, under the protection of his name, Kurochkin pursues his own aims . . ." (1901:420).

The encoding of resistance, however, is not always so easily read from outside the culture or subculture that produces and consumes the translation. For example, in the early nineteenth century, a number of translations were done of the poetic miniature "La Feuille," written by the French dramatist and poet Antoine Vincent Arnault. Vasilii Zhukovsky, Denis Davydov, Alexander Pushkin, and others translated the short poem, a fact that can only be understood in reference to a "private" set of allegorical associations. The image of the leaf torn from its branch had come in the early nineteenth century to symbolize internal political exile (Etkind 1968:15). In this way the translation of the poem served as a political protest or lament for those who understood the significance of its central motif, which underscores the fact that Russia's second culture had its own interpretive traditions and literary topoi that made possible the recognition and decoding of such acts of resistance among a select audience.

Clearly, in the case of "La Feuille," it is not sufficient to focus on isolated translation decisions in order to understand how Aesopian language is able to hide oppositional content in plain sight. It is necessary to map all of Russia's second culture, that is, to focus on the complex literary system that created the complex web of (oppositional) meanings or meaning potentials within which translations were read. This can be done by examining the significance of a given author, work, or motif within the target culture. Such significance is often reflected in the paratextual material, including commentary on a translation contained in footnotes and prefaces, as well as reviews and reader responses to the translation.

For example, it would be impossible to consider Boris Pasternak's translation of Shakespeare's *Hamlet* (1940) without taking into account the fact that two other translations of the play were also undertaken at almost the same time in the 1930s during one of the worst periods of Stalinist repression. One was by Mikhail Lozinskii (1933–38) and the other by Anna Radlova (1934). It is striking that at such a time all three translators translated a play about a university student—an intellectual, perhaps—who agonizes over what action to take against an immoral ruler, in this case his uncle. It is impossible to classify definitively these translations as acts of resistance without corroboration of the translators' intentions, and in conditions of repression the motivation behind acts of resistance is generally concealed. Pasternak, however, does indicate some of the political implications of translating Shakespeare's drama: "When [Shakespeare] writes about good and evil or about truth and falsehood we perceive a view of the world which would be inconceivable in an atmosphere of *servility* and *obsequiousness*. We hear the voice of a genius, a king among kings, the judge of the gods, *the voice of western democracies to come* whose foundation is the pride and dignity of the toiler and the fighter" (Pasternak 1961:192; trans. Rozencveig 1993:645–46; italics mine). Anna Kay France (1978:39) contends that Pasternak took liberties with Shakespeare's text in order better to support his ennobling vision of the prince.

For an elaboration of what *Hamlet* might have meant to Pasternak, we can look to other evocations of the Danish prince in Pasternak's work. In *Doctor Zhivago*, for example, the main character of that novel is both a doctor and a poet, and Pasternak includes poems by Zhivago at the end of the novel, the first of which is entitled "Hamlet." The lyric subject of the poem, however, is not the Danish prince; rather, he is an actor about to go on stage to play the role of Hamlet. By choosing an actor as his character's lyric hero, Pasternak not only reminds us of the play within the play in Shakespeare's drama but also offers an image of someone (like the translator) who is constrained to express himself through the words of another. That theme is further suggested by the fact that the poem is presented as the work of the fictional Zhivago. Moreover, it contains two easily recognized citations. The first citation is from Jesus Christ, awaiting his crucifixion in the garden of Gethsemene: "Esli tol'ko mozhno, Avva Ochi, / chashchu etu mimo pronesi" (Pasternak 1989–92:3.511; If it be only possible, / Abba, Father, let this cup pass from me). The second is a Russian folk saying: "Zhizn' prozhit' ne pole pereiti" (Pasternak 1989–92:3.511; Living life is not like crossing a field). Like his lyric hero, Pasternak speaks through the words of many others: the fictional poet Zhivago, the playwright Shakespeare, Christ, and the Russian folk.[3]

Furthermore, in lines three and four, the poet instructs his readers in how to decode Aesopian language: "I lovliu v dalekom otgoloske / Chto sluchitsia na moem veku" (Pasternak 1989–92:3.511; And I try to catch in the distant echo / What will happen in my time). The reader is encouraged to make a connection between the events portrayed in the distant past and those of the present time. Pasternak makes a similar point in his essay "On Translating Shakespeare" in 1956, when he discusses Shakespeare's use of historical materials for his dramas: "why should Shakespeare seek the inspiration of his realism in such remote antiquity as Rome? The answer—and there is nothing in it to surprise us—is that just because the subject was remote it allowed Shakespeare to call things by their name. He could say whatever seemed good to him about politics, ethics, or any other thing he chose" (1959:138). Pasternak continues, "Shakespeare's chronicles of English history abound in hints at the topical events of his day. . . . Drama spoke in hints. Nor is it surprising that the common people understood them since they concerned facts which were close to everyone" (1959:139).

The 1930s and 1940s were a time of great despair and frustration for Pasternak, who saw his literary friends persecuted by the regime. Some accused him of accommodation during the Stalinist era, going to Paris with an official group of writers to represent the Soviet Union, failing to intervene with Stalin to save Mandel'shtam, and in general enjoying freedom from persecution. Pasternak claimed he took "refuge in translation" (qtd. in Rozencveig 1993:643) and may have felt guilty for doing so; he lamented, "Mayakovsky shot himself while I translate" (qtd. in Friedberg 1997:115). Nonetheless, his feelings about the tragedy occurring around him and about his own personal responsibility to act were reflected not only in his translation of *Hamlet* but also in his translations of Shakespeare's sonnets. Pasternak translated only three of the bard's 154 sonnets, making his selection rather marked. Moreover, he eschewed the sonnets on romantic themes, choosing instead more melancholy and metaphysical ones. One of his most acclaimed translations is of Sonnet 66, "Tired with all these, for restful death I cry . . ." (Budberg 1971:149). This sonnet consists of a litany of complaints (lines 3–12) regarding the moral and political corruption of contemporary society, and it includes a line that must have had particular resonance for Pasternak in the 1930s: "And art made tongue-tied by Authority."[4] What little romance the sonnet does contain is attenuated by Pasternak's decision to translate "my love" in the final couplet with the Russian word *drug*, which, though it can refer to a romantic partner, has as its first meaning "a close friend."

The full meaning of Pasternak's translation of Shakespeare's *Hamlet* cannot be fathomed, however, without consideration of the long tradition of the Russian reception of the play. Beginning in the nineteenth century, the character of Hamlet served as a vehicle for posing certain questions about art and political engagement. The great nineteenth-century literary critic Vissarion Belinsky, for example, attacked what came to be known as Hamletism shortly after the publication of Nikolai Polevoi's translation of the play that premiered in 1837, in which Hamlet was presented as weak and vacillating. Peter Holland notes that "Hamletism was seen as a retreat into the self from the pressures of social action and civic responsibility" (1999:322). The writer Ivan Turgenev reinforced this view of Hamlet in his 1859 lecture, "Hamlet or Don Quixote." In that essay Turgenev uses the literary characters of Hamlet and Don Quixote to describe two fundamental peculiarities of man's nature. In Turgenev's view Don Quixote is not a ridiculous character but a man who dares to act in the world with straightforward enthusiasm; Hamlet by contrast is weak and egotistical. Turgenev laments that in Russian society "Hamlets outnumber Don Quixotes, though Quixotes are still to be found" (Turgenev 1972:11).

We must place Pasternak's *Hamlet*, generally regarded as offering a sympathetic portrait of the young prince, within this tradition. Edited and updated, Pasternak's translation appears to be motivated by a sincere empathy for the character and his predicament. Although unable to act, Pasternak's Hamlet is not presented as selfish and egotistical. Perhaps like Pasternak himself, this Russian Hamlet is in search of a solution to the moral or ethical problem of how to react to and resist injustice and tyranny. In his 1956 article "On Translating Shakespeare," Pasternak states unequivocally, "This is not a drama of weakness, but of duty and self-denial" (1959:130–31). His *Hamlet* is a defense of Hamletism, and Pasternak's ordeal over the publication of *Doctor Zhivago* abroad was later described by Czeslaw Milosz as Pasternak's "Hamletic act" (1977:75), an expiation for many of the sins associated with his previous prevarication. Avoiding a call to political engagement on the one hand and total surrender to apathy on the other, in his *Hamlet* Pasternak paints the moral predicament of members of the Soviet-era intelligentsia in noble, if not heroic, terms. For Pasternak and his contemporaries, "Hamlet offers an apt metaphor for the situation of the Soviet intellectual, particularly during the Stalin era" (Ziolokowski 1998:150).

A discussion of the political subtext of Pasternak's translation of *Hamlet* cannot end with an analysis of the translator's intentions or his strategies of encoding, for any successful act of resistance requires a reader or readers willing to decode that act as subversive. In fact, authorial intention—so difficult to determine even outside conditions of censorship—is far less important than reader response, and Soviet audiences and the government alike were sensitive to the potentially subversive themes in the play. A production of *Hamlet* using Pasternak's new translation at the Moscow Art Theater under the direction of one of its founders, Vladimir Nemirov-Danchenko, was in fact banned for several years. Such censorship of Shakespeare's plays had in fact a rather long history in Russia, for Shakespeare often presents monarchs as all too human by Russian standards. In the eighteenth century, for example, an anonymous Russian translation of *King Lear* excised the king's madness entirely, for it was considered unthinkable that a royal personage could be mad (Ginsburg 1971:356). Aleksandr Sumarokov's translation of *Hamlet* disappeared from the stage in 1762 after Catherine II assumed the throne, as the murder of Hamlet's father by Claudius might have encouraged audiences to draw parallels with Catherine's own rise to power, involving the murder of her husband, Peter III.[5]

In any case, once Pasternak's *Hamlet* was allowed to be performed again in Soviet Russia, audiences applauded when the line "Something is rotten in the state of Denmark" was spoken, clearly interpreting it as a commentary on contemporary society (Holland 1999:334). The response of Soviet audiences in the darkened hall of a Moscow theater created a site of resistance. In a later production directed by Nikolai Okhlopkov in 1956 at the Mayakovsky Theater in Moscow, the play was staged in such a way as to comment even more directly on the state of things in Soviet Russia at the time. A front drop of a massive iron grille suggesting prison bars made Hamlet's world into a prison. In effect the director declared, "Here even to exist is to suffer oppression" (Holland 1999:334). And in Grigorii Kozintsev's critically acclaimed film version of *Hamlet* (1964), "images of armed guards recur frequently in the film: patrolling, escorting, watching, and spying, they represent the repressive mechanism of the State" (Semenenko 2007:130).

Embodying Resistance

The resistance performed by translators in the Soviet Union was not, however, restricted to the encoding of oppositional content. The act of literary translation itself had a place within the highly nuanced system of moral and ethical values constructed by the Soviet-era intelligentsia. The Russian poet Sergei Gandlevsky discussed the moral predicament of the Soviet intellectual in the following terms: "We were constantly taking things apart into what's honest and what's not, like medieval priests struggling to figure out how many angels can dance on the head of a pin. To work is to participate, which is dishonest, but to work as a night-guard making 70 rubles a month—that seems honest because you can't make any less and we don't want to kill ourselves. When I finally got to make money translating, I thought it was honest because I was merely translating, but then I translated a propaganda poem from the Ossetian, and that was dishonest" (qtd. in Gessen 1997:14). The moral categories invoked by this translator are clearly derived from Solzhenitsyn's influential tract "Not to Live by Lies" (1974), in which the writer advocates not open dissent but the "individual refusal to participate in lies" (qtd. in Etkind 1978:150).

Many Soviet intellectuals viewed translation as a relatively ethical undertaking because they considered it to be more or less apolitical. In fact, literary translation, children's literature, and the art of chess witnessed an unprecedented flowering in the Soviet period precisely because they were thought to be politically neutral for the most part while at the same time creatively and intellectually demanding (Etkind 1997:49). Although literary translation may have been considered as lying outside of politics in the narrow sense of the word, it was often viewed within the subculture of the intelligentsia as a highly moral or even ethical undertaking. Discussions of literary translation often celebrated the officially suspect concept of individuality, specifically the unique talent and genius of the literary translator. Samuil Marshak famously describes this highly subversive and individualist aspect of translation in his 1962 essay "Poeziia perevoda" (The Poetry of Translation): "The translation of lyric poetry is impossible. Every time is an exception" (1990:4.216). Such beliefs contributed to a cult of the literary translator who was set in opposition to the party hack and the cultural *apparatchik*. This celebration of the miraculous and unique in every successful translation may also have been an act of resistance aimed at the tenets of the official Soviet translation school that viewed translation as a science and insisted that anything could be translated (Leighton 1991:12).

Literary translation assumed a moral and ethical value for the Soviet-era intelligentsia through the literary translator's dedication and even slavish devotion to a traditional high-culture aesthetics that celebrated complexity and innovation. These translators were seen—often in heroic terms—as serving the "eternal" or universal values of art in preference to the fleeting and shifting political values of the party or state. The sociologists Lev Gudkov, Iurii Levada, Aleksandr Levinson, and Lev Sedov assert in their 1988 study of Soviet bureaucracy, "It is difficult not to admire that in the hardest times, in the atmosphere of humiliation and pinches, the people of high culture decently served the ideals of truth, continued the traditions of our intelligentsia, creating rational, good, eternal things" (qtd. in Shlapentokh 1990:57).

For members of the Soviet intelligentsia, the trial of Joseph Brodsky—transcripts of which circulated in *samizdat* (and in fact gave birth to the phenomenon of samizdat)—represented in the starkest terms imaginable the fundamental opposition between the values of Russia's "second culture" and those of its official, state-sponsored culture. Then working "freelance" as a poet and translator, Brodsky was charged with social "parasitism." The following exchange at his first appearance in court evoked the New Testament scene of Christ before Pontius Pilate:

> *Judge:* But what is your specialist qualification?
> *Brodsky:* Poet. Poet-translator.
> *Judge:* And who declared you to be a poet? Who put you on the list of poets?
> *Brodsky:* No one. (Spontaneously.) Who put me on the list of human beings?

Judge: And did you study for this?
Brodsky: For what?
Judge: For being a poet. You didn't try to take a course in higher education where they train . . . teach . . .
Brodsky: I don't think it comes from education.
Judge: Where does it come from then?
Brodsky: I think it comes . . . (embarrassed) . . . from God. . . .

(qtd. in Etkind 1978:95)

When the hearing ended, the judge expressed surprise at the number of onlookers present, at which point a voice from the crowd cried out: "It's not everyday they try a poet" (qtd. in Etkind 1978:97).

Brodsky had dropped out of school after seventh grade and at his second hearing witnesses for the defense painted a picture of the poet-translator as a talented autodidact who dedicated himself selflessly to his higher calling. One witness, the poet Natalia Grudinina, testified, "From conversations with Brodsky and some of his acquaintances, I know that he lives very modestly, denying himself new clothes and entertainment and spending most of his time at his desk" (qtd. in Etkind 1978:250). Grudinina went on to explain to the court that "Verse translation is extremely difficult work, calling for devotion, knowledge, and poetic talent. . . . Such labour calls for an unselfish love of poetry and of work itself" (qtd. in Etkind 1978:252).

The public prosecutor and witnesses for the prosecution were enraged that this discourse of heroic self-sacrifice was applied to Brodsky. A witness named Romashova, for example, expressed amazement that "my colleagues create such a halo around him" (qtd. in Etkind 1978:256), and the prosecutor Sorokin declared, "he must be expelled from the hero-city [of Leningrad]. He is a parasite, a ruffian, an ideologically filthy individual. Brodsky's admirers drool over him. But Nekrasov wrote: 'You do not need to be a poet, / But you must be a citizen.' Today we are trying a parasite, not a poet" (qtd. in Etkind 1978:259).[6] Ironically, Sorokin invoked the words of a revered Russian poet in an attempt to denigrate the poet's calling. Circulated in samizdat, these transcripts reinforced for intelligentsia readers the age-old opposition between God and Caesar, or, in its romantic iteration, the opposition between the artist and the law. Pasternak reflects the sentiment in his poem "Hamlet": "Ia odin, vse tonet v fariseistve" (1989–92:3.511; I'm alone. Everything is drowning in Pharisaism). Similarly Roziner includes direct citations from the transcripts of Brodsky's trial in his depiction of the prosecution of his genius poet Finkelmeyer as a "parasite."

An alternative pantheon of heroes emerged from within the Soviet Union's second culture, individuals whose heroism was defined by sacrifice not to the party or the nation but to the eternal, universal values of high culture, often associated with the classics of Western European literature. Literary translators figured prominently within that pantheon and came to embody resistance for a Soviet-era intelligentsia that often viewed opposition to the regime in terms of non-participation rather than open dissent. The translator's heroism was defined by a selfless devotion to the cult of the "tsarstvennoe slovo," the "kingly word," to borrow a phrase from Akhmatova (1967–68:1.285).

The telling and retelling of their stories of sacrifice at the altar of high culture played a role perhaps no less significant in the social reproduction of intelligentsia values than the encoding and decoding of Aesopian language. In his 1963 *Poeziia i perevod* (Poetry and Translation), for example, Etkind relates the story of Tatiana Gnedich and her translation of Byron's *Don Juan*. Etkind recounts how Gnedich, a teacher of English and a translator, was arrested in 1945 and held in a KGB jail awaiting trial. While in her cell she began to translate Byron's *Don Juan* into Russian. She was able to do so because she had memorized the first two cantos, some two thousand verses out of a total of seventeen thousand. This greatly impressed her investigator, so much so in fact that he arranged for Gnedich to have a private cell, a copy of Byron's *Don Juan*, and a Webster's dictionary. She finished the translation in two years, after which she was sent to a prison camp to complete her sentence. Fortunately Gnedich was able to preserve a copy of her translation that she had typed up on a prison typewriter. When she was released in 1956, a publishing house accepted her translation and issued it in a first printing of 100,000 copies, and critics praised the work as the finest translation of Byron into Russian.

Constructed around two oppositional commonplaces, Gnedich's story is a perfect parable for an intelligentsia audience. The first opposition is embedded in the story itself and involves the translation of *Don Juan*, a thoroughly apolitical text (using political here in the narrow sense of the word) in the thoroughly politicized context of the gulag. This prompts the interpretation of Gnedich's feat as an act of moral rather than political resistance. The second opposition is suggested by the ending of Etkind's tale:

"Love produces inspiration which pushes us to perform great feats" (1963:179–80). There is an implied opposition here between cultural work done out of love and cultural work done on command. That same opposition was dramatically portrayed in the predicament of Brodsky, one of the most talented poets of his generation, who could not or would not find a place for himself within the Soviet literary establishment.

Tatiana Gnedich was not the only translator to pursue her art in a Soviet prison. During a fifteen-year stay in a prison camp, Ivan Likhachev translated Baudelaire's *Les Fleurs du mal*, which he had committed to memory. For Etkind, Likhachev's translations clearly comprised a moral act, a refusal to be broken by the regime, something that allowed the translator to survive his incarceration. Etkind writes: "This refined member of the intelligentsia who had mastered nearly all of the European languages, a connoisseur of German music, Portuguese poetry, and French causerie, worked chopping wood in temperatures that reached fifty degrees below zero, while laboring for himself over the verses of Baudelaire and the lines of his Russian translations, which were stored in his consciousness and expressed perhaps his own despair" (1997:47).

Similarly, Sergei Petrov, like Likhachev, had committed to memory an enormous number of French and German poems. These poems he translated while in prison, at times going so far as to introduce prison slang into his translations, thus leaving a trace of his incarceration within the translated text, and they provide yet another example of encoded resistance.[7] This view of literature as a site of moral resistance against the repression and censorship of the Soviet regime constituted one of the defining features of the Russian intelligentsia right down to the fall of the Soviet Union. As Etkind indicates, poetic translation was a means of salvation in the prison camps (1997:47).

Although never incarcerated, the great Soviet translator Mikhail Lozinskii earned a place for himself in the intelligentsia's pantheon of heroes through his unwavering devotion to world literature in spite of a debilitating physical illness. In her 1966 essay "Slovo o Lozinskom" (A Word on Lozinskii), Anna Akhmatova paints the following heroic portrait of the translator: "In his work Lozinskii was tireless. Suffering from a serious illness that would have broken another, he continued to work and to help others . . . and the terrible, torturous illness proved powerless in the face of his superhuman will. It is terrible to think that it was at just that time that he undertook the great feat [*podvig*] of his life: the translation of Dante's *Divine Comedy*"

(1967–68:2.188). Translation as a *podvig* is a recurring motif among Russian intellectuals. For example, Etkind underscores the heroic nature of the translator's task by using the term *podvig* to describe Gnedich's gulag translation of *Don Juan*, and Marshak describes the great feats of Russian literary translation as "bogatyrskie" (heroic), from the Russian word *bogatyr'*, a hero of Russian folklore (1990:4.213).

No less heroic than Akhmatova's picture of Lozinskii is the one painted by his granddaughter, the contemporary Russian writer Tatiana Tolstaia, in her essay "Perevodnye kartinki" (Transferable Pictures). She writes, "My grandfather, Mikhail Leonidovich Lozinskii, was a great translator, who spoke six languages fluently and translated, in addition to almost everything else, *Hamlet* and the *Divine Comedy* into Russian. I do not remember him. He died when I was four, a bitter sorrow in my life. In our house, however, it was as if he were alive. . . . They said he worked all the time, all day long, despite infernal pain that tortured him for years; and during breaks from his work, as our elders remember, he would read Flaubert's letters—in French, of course—to relax. Such Titans used to roam the Earth in ancient times! My father, who adored his father-in-law, would read his translations aloud for us, sometimes with tears in his eyes" (2002:250–51).

Conclusion

In the introduction to *Cultures of Letters* (1993), Richard Brodhead states that "writing always takes place within some completely concrete cultural situation, a situation that surrounds it with some particular landscape of institutional structures, affiliates it with some particular group from among the array of contemporary groupings, and installs it within some group-based world of understandings, practices, and values" (1993:8). This is of course no less true of literary translation, which in Soviet society was not merely "affiliated" with an intelligentsia that defined itself largely by its opposition to the official culture of the regime but also provided the rituals and folklore that produced and sustained the intelligentsia's subculture. Literary translation was in turn installed within the intelligentsia's "world of understandings, practices, and values," acquiring a distinct ethical weight and unprecedented visibility.

Resistance must be understood within its specific context insofar as resistance acquires meaning only in relation to that which is being resisted.

Thus, in order to understand how the translation of more or less canonical literary texts could serve as acts of resistance, it is necessary to situate such acts within specific literary-cultural contexts. In very general terms the dogmatic Marxism of Soviet cultural policy, especially after Stalin's consolidation of power in the late 1920s, generated resistance aimed at preserving literature's pretensions to timeless esthetic and moral values. Moreover, the concept of world culture held by the Soviet-era intelligentsia gave pride of place to many of the great writers of the Western literary canon, including Shakespeare, Dante, and Lord Byron (a Russian favorite). What made such acts of resistance possible was in part the prestige accorded to translation in Russian culture in general and in Soviet cultural policy in particular, which was closely related to the prestige accorded to knowledge of foreign languages and cultures overall. In many ways the resistance of the Soviet-era intelligentsia was aimed at preserving their cultural heritage in the broadest sense, that is, not only Russian culture, but all of Western European cultural heritage, which they saw as their own.

The special place of literature, however, has not survived the change of context brought about by the fall of the Soviet Union and the emergence of the new context of post-Soviet Russia. Members of the Soviet-era intelligentsia lament the capitulation of high literature before the onslaught of boulevard literature: romance novels, action thrillers, and detective fiction. Lev Gudkov has characterized the context of the contemporary intelligentsia: "Young people are openly scornful of intellectual pursuits, 'big' literature and good cinema are losing their audiences, and fewer and fewer people are concerned about the future of our cultural heritage" (1995:170). No longer a selfless intellectual toiling at the altar of high culture, the literary translator has been fictionalized in post-Soviet popular fiction in an altogether different light. The translator-detective has become an enormously popular character in post-Soviet culture through the best-selling works of Aleksandra Marinina, Boris Akunin, and Polina Dashkova.[8] Evicted from his ivory tower, the translator-detective works on the street, no longer resisting the official ideology of the regime, but the crime and corruption of a new capitalist Russia.

Notes

1. All translations in this article are my own, unless otherwise noted.
2. For more on socialist realism see Ermolaev (1963) and James (1973).

3. For more on the relationship between *Doctor Zhivago* and Shakespeare, see Glazov-Corrigan (1994).

4. The entire text of Sonnet 66 reads:

Tired with all these, for restful death I cry,
As, to behold desert a beggar born,
And needy nothing trimmed in jollity,
And purest faith unhappily forsworn,
And gilded honor shamefully misplaced,
And maiden virtue rudely strumpeted,
And right perfection wrongfully disgraced,
And strength by limping sway disabled,
And art made tongue-tied by authority,
And folly (doctorlike) controlling skill,
And simple truth miscalled simplicity,
And captive good attending captain ill.
Tired with all these, from these would I be gone,
Save that to die, I leave my love alone. (Shakespeare 1957:4.1427)

5. For more on the political implications of Russian translations of Shakespeare's dramas, see Diener (1984).

6. Nikolai Nekrasov was a famous nineteenth-century poet, known for the social consciousness of his verse.

7. Ironically, Gnedich, Likhachev, and Petrov appear to have unwittingly followed the advice that Lenin gave in the prerevolutionary period to political radicals doing time in czarist prisons. The best way to keep busy in prison, he wrote, was to translate and then backtranslate entire novels (Komissarov 1998:109).

8. For more on the motif of the translator-detective in Russia, see Baer (2005).

PAUL F. BANDIA

Literary Heteroglossia and Translation: Translating Resistance in Contemporary African Francophone Writing

IN postcolonial translation studies most analyses of modes of resistance have dealt mainly with the ways that postcolonial subjects subvert the colonial language either to assert identity or to construct a counterhegemonic discourse against discourses of colonialism (see Venuti 1992, 1995, 1998; Rafael 1993; Mehrez 1992; Bassnett and Trivedi 1999; Simon and St-Pierre 2000). With respect to the African context, Chantal Zabus (1991) has discussed the concept of relexification as a resistance strategy of indigenizing European languages, and Moradewun Adejunmobi (1998) has distinguished between compositional translations, authorized translations, and complex translations to reveal the power relations at work in shaping the identity of African literature.[1] In earlier works I have discussed the impact of African oral narratives on resistance in writing and translation (Bandia 1993, 1996; cf. 2006). These analyses have dealt for the most part with language *in situ* as the defining factor of the autonomy and authenticity of African literature. I claim that some aspects of African creative writing practice can be likened to translation in both a metaphorical and a denotative sense, in which African writers mediate between a culture of orality and a Western written language in a process of translation informed by ideological concerns related to representation, identity, and resistance to colonial domination.

In this essay I seek to alter the terms of the study of resistance by connecting postcoloniality and translation in a new way. Rather than dwell on the binarism of colonized versus colonizer, I introduce the paradigm of class and power into discourses about postcoloniality, indicating that resistance in contemporary postcolonial society is internal rather than external, centripetal rather than centrifugal. Resistance seems to have shifted from a counterimperialist struggle against colonizing forces to the dialectic of class and power within the postcolonial space itself. Expressions of resistance including humor, derision, and reliance on practices of oral manipulation of language variety should be highlighted where strategies of resistance in former colonies are now pitted against internal rather than external sources of oppression. In this article, therefore, I call for a new program of translation whereby priority is given to translating modes of resistance within the specific situations of the postcolonies, including heteroglossic linguistic practices, as determined by struggles of class and power.[2]

Expressions of Resistance in Contemporary Postcolonial Fiction

Recently some postcolonial writers have drawn attention to an important paradigm in postcolonial studies, namely the importance of the reality "on the ground" in postcolonial societies, the lived experience of postcolonial subjects. A close reading of the works of these writers reveals the superficiality and reductionism in systematically assuming that topics pertaining to postcoloniality automatically imply resistance or opposition to an external hegemonic force. These writers follow Frantz Fanon (1966, 1967), who had pointed out much earlier that the knee-jerk opposition of the colonizer and the colonized obscures or overlooks the machinations of internal oppression within the colonies. In Fanon's view the rupture experienced by the postcolonial subject and the ambivalence of colonial relations are too complex to be reduced to a simple dual or binary opposition between the colonized and the colonizer. He thus rejected colonial essentialism and suggested other ways of analyzing and understanding the aggression of colonial space.

The novels of African Francophone writers such as *Trop de soleil tue l'amour* (Too Much Sun Kills Love, 1999) by the Cameroonian Mongo Beti and *La vie et demie* (Life and a Half, 1979) by the Congolese Sony Labou Tansi are examples of contemporary African fiction that locate postcolonial preoccupations within the postcolony itself.[3] These contemporary works in French have their Anglophone counterparts, including Ben Okri's *The Famished Road* (winner of the 1991 Booker Prize) and Chris Abani's *Graceland*

(2004). Such contemporary fictions have moved away significantly from topics related to colonial and postindependence struggle for independence and autonomy, and they tackle themes dealing with the everyday struggles of postcolonial subjects. In these contexts the concept of resistance or unequal power relations is understood in terms of internal dynamics within the postcolonial space which, although it may still involve the deft hand of the colonial metropole, is largely directed at a local elite. This shift in focus introduces important paradigms pertaining to class and power, thus enhancing the purview of postcolonial resistance studies and requiring different parameters for understanding forms of resistance in writing and translation.

In *On the Postcolony* (2001), Achille Mbembe calls attention to the importance of the actual situations in postcolonial societies; he contests binaries such as external oppression versus resistance and autonomy versus subjection, that have characterized discourses in postcolonial studies.[4] Mbembe laments the fact that as a continent of postcolonies, Africa is never really studied in and of itself. Instead Africa is often used as a foil or a sounding board for the West, representing all that the West is not, including the failures of the West. When everything African is reduced to resistance or opposition to the West, thus ignoring the complexity of human action within postcolonial societies, it is inevitable that knowledge of Africa and the understanding of its realities will be impoverished. Hardly any attention is paid to the economic explanations of contemporary social and political phenomena, and "all struggles have become struggles of representation" vis-à-vis the West (Mbembe 2001:6).

According to Mbembe most contemporary works on issues of representation, agency, and resistance have systematically side-stepped questions related to the materiality of postcolonial subjects. Rather, the questions posed emphasize matters of discourse and language, often in relation or in contrast to their Western metropolitan counterparts, as if language and discourse were detached from the acts and practices that construct the social realities in postcolonial contexts. This tendency to focus on representation and discourse is connected with the apprehension of Africa mainly in terms of a dualist and agonistic relationship involving emancipation from colonialism and assimilation into Western modernity. Contemporary postcolonial fiction, such as Beti's *Trop de soleil tue l'amour*, tends to move away from such externalized opposition and the preoccupation with asserting Black humanity.

Trop de soleil tue l'amour is a searing depiction and critique of African society in the late twentieth century. It highlights the failure of the democratization process and paints the picture of a continent adrift. Returning in 1991 to his home country, Cameroon, after decades of exile in France, the author was disillusioned and embittered by the state of affairs in his country, which was supposedly independent and consequently under the rule or control of the local elite. In this satirical novel written after his return, Mongo Beti laments the complete degeneration of society, the social dysfunction, the moral vacuum, and the general lassitude, stupor, and inaction of the populace. Beti had always been an anticolonial militant, critical of the effects of colonialism and slavery on Black people, viewing the struggle as mainly a Black-versus-White affair and considering the heads of postcolonial states as puppets of the former colonial powers. His writing as a whole is subversive and deals intimately with Africa's sociohistoric contexts, so much so that one can glean Africa's contemporary history through it.[5] When Beti returned to Africa, he noted the stark difference between the highly militant discourses about African development articulated in Europe and the complacent attitudes of the local elite who did not seem interested in the future of Africa and were indifferent to the plight of the poorer members of society. *Trop de soleil tue l'amour* is not so much anticolonial as it is antiestablishment, and it highlights forms of resistance to internal oppression, focusing on materiality, power, and class through content, style, and language.

Hybridity and Resistance

Homi Bhabha's (2004/1994) critique of binary conceptualizations and his concept of hybridity provide a critical framework for understanding the current tendency to avoid colonialist dualisms in favor of emphasizing the complex nature of today's postcolonial reality. Such a critical framework is also conducive to integrating the paradigms of class and power into discourses about postcoloniality. Bhabha's concept of hybridity allows one to go beyond binary oppositions to an understanding of postcolonial society as a space of negotiated identities, a space of translation (Bhabha 2004/1994:37). Bhabha points out the ambivalence of postcolonial discourses that construct an identity for colonized subjects based on colonial values on the one hand; on the other hand these same discourses deny colonized subjects full participation in those values, leaving them in a hybrid state, incomplete and partial, hence signifying an inappropriate difference to be closely controlled (2004/1994:122–23). In the essay "Signs Taken for Wonders," Bhabha presents the English book—supposedly a signifier of colonial authority, desire, and discipline—paradoxically as an emblem of ambivalence revealing the weakness of colonial discourse and its susceptibility to mimetic subversion (2004/1994:145–74). The colonized subject's mimicry or repetition of the English book invariably involves a change in its nuances, in other words a subversion that translates eventually into political insurgence.

Bhabha's concept of mimetic subversion that in effect gives credit to the colonized subject's semiotic agency can be applied to the postcolonial subject's mimicry and subversion of the discourses of dominance and power used by the local elite of the postcolony. Bhabha argues that hybridity is a strategic reversal of the process of domination through disavowal: "It unsettles the mimetic or narcissistic demands of colonial power but reimplicates its identifications in strategies of subversion that turn the gaze of the discriminated back upon the eye of power" (Bhabha 2004/1994:159–60). Contemporary postcolonial practices of hybridity are often deployed to evade the eye of the authority or to escape surveillance, as well as to highlight the disproportion between the grandiose rhetoric of the ruling elite and the real economic and political situation facing the lower classes. The display of hybridity, through linguistic interventionism or other modes of resistance, is meant to "terrorize" the elite by way of mimicry or even mockery. We see below how mimetic subversion is enacted through humor and derision as forms of resistance to power. Bhabha states aptly, "To the extent to which discourse is a form of defensive warfare, mimicry marks those moments of civil disobedience within the discipline of civility: signs of spectacular resistance" (2004/1994:172).

In today's postcolonial societies hybridity has become the norm and is no longer viewed by postcolonial subjects as an incomplete, partial, or inappropriate reflection of the metropole. Hybridity here is not just a state of refuge from colonial aggression but rather a fact of life with its own internal machinations for survival. Unlike *métissage*, hybridity is not made up of equally constituted parts; it is a state in which blending seems to occur mainly within the instituted colonial matrix "so that other 'denied' knowledges enter upon the dominant discourse and estrange the basis of its authority" (Bhabha 2004/1994:162). Colonial language is thus subverted and in its various manifestations becomes a powerful weapon in the hands of the dominated, as well as an important component of the linguistic fabric of postcolonial society.

Translating Modes of Resistance: Humor and Derision

The subversive writing strategies employed in novels dealing with current postcolonial realities, which I refer to as the esthetics of resistance, are expressed in ways that are significantly different from those in novels about decolonization or fiction that seeks to reveal the imperial subtexts of colonial discourses. As mentioned above, resistance in today's postcolonial society is less about resistance to the colonizer than it is about resistance to neocolonial regimes of domination and oppression. By neocolonial regimes I mean those power structures that are based on a reappropriation (or mimicry) by Africans of colonial state forms and colonial mannerisms and mentalities. These regimes thrive in so-called independent postcolonies that now have to contend with neocolonial forms of subjugation and oppression such as expanding capitalism, globalization, and the spread of multinational corporations. Postcolonial societies are invariably chaotically pluralistic and therefore should be appraised in all their complexities.

In view of this complexity, postcolonial power relations can be explained not primarily in terms of oppositional resistance or lack thereof or even collaboration but rather in terms of a state of "conviviality" between the dominant and the dominated, as both parties are forced to share the same living space (Mbembe 2001:104).[6] The result is what Mbembe refers to as a form of "intimate tyranny" that transcends the binary opposition of oppressor and oppressed. In this context postcolonial subjects learn to bargain and survive against all odds, adopting varying identities flexible enough to negotiate in or exit from situations of entanglement with authority. Therefore power relations in postcolonial contexts are accompanied by a kind of familiarity and domesticity, which may explain why, contrary to expectations, overt resistance has given way to covert responses or contradictions between overt acts and underground activities. Postcolonial subjects have devised other subtle means of registering discontent, disengagement, and resistance.

Although actual experience is symbolically structured by language (and from a translation perspective experience can be grasped and transmitted only through language), struggles of representation, identity, and resistance take many different forms in what can be referred to as the languages of life. Lived experience in postcolonial Africa is made up of socially produced and objectified practices that cannot all be viewed simply as matters of discourse and language. There are some meaningful expressions that, though molded in language, can be better understood as specific instances of practices imbued with embodied meanings. For instance, humor and derision are powerful weapons used to counter oppression or to subtly undermine authority. Many contemporary African novels have represented humor and derision as strategies of resistance, protest, and survival in the former colonies (see Kourouma 1998; Labou Tansi 1979, 1988). What is significant about these novels is that they depart from the early postcolonial, anticolonialist discourses and embrace more antineo-colonialist, antiestablishment discourses in a quest for social and economic justice and autonomy.

Humor and derision flow from the use of the grotesque and the obscene as strategies for deconstructing regimes of violence and domination. In his discussion of what he calls the banality of power in the postcolony, Mbembe underscores Mikhail Bakhtin's (1984) claim that the grotesque and the obscene are above all the province of ordinary people (*la plèbe*); moreover, "as a means of resistance to the dominant culture and as a refuge from it, obscenity and the grotesque are parodies that undermine officialdom by showing how arbitrary and vulnerable is officialese and by turning it all into an object of ridicule" (Mbembe 2001:103–4). Although Mbembe takes his cue from Bakhtin here, he extends the notion of the grotesque and the obscene beyond "nonofficial" cultures to include the means by which all systems of domination are confirmed or deconstructed. For Mbembe the grotesque and the obscene are two essential elements that identify and are characteristic of postcolonial regimes of domination. These regimes engage in daily rituals whose sole purpose is to institutionalize themselves as symbols or fetishes to which the subjects are bound. The fetishization of power (through the display of wealth and ostentation, pomp and ceremony), as well as the spread of fear (through violence and unpredictability), results in discourses that are integral to political cultures within former colonies.

There is nevertheless considerable disparity between the images the state projects of itself and the way people play with and manipulate those images, undermining the state and eluding control in the process. To avoid trouble or overt conflict, ordinary people locate the fetish of state power in the realm of the ridiculous. Laughter, derision, and humor thus become strategies for deconstructing regimes of violence and domination in the ex-colonies, and these resistant strategies have been carefully "translated" or carried over into African literature in European languages. Representing this political otherness of neocolonial Africa in literature results in a measure of violence or disruption of discourse in what I call the post-postcolonial text. Such subversive writing makes use of specific strategies of humor and derision, as well as various specific language practices, that must be preserved in translation in order to reproduce the subversive character of the source text, including its subtexts. A successful poaching of meaning from African novels about the postcolonial condition or the neo-colonial state relies on understanding popular humor as a powerful ex-pression of resistance. Popular humor as a type of resistance to state power can take the form of deliberate mistranslations and misrepresentations of the discourses of the elite, for example the deformation of speeches or slo-gans of political parties.[7]

In *Trop de soleil tue l'amour*, for example, Beti portrays state power in the postcolony as grotesque and obscene, as a regime of simulacrum, and he reveals how ordinary citizens use humor and derision to resist or circumvent state control. The author satirizes governmentality in the post-colony and shows how postcolonial subjects can simulate adherence to bureaucratic rituals, while undermining state authority. Translating the humor in this novel is tantamount to translating various expressions of resistance to state power, in terms of both content and language. At the same time the humor is often embedded in disruptive and innovative uses of French, calling for subversive translation practices that are highly de-pendent upon the inventiveness and creativity of the translator.

Unlike early postcolonial writing that often resorted to a form of writing as translation in order to subvert or modify the colonial language, contemporary African literature does not seek to assert identity mainly through a peculiar use of language per se. In Beti's novel, for example, his goal is not to use the French language differently in order to assert Afri-canness or to express resistance to Western hegemony. In fact, the narra-tive voice of the novel is written in a popular but standard style of French, and Beti does not deliberately seek to deform the structures of the French language. Rather, the novel reveals variations on the "colonial" language in its diverse manifestations within contemporary African society, particularly in the passages of dialogue. The diverse registers and varieties of language convey a sense of the internalization of French on a cultural level and its consequent mapping on a landscape in the postcolony that is characterized by a social hierarchy reflected in part in language.

Zam the journalist, the main protagonist, uses a fairly mainstream popular French, while his friend Eddie, the (fake) lawyer, is given to Parisian argot for a variety of reasons, including the fact that it is a language befitting the chaos and mess of the postcolonial world. Consider for example the following passage which occurs after a few bureaucratic words spoken by Eddie result in sudden fear on the part of a corrupt police official:

> —Qu'est-ce qui lui a pris tout . . . à coup de capituler comme ça, en rase campagne? demanda Zam . . . à son avocat dès qu'ils furent dehors.
> —Je suppose, fit l'avocat, que tu veux parler de cet *enculé de flicaillon de merde*, que je n'avais d'ailleurs jamais vu auparavant, ce qui ne laisse pas de m'étonner? *Tu as vu comment il cause?* On dirait un acteur qui a longtemps *répété les répliques*. Et comment il te reluquait, tu as vu? *Et si, c'était un pédé?* (Beti 1999:37, emphasis mine)

> "What came over him all of a sudden to toss in the towel in the middle of a round like that?" Zam asked his lawyer as soon as they were outside.
> "I suppose," answered the lawyer, "you're referring to that shitty asshole of a small-time cop, who in any case, I'd never seen before? Which doesn't make it any less surprising. Did you just hear him chat? Like he's an actor who has spent a long time rehearsing his lines. And how he ogled you, did you see? And what if he was queer?"

Zam's question here draws attention to the humor implied in the way bureaucratic words can have a dramatic effect in the culture. Zam uses the expression "capituler comme ça, en rase compagne" (literally, 'capitulate like that in open country') playfully or facetiously to describe the policeman's act of cowardice. The translation, "toss in the towel in the middle of a round like that" reproduces the implied humor by taking up the playfulness implied in an English idiomatic expression drawn from the pugilistic domain to underscore the struggle between the dominant state power and ordinary citizens. This kind of modulation in translating from one domain to another is meant to achieve a similar effect in the target language. Moreover, Eddie's Parisian argot ("cet enculé de flicaillon de merde"; literally something like 'that asshole of a trashy little piece of cop shit') indicates his disdain for the agent of the state and is captured in a comparable English phrase "shitty asshole of a small-time cop" which also stresses disdain for and animosity toward state authority. Furthermore, when Eddie asks, "Tu as vu comment il cause?" (instead of the standard, "Tu as vu comment il parle?," literally, 'you saw how he speaks?'), he employs the word *cause* (chatter, yack) to ridicule or poke fun at the policeman's manner of speech and to undercut his authority by demoting his official pronouncements to the status of gossip, a connotation captured in the translation. Translation of this type seeks to replicate the use of humor as a strategy of resistance to state oppression, even if this means providing a dynamic equivalent to enhance the intensity of the power differentials.

From the standpoint of writing and translation, we are not dealing here with the kind of linguistic innovation or formal experimentation aimed at enacting resistance to the colonial metropole or asserting identity per se, typical of earlier postcolonial writing, but rather with a situation of literary heteroglossia prevalent in contemporary African fiction because it reflects resistant African cultural practices in the postcolony. There is the deliberate alternation between the reasoned and standard variety of French spoken by Zam the journalist and the gruff Parisian argot used by the tough-talking Eddie. The plurivocity and heteroglossia woven into the novel throughout reveal a dark humor and echo the chaotic pluralism of the postcolony, directing the reader's attention to deliberate attempts to create discord and block communication between the discourses of the elite and those of the populace. They are a means of expressing resistance to oppression and of exposing the imbalance of power. When a translator attempts to transpose such representations of the plurivocity of the postcolony, this writing practice changes the terms of translating from a constant search for foreignizing linguistic equivalents to a strategy for reproducing the multiple and conflicting voices of the same source language. The translator must seek to capture these multifarious voices in a heterogeneous language reflective of the implied chaos and the various strategies of dissension and resistance employed in postcolonies by the oppressed to counter state hegemony and dominance by the elite.

There are several distinct "languages" to deal with in Beti's novel. They include at a minimum the standard French of the narrative voice;

Zam's mainstream popular French; the language spoken by Eddie and to-day's been-tos[8] or deportees (Parisian argot, tough talk, and coarse language reflective of harsh experiences in the seedy underworld of illegal immigrants in the metropole); the *français africain* or African French Vernacular used by the character named Bébète, as well as other semi-literates (marked by frequent code-switching and code-mixing involving indigenous languages and a local variety of French);[9] and African officialese. The language of state control is thus alienated from its colonial mantle of power and challenged by the oral speech of the illiterate or semi-literate proletariat in the postcolony. Moreover, the heteroglossia in Beti's novel has a materialist basis. The language varieties position the characters socially and economically with respect to class and power, revealing tensions and conflicts within the postcolony.

Translation of such a text must therefore become heteroglossic, paying particular attention to language varieties correlated with class and power inequalities in an attempt to capture the various vernacular expressions of resistance. There is a semblance here of what Samia Mehrez has characterized as "a perpetual migration of signs" (1992:134), an emphasis on the unequal and noncommunicating dialogue between various languages within the postcolonial space. The task of the translator in this context is not merely to cope with different linguistic registers, but rather to represent what amounts to a collection of linguistic varieties, representing distinct language groups and language practices, even though they are rooted in more or less the same code. That is, although they occur within the same European language, these hybrid languages vary according to the native languages of the speakers. It should be pointed out that this form of intralinguistic heteroglossia, where various "languages" coexist within the frame of a major code, should be distinguished from the situation of pidgins and creoles in relation to their substrate languages: the language varieties in contemporary postcolonies cannot be extricated from the source code or given autonomy as in the case of creoles. Also, it is difficult to find direct equivalents in the receptor language for those "languages" as they are used in postcolonial Africa. Intralinguistic heteroglossic practices in English have not evolved in the same way or for the same reasons as corresponding French practices in contemporary Africa. For instance, West African Pidgin English is a creole that is used almost uniformly across West Africa but for translation purposes there is no French equivalent of similar linguistic stature.

Heteroglossia, Translation, and the Politics of Resistance

Contemporary literature dealing with the postcolony or neocolonialism exploits existing forms of language to address the immediate concerns of postcolonial society. In *Trop de soleil tue l'amour*, for example, the use of officialese by representatives of state power, who desire its majesty or power as a fetish, is borrowed and subverted by ordinary people in ways that locate officialdom in the realm of ridicule. Consider the following statement by Eddy.

> T'as vraiment pas pigé, journaleux de mes fesses? Pour leur foutre la pétoche, . . . à ces enfoirés, y a des mots fétiches aujourd'hui. Tu prononces, par exemple, *fanatiques, initiatives incontrôlées, individus vindicatifs*, et le tour est joué. (Beti 1999:39, emphasis mine)

> You really don't get it, do you, hack of my ass? And you call yourself a journalist? If you want to scare those assholes shitless, all you need these days are a few magic words like fanatics, uncontrolled initiatives, vindictive individuals, and the game's over.

Eddy uses the argot expression "journaleux de mes fesses" (literally, 'journalist of my ass'), to mock Zam the journalist about his ignorance of the ways of corrupt policemen and the importance of officialese; in translation the expression has been expanded as "hack of my ass. And you call yourself a journalist?" The translation takes up Eddy's humorous use of argot while highlighting his sense of pride as a streetwise individual who has more savvy than a local journalist about the inner workings of the corrupt state apparatus. Eddy evokes the power of officialese in the words emphasized above to illustrate the humbling effect such words can have even on an agent of the state, the corrupt policeman alluded to above. The humor underscores for the reader that these words meant to intimidate ordinary citizens can also have such a deterring effect on a policeman. On the whole, Beti's text reveals the hollow pretense of officialdom in the former colonies and the strategies actually employed to subvert it. Officialese is a common phenomenon in most postindependence governments in Africa, a leftover from colonial rule, that was designed to impress upon the natives a sense of awe and deference to the colonial administration. The mimicry of this practice by local governments has been a frequent source of derision and mockery in contemporary postcolonial literature.

Mongo Beti's novel also foregrounds français africain (African French Vernacular), a language variety that in reality betrays failed attempts to mimic metropolitan French but is used strategically in the novel to under-mine state power. Beti's attitude toward African French Vernacular can be explained in light of his hostility toward "la Francophonie," the umbrella concept promoted (especially by France) to bring together and heighten the affiliation of all French-speaking countries. Beti attributes what he considers to be the poor state of the French language in Africa to the ambiguity and hypocrisy of "la Francophonie," which he views as an instrument of neoco-lonialism and a forum for exploitative collaboration between the former colonial power and the local elite. In his novel Beti uses français africain as a double-edged sword. On the one hand he seeks to expose the elite as fake, a false elite who engage in a hyperbolic language of control and domination, emulating the colonial power, yet who remain incapable of using the colo-nial language properly. On the other hand while exposing the general laxity of the African elite, he highlights the linguistic resourcefulness of ordinary people in their struggle for survival and their resistance to oppression.

Beti regrets the fact that very few people use indigenous languages in the nation's capital and speak instead the hybrid français africain, as can be seen in the passage below. He therefore makes it a point in *Trop de soleil tue l'amour* to translate statements made in the indigenous languages into standard French, irrespective of the character's social class or level of edu-cation.[10] This seems to be Beti's way of foregrounding the authenticity of native vernaculars that he holds in higher regard than hybrid languages derived from the colonial tongue.

> Zam et Bébète se regardèrent; le taximan avait l'air d'un brave garçon; de plus, on résiste difficilement ici à qui vous parle en langue maternelle, tel-lement c'est devenu rare dans la capitale.
> —Quelle chance est la vôtre, répétait-il. Pourquoi hésiter? Suivez-moi, vous ne regretterez pas. Quelle coïncidence, un vrai miracle . . .
> —Ils se laissèrent séduire et dormirent le soir même dans une élégante villa, construite en rotonde, avec jardin, téléphone, piscine et dépendances. . . .
> —N'aie pas peur, mon joli bébé. De toute façon, on saura bientôt si c'est du lard ou du cochon, comme disent les Français.
> Normalement, Bébète aurait dû répliquer, dans le français africain où elle excellait, quand elle voulait bien:
> —Ça veut même dire quoi là?
> Mais elle ne disait rien, et Zam ne se formalisait pas de ce mutisme. (Beti 1999:61)

Zam and Bébète looked at each other; the cab driver seemed an honest lad; what's more, it's difficult not to trust someone who speaks to you in the mother tongue, which has become so rare in the capital.

"You are so lucky," he repeated. "Why hesitate? Come with me, you won't regret it. What a coincidence, it's a real miracle . . ."

They let themselves be persuaded and spent that same night in an elegant villa, of circular shape, with a garden, telephone, pool, and outbuildings.

"Don't be afraid, my lovely baby. In any case we'll soon find out whether it's lard or pork, as the French say."

Normally Bébète would have retorted in African French, in which she excelled when she chose to speak it:

"That there even means what?"

But she said nothing and Zam didn't make much of her silence.

After stating that regrettably the native tongue is rarely heard in the capital city, the author represents the cab driver's statements made in the native language in standard French. Generally cab drivers in postcolonial urban sprawls are illiterate or semi-literate in the colonial language and tend to use hybrid varieties of the colonial language in dealing with their customers from various ethnic backgrounds. It is therefore significant that Beti represents the cab driver's speech in the vernacular as a translation into standard French. In keeping with the author's strategy, I have translated the cab driver's statement into standard English.

When juxtaposed with oral statements in African French Vernacular on the same page, such as "Ça veut même dire quoi là?," Beti makes a point about the "authenticity" of the indigenous languages and the impoverishment of hybrid, creolized versions of the colonial language. There is implied humor couched in the sarcastic phrase about Bébète's command of African French Vernacular "in which she excelled," which must be captured in the translation. The humor is enhanced by Beti's deliberate misuse of the French idiomatic expression "si c'est du lard ou du cochon," which normally means "you never know where you are with someone, whether or not someone is being serious." I have chosen to translate the expression literally as "whether it's lard or pork" in order to retain the humor and replicate Beti's use of the expression to underscore the uncertainty and precariousness of life under a neocolonial regime.

Although Beti regrets the scarcity of the use of indigenous languages in the capital city, he understands the people's recourse to hybrid languages derived from the colonial tongue for purposes of interethnic communication, in-group solidarity, and resistance to oppression by the political elite.[11] He also acknowledges the communication value of such hybrid languages in contexts where there is a language difference between the masses and the cloned Westernized elite. He is therefore firm in his condemnation of the elite whom he sees as puppets trying to emulate colonial attitudes, including the use of colonial languages that they themselves master so imperfectly. Beti takes issue with those members of the elite who despise the masses for speaking local hybrid varieties of the colonial language, but who themselves have a poor command of the standard language. This elite class insists on the use of colonial languages rather than native vernaculars in schools and other official spheres. Local varieties such as français africain are therefore the consequence of such linguistic imposition, oppression, and alienation, which understandably have now become conduits for acts of resistance to state power.[12]

There is a deliberate contrast between the African French Vernacular used by illiterate or semi-literate individuals such as Bébète, as well as various state agents and politicians, and the Parisian slang used by Eddie, the postcolonial subject who has been to the capital of the colonial metropole and has come back home with only negative attributes. The following exchange between Eddie and an opposition leader is an example of linguistic confrontation in the postcolony and its significance for the subtext of class-based resistance and subversion in contemporary African fiction.

> —D'abord tu es quoi? lui objecta un leader bien connu de l'opposition, celui dont on disait qu'il aurait pu organiser un congrès de son parti dans une cabine téléphonique, tant ses troupes étaient évanescentes, sinon inexistantes. Oui, tu es quoi même? Tu es journaliste? Tu es leader politique? Tu es quoi? Tu fais quoi là même? Au nom de quoi tu prends la parole ici?
>
> C'est le genre d'attitude qu'il valait mieux ne jamais adopter avec Eddie, qui répliqua aussi sec :
>
> —Et toi, qui es-tu, espèce de trou de cul? Petit pédé merdeux, enfoiré de connard de bougnoul, où sont tes troupes? Qui représentes-tu? (Beti 1999:74)

In this passage Beti uses nonstandard forms of interrogatives such as "tu es quoi?" (literally, 'you are what?', as well as the familiar *tu*, to highlight the politician's poor knowledge of French and crude manners. Although interrogatives without syntactic inversion are common in conversational metropolitan French, the practice is more prevalent in African French, and these affirmative-interrogatives are often accompanied by "empty" or unnecessary words or particles such as *même* (even), *là* (there), or a combination of the two, *là même* (there even).[13] Although this nonstandard use of French is characteristic of African French Vernacular, the author's aim is not to put down this dialect but rather to expose the pretense and self-delusion of the politician who during a heated debate slips into the hybrid language all the while thinking he is speaking standard French. Eddie replies by using the familiar *tu*, as well as a series of insults in Parisian argot: "espèce de trou de cul," "petit pédé merdeux," "enfoiré de connard de bougnoul," translated below. This confrontation between the elite politician and Eddie is an allegory of class conflict played out in linguistic terms. Here the humor is embedded in the politician's laughable and delusionary use of nonstandard French, as well as Eddie's unbridled use of argot to enact resistance by undermining the politician's authority.

Traces of français africain in this dialogue, such as "tu es quoi même?" (literally, 'you are what even?') and "tu fais quoi là même?" (literally, 'you are doing what there even?'), abound in the novel. They occur in a variety of situations from arguments in casual conversations to heated debates involving government officials or semi-literate individuals. The tendency to pose questions in the affirmative in français africain reflects the influence of indigenous African languages, for the interrogatives seem to be literal translations from the vernaculars (see Kom 2000; Noumssi and Fosso 2001). The grammatical particles *là* and *même* are used frequently as emphasis, as interjections, as grammatically empty categories, as mere tags, or as hypercorrective attempts to emphasize Frenchness employed by French-speaking Africans. As simple as these markers of français africain might appear, it is not always easy to translate them while maintaining their metalinguistic significance as expressions of subversion or resistance to authority.[14] The following translation seeks to retain these qualities.

> "First of all, you are what?" objected a well-known leader of the opposition, whose party membership, rumor had it, was so evanescent and so nonexistent that he could easily hold a party congress in a telephone booth. "Yes, you are what even? You! A journalist? You! A political leader? You are what? You are even doing what here? In the name of what do you speak here?"

It is the kind of attitude one was better off never adopting toward Eddie, who retorted dryly:

"And you, who are you, asshole? Shitty faggot, poor little wog of a nigger, where are your militants? Who do you represent?"

Here the nonstandard interrogatives have been translated by similar nonstandard forms in English to indicate the divergent and subversive character of Eddie's speech. For example, "tu es quoi?" is rendered as "you are what?" (rather than the idiomatic "what are you?"). The English translation attempts to give an approximate rendition of the context and manner of enunciation of a comparable semiliterate, English-speaking West African. The nonstandard syntax of the French is mirrored in the disrupted English syntax of the translation, and the peculiar use of grammatical particles such as *là* and *même* are retained in the translation, calling the reader's attention to their significance as forms of resistance to the imposed metropolitan language. At the same time no specific dialect of English is chosen as an equivalent of African French Vernacular. The implied humor in this passage is enhanced by Beti's deliberate interventionist writing that allows the translator the liberty to subvert the target language in an attempt to capture the already subverted discourse of the novel. The subversive translation (Levine 1991) plays with language registers, dialects, and varieties in much the same way that Beti's writing does to enact resistance.

As mentioned above, because français africain is neither a pidgin, nor creole, nor standard French, it has no established Anglophone equivalent. It is an unstable variety of French, often calqued on the syntax of diverse indigenous languages, betraying the speaker's approximate knowledge of standard French. The humor here is enhanced by the contrast between the politician's poor use of French and Eddie's tirade of insults in fluent Parisian argot. My translation seeks to reproduce this sociolinguistic reality by disrupting the English syntax and the grammaticality of interrogatives, as well as by using tags to approximate the particles in the French text. Lawrence Venuti notes that "foreign texts that are stylistically innovative invite the English-language translator to create sociolects striated with various dialects, registers and styles, inventing a collective assemblage that questions the seeming unity of standard English" (1998:11). The translation of Beti's text here is disruptive of language not merely in order to question the "seeming unity of standard English" but also to reflect societal chaos and the subversion of language as a strategy of resistance in the African postcolony of Cameroon.

Translation and Resistance: A New Direction

This study calls for a new program of translation to deal with modes of resistance characteristic of contemporary postcolonial societies where various strategies of resistance can be understood in terms of opposition to internal rather than external forms of oppression. Resistance to state forms of oppression more than resistance to colonial domination commands attention in contemporary African writing. Resistance in contemporary Francophone African fiction is expressed in both content and form, and hybridity is used deliberately to disrupt the flow of the novel, which is generally written in standard metropolitan language but includes heteroglossic elements contesting the authority of that colonial norm. There is subversion of language reflecting subversive social transactions marking the tension between the populace and the elite, as well as other internal contestations.

My analysis of contemporary postcolonial narrative strategies uses a critical framework that introduces class and power as pivotal elements in discourses about postcoloniality. The study shows how resistance is shaped by the internal dynamics of class and power in postcolonial society. Because of inequalities in power, resistance can take many subtle forms including humor, derision, laughter, and the interplay of language varieties. In literature these modes of resistance are expressed in language, but language is often secondary to images of the grotesque or the obscene that serve as conduits for humor and derision and that are played up as strategies of resistance to state power. The linguistic situation in contemporary postcolonial societies has become even more complex than that represented in early postcolonial fiction which opposed mainstream European language to colonized varieties or to vernaculars. The bidirectional opposition between the language of empire and its colonial derivatives has been supplanted by a multidimensional linguistic reality with strong sociolinguistic indicators pertaining to economic stratification, class, and differentials in power. The linguistic hybridity and literary heteroglossia characteristic of today's postcolonial societies result from both incomplete mimicry of colonial discourses and deliberate attempts to negotiate or circumvent state authority and neocolonial realities. Writing this hybridity and heteroglossia is metaphorically to translate the languages of resistance with their multiple voices and representations.

The many new forms of resistance found in contemporary African literature call for new programs of translation. If the translator is to transpose the author's own resistance and the author's representations of resistance, the translator must carry over conflicts of class and power internal to postcolonial societies. It is essential for the translator to grasp the modes of resistance within the specific situations of postcolonies and then represent this resistance through translation strategies that mirror and account for the various forms of expression in the source texts. In particular translation must seek to recreate the subversive character of contemporary postcolonial literature by paying close attention to the various intersecting registers and language varieties used to position characters and to draw a portrait of the society as a whole. If political resistance in the postcolony involves a class struggle expressed in part through the play of language, then resistance in translation cannot involve homogenization of language in the translated text. The translation of popular vernaculars and dialects is a thorny issue especially in postcolonial contexts where colonial policies have resulted in differing dialectal practices. These vernaculars and dialects are often distinguished by their lack of mutual intelligibility, indicating the incommensurability of dialects across languages, hence the tendency either to exaggerate or to obliterate dialect markers in translation.[15] No uniform textual strategy (including foreignization) can suffice for translating contemporary texts from the postcolonies and contemporary postcolonial writers.

Resistance is achieved not by foregrounding foreign elements of the source text in translation or by disrupting target language norms by reproducing source language items, as Venuti suggests (1992, 1995, 1998), but rather by deliberately attempting to capture the already subversive and defamiliarized heterogeneous language of the source text. In other words translating resistance in the postcolony deviates from Venuti's concept of resistant translation in that the translator seeks to resist oppressive norms not by foreignizing the target language but by being attuned to the subversive and defamiliarizing language of the source text. Beti's prose is already resistant because it plays with various forms of language, notably the many forms of heteroglossia, including dialects, characteristic of the urban neocolonial setting. His writing is already a translation insofar as it involves an interventionist strategy to decenter the French language and to disrupt the transparent use of language as a whole in his representations. The translator of such resistant writing should therefore strive to reinforce the writer's stylistic peculiarities and heterogeneity, as well as to sustain the underlying ideological program. The translation must reflect the dialogism of the source text (cf. Bakhtin 1981), not merely so as to disrupt the reader's complacency and presuppositions but to convey the author's cultural vision as well. Heteroglossia serves to convey authorial strategies, including the humor, derision, and parody that express resistance in Beti's novel.

The translation choices commanded by a discourse of resistance based on class conflict and the particular situation in the postcolony discussed here are similar to those suggested in Gayatri Spivak's (1993) concept of "strategic essentialism," whereby the translator as postcolonial mediator is called upon to pay particular attention to the forms, the language, and the specific context of the postcolonial reality. Translation here is not about reviving some lost essence of a pristine precolonial past or undoing a colonialist hegemonic discourse. Instead translation enacts a mirroring effect of reproducing and perpetuating the already resistant and subversive discourses of the postcolony expressed in the source text. Translation participates in exposing the consequence of colonialism and neocolonialism in a specific historical situation. The translator should therefore be conversant with the "history of the language, the history of the author's moment, the history of the language-in-translation" (Spivak 1993:186). This awareness allows the translator to assume an active role as a mediator who reinforces the author's expressions of resistance in the target language culture, creating and constructing structures of resistance in the target text rather than subsuming them. The translation approach is interventionist in that the target language resources are mobilized in order to reproduce similar source language resistant effects.

This sort of interventionist translation is neither wholly foreignizing nor wholly domesticating, nor does it involve a systematic quest for dynamic equivalence or formal equivalence, for it does not concern itself with issues of transparency or fluency. The translator's main concern is to convey the aesthetic effect of the source and to participate in the construction of a discourse of resistance across linguistic borders as determined by the variables of class and power (cf. Lane-Mercier 1997). Linguistic interventionism is taken up in such translations by employing strategies that disrupt the target language and reproduce the intended effect of resistance to state power and other local forms of oppression. The case of Francophone African literature demonstrates how the study of translation and resistance stands to benefit from discourses on postcoloniality that include the important paradigms of class and power as they pertain to specific situations in contemporary postcolonial societies.

Notes

1. Compositional translations refer to European-language texts for which there are no obvious originals in indigenous African languages; authorized translations occur when a European-language text is inspired by several existing versions of an indigenous text; complex translations are not a method for Africanizing European languages but rather a process in which the movement between languages is deliberate and becomes an end in itself.

2. The term *postcolony* is borrowed from Achille Mbembe's *On the Postcolony* (2001) and refers to the current context of former colonies.

3. All translations are my own unless otherwise noted.

4. *On the Postcolony* (2001) is a translation of *De la postcolonie: Essai sur l'imagination politique dans l'Afrique contemporaine* (2000). Both books came out about the same time; the French original has six chapters while the English translation has five.

5. See especially Beti (1971, 1985, 1987; cf. 1984, 1993, 1994).

6. Mbembe uses the term *conviviality* in its gallicized sense, translated literally from the French *convivialité*, meaning warm and friendly relations.

7. See, for example, Toulabor (1981). Writing about political derision in Togo, he shows how under a one-party dictatorship, citizens devised means to undermine state authority by giving new meaning to words or phrases drawn from government speeches or slogans.

8. A *been-to* is an African who has lived in Europe. It is often used derogatorily to mean someone who came back to Africa after a long stay in Europe with nothing to show for it (no academic degrees, diplomas, or valued professional training, and no measure of wealth).

9. The term *français africain* refers to a variety of French spoken by uneducated or semi-literate individuals in Francophone Africa. This language variety is distinct from the standard French spoken in Africa called by some linguists *le français d'Afrique*. As there is no known equivalent in English in Africa, I have chosen to translate *français africain* as "African French Vernacular," by analogy with Black English Vernacular (BEV).

10. There are more than 250 native vernaculars representing ten major language groups in Cameroon, including the language Beti foregrounds in this novel.

11. See the comments in Beti (2003).

12. It is rather surprising that Beti became a defender of indigenous languages, as it is generally known that he vehemently opposed the teaching of native languages in schools in the decades following independence. At the time he argued that education in indigenous languages would prevent African youth from mastering the French language and from being competitive on the world stage. Beti's about-face could be the result of his personal sense of alienation and frustration after spending almost half a century in exile in France.

13. The use of the familiar *tu* instead of the formal *vous* is also a deliberate mark of disrespect on the part of both speakers.

14. Cf. Even-Zohar (1990:219–45) who discusses similar problems related to what he calls "void pragmatic connectives."

15. A discussion of the problem of flattening dialects is found in Simon and St-Pierre (2000:256, 285); cf. Lane-Mercier (1997) on problems of incommensurability of dialects.

JOHN MILTON

The Resistant Political Translations of Monteiro Lobato

Iₙ this article I examine the translations and adaptations of José Bento Monteiro Lobato (1882–1948), a prolific writer of fiction, children's books, and treatises, most of which focus on bringing a more forward-looking mentality to Brazil. As a publisher initially with Monteiro Lobato e Cia. and then with Companhia Editora Nacional, Monteiro Lobato was also a key figure in the development of the Brazilian publishing industry. He was the first publisher in Brazil who attempted to develop a mass market for books and to turn the book industry into a consumer industry. Until Monteiro Lobato most publishing was in the hands of Portuguese or French-owned companies, and the target market was very much that of the Francophile middle-class elite. Monteiro Lobato used his translations, retellings, and writing, as well as his work as a publisher, to advance his political views and criticisms of the government (1930–45) of the populist dictator of Brazil, Getúlio Vargas (1882–1954), and to shift power structures. Monteiro Lobato's domesticating strategies and his complex manipulation of the place of enunciation in his writing and his translations alike combined with his contemporary colloquial Brazilian Portuguese to create effective tools of political resistance.

Monteiro Lobato's initial success as a writer was with *Urupês* (1918), stories about rural life inspired by his experience as a farm owner near São Paulo, which featured Jeca Tatu, an indolent yokel, who for Monteiro Lobato represents rural backwardness and ignorance. This book was followed by his first collection of children's stories, *A menina do narizinho arrebitado* (The

Girl with the Turned-up Nose, 1921), in which he introduced his cast of children and dolls at the Sítio do Picapau Amarelo (Yellow Woodpecker Farm). The success of both books was phenomenal and in many ways started the book industry in Brazil.[1] By 1920 more than half of all the literary works published in Brazil were published by Monteiro Lobato e Cia., and in 1941 a quarter of all books published in Brazil were produced by Monteiro Lobato's Companhia Editora Nacional (Koshiyama 1982:133).[2] Monteiro Lobato believed that a growing book industry would significantly aid the development of Brazil; he proclaimed, "Um país se faz com homens e livros" (A country is made by people and books; qtd. in Koshiyama 1982:99).[3] He believed that people act responsibly in virtue of knowing the human experience of other people; such knowledge is found in various forms of communication, especially books, and results in action.

Despite his exaltation about books, Monteiro Lobato had a hardheaded attitude toward selling them. He saw books as commercial objects that could be sold just as other goods were, at a variety of sales outlets: "livro não é género de primeira necessidade . . . é sobremesa: tem que ser posto embaixo do nariz do freguês, para provocar-lhe a gulodice" (books are not staples of the diet . . . they are desserts: they must be put under the nose of the customer to excite his sweet tooth; qtd. in Koshiyama 1982:72). He managed to increase the points of sale for his works from 40, the total number of bookshops in Brazil when he began publishing, to 1,200, including drugstores and newsstands (Hallewell 1985:245). He was also innovative in terms of the visual presentation of books, becoming responsible for more attractive covers than the featureless yellow ones that followed French fashion.

Monteiro Lobato stressed the importance that Brazil should give to its own culture, consistently opposing dominant Francophile tendencies that copied the latest Parisian fashions in art, music, and literature. He wanted to open Brazil outward to German, Russian, Scandinavian, and Anglo-American literature. Accordingly, he became a prolific translator, adapting such works as *Peter Pan, Alice in Wonderland, Robinson Crusoe, Tom Sawyer, Huckleberry Finn*, and *Gulliver's Travels*. Monteiro Lobato's Companhia Editora Nacional opened in 1925 after the bankruptcy of Monteiro Lobato e Cia., which over-invested in printing presses. This second publishing house issued works by Conan Doyle, Eleanor H. Porter, Ernest Hemingway, H. G. Wells, Herman Melville, Jack London, John Steinbeck, and Rudyard Kipling. Thus Monteiro Lobato helped initiate a movement toward the importation of works written originally in English, that continued right up to World War II, when English began to oust French as the primary foreign language studied and spoken in Brazil. His companies also published unknown Brazilian authors, thus democratizing access to the publishing industry, because being published had previously depended on having either money or influence in high places.

At the time Monteiro Lobato was writing, very little had been translated into Brazilian Portuguese. In his 1923 essay "Traduções" ("Translations"), he emphasized the spiritual enrichment that translations—and not only translations from French—could provide, and he specifically noted the scarcity of good translations from languages other than French (Monteiro Lobato 1951:125–30). Monteiro Lobato mentioned the lack of translations into Brazilian Portuguese of Homer, Sophocles, Herodotus, Plutarch, Aeschylus, Shakespeare, Goethe, Schiller, Molière, Rabelais, and Ibsen. He argued that Brazilian readers needed light and air, new horizons and wide-open windows, to escape their dark prison.

Promoting another type of resistance to French cultural tastes, Monteiro Lobato believed that Brazil should look to itself: to its interior, to its own folklore, and to its own traditional myths (see Azevedo 1997:63 and passim). But he also believed that rural Brazil needed reawakening. Always the practical man, Monteiro Lobato encouraged vaccination campaigns and improvements in basic sanitary conditions. He thought that the government needed to stimulate investment in the interior, and he criticized the country people themselves for their indolence, typified in his picture of the idle yokel, Jeca Tatu, who contrasts radically with the idealized and romanticized rural figures found in the works of the late nineteenth-century Brazilian novelist José de Alencar, for example. Monteiro Lobato's translation, literary, and publishing activities were thus part of engagement with economic and cultural reforms, and his activist undertakings related to public policy.

Monteiro Lobato and the United States

From 1927 to 1931 Monteiro Lobato was commercial attaché for the Brazilian government in New York and he became greatly impressed by the economic organization and efficiency of the United States. He was an enthusiastic admirer of Henry Ford and visited Detroit, where, he said, his week there was "a mais notável de minha vida" (the most important in my life;

qtd. in Azevedo 1997:256). The way in which the United States had taken advantage of its mineral wealth, particularly its iron ore, coal, and oil, showed him what Brazil might be capable of if the country took the correct steps and developed its own iron and oil industries rather than leaving them to the mercy of trusts, such as the Standard Oil Corporation in particular.

In 1926, even before going to the United States, Monteiro Lobato wrote a series of articles for the newspaper *O Jornal* that were then translated into English by Aubrey Stuart and published in Rio de Janeiro in 1926 in pamphlet form under the title *How Henry Ford Is Regarded in Brazil*. In the same year the Companhia Editora Nacional published Monteiro Lobato's translation of Ford's *My Life and Work* (*Minha vida e minha obra*) and in 1927 Ford's *Today and Tomorrow* (*Hoje e amanhã*). Monteiro Lobato saw Ford as an "organic idealist," who by "ensinando a trabalhar, provando que o trabalho é o supremo bem e demonstrando a altíssima significação da palavra indústria" (teaching people how to work, proving that work is the supreme good, and showing the highest meaning of the word *industry*; qtd. in Azevedo 1997:206).

Fordism and U.S. efficiency were venerated by Monteiro Lobato. He saw them as offering a stark contrast to the lack of efficiency in Brazil. Interestingly, perhaps because of the fact that he came from a country that had as yet virtually no urban proletariat, Monteiro Lobato could see few of the evils that might accompany Fordism. He had nothing but praise for Ford, writing "um dia de Nova York vale uma vida no Brasil—pelo menos ensina mais que ela" (one day in New York is worth a life in Brazil—at least it teaches more; qtd. in Azevedo 1997:243). Monteiro Lobato believed that Fordism would improve the welfare of the entire country, providing a wealth of goods that would be available for all. He argued that Brazil should copy the United States, making use of its natural resources and improving communications and information systems. Monteiro Lobato suggested that a Brazilian cultural center should also be established in New York to provide cultural and commercial information, and that Brazil should provide more information about its goods, present them better, improve quality control, and increase tourism from the United States.

Monteiro Lobato idealized U.S. society throughout the Roaring Twenties. He thought that a desirable level of wealth and happiness had been achieved: "Aqui vejo todos os problemas resolvidos e uma média de felicidade individual que nunca nenhum sociólogo julgou possível. É positivamente o primeiro país que acertou a mão na ciência do viver coletivo" (Here I can see that all problems have been solved and that there is an average level of individual happiness that no sociologist ever thought possible. It is quite definitely the first country that has got the science of collective living right; qtd. in Azevedo 1997:238). In *Mr. Slang e o Brasil* (Mr. Slang and Brazil; 1927), a pamphlet consisting of conversations between an Englishman who is a "philosopher" living in Rio de Janeiro and an average Brazilian, Monteiro Lobato also praises Ford's policy of employing the blind and physically handicapped, making them feel useful to society and paying them well at six dollars a day. Monteiro Lobato also appreciated the freedom enjoyed by women in the United States: "O mais curioso da América é o grau da independência que se alçou a mulher. Estão no seu paraíso. Riem-se do puro bem-estar. São donas do homem. Fazem as leis. Dirigem o país. E que lindas pernas têm!" (The most interesting thing about America is the level of independence that women have attained. They are in paradise. They laugh as a result of pure well-being. They own the men. They make the laws. They direct the country. And what lovely legs they have!; qtd. in Azevedo 1997:238). The United States had other lessons for Brazil, according to Monteiro Lobato, and he promoted them in his writings and translations. Brazil should learn from American reforestation and replant the lands that had been cleared for coffee but that were now idle; it should develop alternate fuels because Brazil was dependent on imported oil; and it should open up coffee exports to the Soviet Union (cf. Azevedo 1997:238). All these views help to delineate Monteiro Lobato's program for Brazil and the social criticism of his own culture that permeate his translations and publications. The translation and importation of Ford's ideas served to counter the elitist policies and cultural hierarchies established by the traditional oligarchical regime.

Monteiro Lobato and Oil

Monteiro Lobato inscribed his social programs in his publication projects. His activities with respect to iron and oil in Brazil serve as an example of the interrelationship between his political actions, his writing, and his translations. Though no longer commercial attaché after 1930, he tried to interest President Getúlio Vargas in the idea that Brazil should produce iron, writing pamphlets and articles on the Smith furnace process; these articles were later collected in *Ferro: Solução do caso siderúgico da Brasil pelo processo*

Smith (Iron: The Solution to the Problem of Steel in Brazil through the Smith Process; 1933).

On his return from the United States in 1931, Monteiro Lobato invested all his efforts and capital in oil prospecting in Brazil. As with his other campaigns, he published books tied to his activities and his positions, and translation played a vital role in these efforts. For example, he published *A luta pelo petróleo* (1935), a Portuguese translation by Charlie W. Frankie of *Blood and Oil in the Orient*, written by Frankie's fellow prospector Essad Bey. The book chronicles the Bolshevik takeover of Baku and includes a preface by Monteiro Lobato describing the inefficiency of the Brazilian Geological Service and its collusion with international trusts. Ironically the nationalist populist regime of Vargas had sold itself to the international trusts and would not allow Brazilians (like Monteiro Lobato) to exploit the country's resources. According to Monteiro Lobato the policy of the Geological Service was "não tirar petróleo e não deixar que ninguém o tire" (neither to extract oil nor to allow anyone else to extract it; qtd. in Azevedo 1997:285). These ideas were repeated in Monteiro Lobato's own book *Escândalo do petróleo* (The Oil Scandal; 1936) and again in his children's book *O poço do Visconde* (The Well of Visconde; 1937), in which oil is discovered at the Sítio do Picapau Amarelo.

As it happened Monteiro Lobato's plans to find oil were foiled by the hardening of the Vargas regime in 1937 and the advent of the hard-line dictatorship of the Estado Novo (1937–45).[4] During the Estado Novo all prospecting plans were centralized and placed under the control of the government. Monteiro Lobato had lost much of his wealth in the 1929 Wall Street crash, and he suffered further heavy financial losses under the Estado Novo. For the rest of his life, he was financially dependent on the royalties from his writings and translations.

Monteiro Lobato's Children's Literature and Adaptations for Children

When Monteiro Lobato began writing for children, all the children's literature available in Brazil was written in the Portuguese of Portugal. The desire to provide stories that his own and other Brazilian children could read stimulated him to write books for children. He believed in developing the Brazilian language; he thought that after 400 years of subservience to

Portugal it was time to break away definitively from Lisbon and to develop a separate Brazilian language (Hallewell 1985:242). The relationship with Portugal had never been easy. Until 1822 and the arrival in Brazil of the Portuguese court in flight from Napoleon, no printing press had been permitted in Brazil. Unlike in the Spanish colonies, no university had been established in Brazil, and thus Brazilian intellectuals felt little allegiance to Portugal.

The project of writing children's literature in Brazilian Portuguese became the vehicle to promote many of Monteiro Lobato's own social, educational, political, and economic ideas. In *Translation, Rewriting, and the Manipulation of Literary Fame* (1992), André Lefevere shows the commonalities between all types of rewriting, and he emphasizes "the importance of rewriting as the motor force behind literary evolution" (2). He analyzes the various slants that may be put on a work by translators, editors, historiographers, adapters, and other types of rewriters, including translators. In "Mother Courage's Cucumbers: Text, System, and Refraction in a Theory of Literature" (1982), he gives the example of how Brecht's work was rewritten by translators, noting that the strong ideological element of Brecht's text is softened in English versions and emphasizing that this was the only way Brecht's work could be accepted in the British and U.S. theater in the postwar period. Similarly, in *Translation in a Postcolonial Context* (1999), Maria Tymoczko describes how the Irish nationalist project also rewrote traditional Irish myths, eliminating scatological material and humor from translations of the medieval tales about Cú Chulainn and making him conform to the needs of cultural nationalism. In a similar way, Monteiro Lobato reframes and manipulates the works he translates for children to insert his own social, educational, and political program. His ideological project became so obvious that his supposedly innocuous translation of *Peter Pan* became a target for censorship, as we see below.

In a letter from 1921, Monteiro Lobato mentions his plans to produce a series of books for children "com mais leveza e graça de lingua" ("with more lightness and wit"; qtd. in Vieira 2001:146) than the translations of Carlos Jansen Müller, a Brazilian translator whose versions of classics such as *Gulliver's Travels* and *Don Quixote* were produced for the prestigious Colégio Pedro II secondary school in Rio de Janeiro at the end of the nineteenth century. Monteiro Lobato intended to rework and "improve" these translations, and he remarked, "temos que refazer tudo isso— abrasileirar a linguagem" (we must redo all of this so as to Brazilianize the language; qtd. in Koshiyama 1982:88). He proposed that the translator Godofredo Rangel, his friend, adapt children's classics such as *Gulliver's Travels* and *Robinson Crusoe* by eliminating the stylistic heaviness and literariness of the Jansen Müller Portuguese translations so as to produce versions with a lighter, more witty, and more Brazilian style, taking the liberty of improving the originals where necessary (Monteiro Lobato 1944:419). Monteiro Lobato's translation technique promotes a more simplified and colloquial language that could immediately be understood by children, the target audience, and this technique allows for interventions with an ideological slant.

His own version of *Don Quixote*, called *D. Quixote das crianças* (The Children's Don Quixote; 1936), clearly illustrates Monteiro Lobato's translation and rewriting techniques. The naughty rag doll, Emília, Monteiro Lobato's alter ego, prises a thick book off the shelf, a Portuguese translation of *Don Quixote* by Visconde de Castilho and Visconde de Azevedo, that Dona Benta begins reading to her grandchildren and the dolls. However, they and Dona Benta herself find the literary style turgid. After hearing "lança em cabido, adarga antiga, galgo corridor" (a lance hanging up in the cupboard, an ancient shield, and a fast dog; Monteiro Lobato 1957:16), Emília, who like Monteiro Lobato is against everything that is old-fashioned and backward, fails to understand the story, loses interest, and wants to go off and play hide-and-seek. Dona Benta decides to retell the story to the children herself in her own words. The result is a text with many translation shifts including abridgments, explanations, and additions, as well as paratextual commentary from Dona Benta, the narrator, and the audience inside the story, namely the children and dolls. *Don Quixote* is thus enlisted in Monteiro Lobato's struggle to change the social and economic structure of Brazil.

This technique of using a frame story to embed the rewriting also takes place in Monteiro Lobato's translation of *Peter Pan* (1930), while his versions of *Robinson Crusoe* (1930), *Gulliver's Travels* (*As viagens de Gulliver*, 1937), *Alice in Wonderland* (*Alice no país das maravilhas*, 1931), and *Alice through the Looking-Glass* (*Alice no país do espelho*, 1931) are adapted without interventions in the form of a frame story, but nonetheless are written in colloquial Brazilian Portuguese, showing simplifications and omissions.

Near the end of *D. Quixote das crianças*, the child Pedrinho asks whether his grandmother Dona Benta is telling the whole story or just parts. Dona Benta replies that only mature people should attempt to read the whole work and that only what entertains children's imaginations should be included in such versions (Monteiro Lobato 1957:152). Monteiro Lobato thus used metacommentary to justify his translation techniques, believing that "literary" qualities had no place in works for children, whose imaginations should be stimulated by fluent, easy language. This is made explicit in a letter dated 1943, where he describes the difficulties he faced:

> extirpar a "literatura" de meus livros infantis. A cada revisão nova mato, como quem mata pulgas, todas as literaturas que ainda as estragam. O último submetido a tratamento foram as *Fábulas*. Como achei pedante e requintado! De lá raspei quase um quilo de "literatura" e mesmo assim ficou alguma . . . (qtd in Abramovich 1982:152)

> extirpating "literature" from my children's books. With each revision I kill, just like someone who is killing fleas, all the literary elements that are spoiling them. The last one I submitted to this treatment was [La Fontaine's] *Fables*. How pedantic and sophisticated it was! I managed to shave off almost a kilo of "literature," but there was still some left . . .

Monteiro Lobato thus had no qualms about making stylistic changes and omissions, and he made a number of additions as well.

In *Peter Pan* and *D. Quixote das crianças*, this intimate contact with the story is emphasized through the interaction the listeners have with the story and the characters. Monteiro Lobato uses the frame technique of the *Arabian Nights*, with Dona Benta becoming a sort of Shahrazad, interrupting the story every night at nine o'clock, bedtime, and promising more entertainment for the next evening. The listeners inside the text get caught up with the stories. In *Peter Pan*, for example, Emília makes a hook to put on her hand.

Monteiro Lobato's rewritings are overtly didactic, and he frequently inserts his pet themes in the middle of the stories. One of the most prominent themes is that of expanding the book market in Brazil. At the beginning of *Peter Pan*, the children, Pedrinho and Narizinho, and the doll, Emília, having heard about Peter Pan in *Reinações de narizinho* (The Pranks of Narizinho, 1931), ask their grandmother, Dona Benta, who Peter Pan is. Dona Benta does not know, so she writes to a bookshop in São Paulo that sends her J. M. Barrie's work in English. Monteiro Lobato thus inserts an advertisement for mail orders to book shops. When the book arrives, Dona Benta retells the story to the children and dolls in Portuguese, thus reenacting within Monteiro Lobato's book the situation of an oral retelling.

There are other didactic elements in Monteiro Lobato's rewritings as well. For example, he introduces vocabulary-building exercises, having Dona Benta explain various difficult words to the children; the liberal Dona Benta also tries to open up the horizons of her grandchildren, for example, in *Hans Staden* encouraging them to read Charles Darwin's *The Voyage of the Beagle* and openly discussing the anthropophagy of the various Indian tribes in Brazil (Monteiro Lobato 1954:29, 52).

Monteiro Lobato's book *Histórias de tia Nastácia* (Stories of Aunt Nastacia; 1937) contains a selection of traditional folktales retold by Tia Nastácia, the black cook at the Sítio do Picapau Amarelo, who is semiliterate, superstitious, religious, and looked down upon by Monteiro Lobato as a representative of the Jeca Tatu type of indolent backward Brazilian mentality. The tales told by Tia Nastácia are a mixture of traditional Portuguese folktales and traditional Brazilian animal fables, often based on those of La Fontaine. Many reflect the retrograde Jeca Tatu mentality, with peasants showing a "natural" obeisance to kings, queens, and their superiors, which Monteiro Lobato is questioning. Dona Benta tells us that the tales have been passed down uncritically from generation to generation, usually by people who are illiterate. Only those who can and do read "bons livros" (good books), "é que se põe de acordo com os progressos que as ciências trouxeram ao mundo" (can keep up-to-date with the progress that the sciences have brought to the world; Monteiro Lobato 1968:81). We see here Monteiro Lobato's problematic view of race, influenced by the eugenic theories of Gustave Le Bon.[5]

After the first tale in *Histórias de tia Nastácia*, Monteiro Lobato introduces a discussion between Dona Benta and the children and the dolls. Emília, the outspoken rag doll, turns her nose up and says "Essas histórias folclóricas são bastante bobas. . . . Por isso não sou 'democrática'! Acho o povo muito idiota . . . (These folktales are quite silly. . . . That's why I'm not "democratic"! I think the people are pretty stupid . . . ; Monteiro Lobato 1968:16). Narizinho also says that she has become much more demanding since reading *Peter Pan*. By contrast Pedrinho, the future intellectual, takes a detached anthropological view, stating that the stories are good in order to study the mentality of the Brazilian people. Indeed, we later discover that Pedrinho has already begun to read Darwin, and he talks about the survival of the fittest (Monteiro Lobato 1968:95). This kind of liberal secular education is encouraged by Monteiro Lobato through Dona Benta, who is pleased that the group is openly discussing concepts such as "democracy," "folklore," and "mentality": "Neste andar meu sítio acaba virando Universidade de Picapau Amarelo" (Now the farm will turn into the Yellow Woodpecker University; Monteiro Lobato 1968:17). Tia Nastácia is bewildered by such open talk and suspicious of book culture, but the stories continue. Like Emília, Monteiro Lobato seems to have little sympathy for and to look down upon those like Tia Nastácia who resist modern "book culture." Monteiro Lobato regretted that rural Brazil was dominated by a mentality that resisted modernization and book culture. He believed that social progress, greater availability of books, and basic health facilities would automatically wipe out such "backwardness" in Brazil.

After a story called "O Bom Diabo" (The Good Devil), Dona Benta takes no notice of Tia Nastácia's criticism (couched in popular language and using the regional folksy term *canhoto* for the Devil) that the children are "ficando os maiores hereges deste mundo. Chegam até a defender o canhoto, credo!" (becoming the worst heretics in the world. They even defend the Devil!). Dona Benta shrugs this remark off, saying "se você conta mais três histórias de diabo como essa, até eu sou capaz de dar um viva ao canhoto" (if you tell another three stories about the devil like this one, even I might cheer him; Monteiro Lobato 1968:73). Tia Nastácia then prays. Naturally, neither Dona Benta nor the children and the dolls accompany her.

Monteiro Lobato also uses his translations to criticize the corrupt Brazilian political system and the excessive powers of the large landowners, the *latifundiários*, popularly called *coroneis* (colonels), although they were not part of the military. These ranch and plantation owners were and still are very powerful in much of rural Brazil, particularly in the northeast, and for Monteiro Lobato they represented the paternalistic and backward-looking Brazil he was fighting against. Pedrinho is surprised to find that there were coroneis in the sixteenth century, and Dona Benta replies that there were fewer than nowadays, "e melhores, como esse Tomé de Sousa, que foi um benemérito" (and better ones, like this Tomé de Sousa, who was a worthy man, a philanthropist; Monteiro Lobato 1954:56).[6] Monteiro Lobato also criticizes the way in which the victors write history. Replying to Pedrinho's question of why the Spanish and Portuguese conquistadores are seen as great and glorious heroes, Dona Benta replies that it is they themselves who have written history (Monteiro Lobato 1954:74).

In *Fábulas* (1921), Monteiro Lobato's rewriting of La Fontaine's *Fables*, the lack of social justice in Brazil can be clearly seen. In "Os Animais e o Peste" (The Animals and the Plague), the only animal to be punished and sent to its death is the ass, who is judged to have committed the worst crime of all: "não pode haver crime maior do que furtar a sacratíssima couve do senhor vigário" (there can't be anything worse than stealing the very sacred cabbage of the vicar; Monteiro Lobato 1969:92). After each of the tales, the children make comments and judgments, which serve as a vehicle for Monteiro Lobato's paratextual social commentary. In "A Mosca e a Formiguinha" (The Fly and the Ant), Visconde, the professor-like doll made from a corn shuck, comments: "Mas muitas vezes um planta e quem colhe é o outro" (But often one person plants and another harvests; Monteiro Lobato 1969:100). In "O Lobo e o Cordeiro" (The Wolf and the Lamb), one of La Fontaine's most famous tales, in which the lamb through fear can never contradict the wolf, Dona Benta explains that the fable "revela a essência do mundo. O forte tem sempre razão. Contra a força não há argumentos" (reveals the essence of the world. The strong are always right. There are no arguments against force; Monteiro Lobato 1969:138). And in "O Cavalo e o Burro" (The Horse and the Ass), through the vehicle of Dona Benta's commentary, Monteiro Lobato teaches the meaning of the word *solidaridade* (solidarity; Monteiro Lobato 1969:141).

Beyond the resistant aspect of Monteiro Lobato's framing of his narratives and his metatextual commentary, his translations and rewritings are resistant as a result of his choice of source texts. In this regard both Peter Pan and Don Quixote can be seen as anarchic figures, failing to respect authority. Pedrinho says of Don Quixote, "O que eu gosto em D. Quixote . . . é que ele não respeita cara. Medo não é com ele. Seja clérigo, seja moinho de vento, seja arrieiro, ele vai de lança e espada em cima, como se fossem carneiros" (What I like about Don Quixote is that he doesn't respect anybody. He's not one to be afraid. Whether it's a priest, a windmill, or a mule-driver, he goes at them with his lance and spear as if they were sheep; Monteiro Lobato 1957:91).

The work of Julia Kristeva illuminates the change of emphasis in Monteiro Lobato's translations and rewritings. Kristeva defines a signifying practice as a "field of transpositions"; in turn such a practice is related to the "place of enunciation"; at the same time she notes that the place of enunciation and its denoted object are never single, complete, and identical to themselves but always plural and shifting (Kristeva 1974:314 and passim). Translation will always introduce another voice into the text, and the new voice will always be quoting another, the original author, however invisible the translator attempts to be. "Invisible" translators attempt to maintain the original place of enunciation, though this will never be completely possible. By contrast Monteiro Lobato in his rewritings deliberately introduces a series of new points of enunciation, a series of new voices—Dona Benta, the children, and the dolls, among others. Thus his texts become dialogic and polyphonic (cf. Kristeva 1969:82 passim). These new voices reflect different aspects of Monteiro Lobato's own beliefs; thus, his rewriting and translation methods shift the place of enunciation from the source author to Monteiro Lobato himself.

In the case of *D. Quixote*, the place of enunciation is shifted from Cervantes in Spain at the turn of the seventeenth century, satirizing chivalric novels as well as contemporary social conditions, to Monteiro Lobato, critic of the Getúlio Vargas dictatorship, whose liberal ideals are voiced through the narrative mouthpieces of Dona Benta, the children, the dolls, and many of his other characters. Using Dona Benta as his vehicle, Monteiro Lobato makes the place of enunciation his own in *Peter Pan*, *Histórias de tia Nastácia*, and La Fontaine's *Fables*, all of which come to serve as a critique of the lack of social and economic progress in Brazil. Thus, Monteiro Lobato's project, originally touted as a means of filling a gap in the Brazilian book market where there was almost no children's literature produced in Brazil itself using Brazilian Portuguese, also became an ideological agent promoting a highly critical attitude to the Brazilian status quo during the Getúlio Vargas dictatorship.

The plurality of Monteiro Lobato's texts can also be illuminated by the concept of intertextuality, originally coined by Kristeva in 1967 (see Plett 1991:3). All texts have a "twofold coherence: an intratextual one which guarantees the immanent integrity of the text, and an intertextual one which creates structural relations between itself and other texts" (Plett 1991:5). A translated work will by nature be related to and have a natural intertextual relationship with the original, but Monteiro Lobato opens up his translations to introduce intertextuality with a number of other texts. For example, in *D. Quixote das crianças* there is intertextuality not only with Cervantes's original but also with the Portuguese "literary" translation of Cervantes by Visconde de Castilho and Visconde de Azevedo, thus introducing us to Monteiro Lobato's own relationship (another intertext) with the Portuguese language and his attempts to use a more contemporary Brazilian Portuguese. The retelling of the text and the interpolations of the children and the dolls make for a *mise en abîme* of intertexts: Monteiro Lobato's ideas on education, economics, and politics; his antagonism with the Getúlio Vargas dictatorship; his previous fictional works, nonfiction writing, and translations; and, on a more literary level, works similar in genre to *Don Quixote*.[7]

Particularly after the introduction of the hard-line Estado Novo in November 1937, Monteiro Lobato's adaptations of well-known children's stories, interspersed with critical comments from Dona Benta, the children, and the dolls, became one of the ways of enacting resistance to the Vargas regime. We should note in this regard that works for children are often read aloud and thus have a complex dual audience, that of the reader (usually a parent, teacher, relative, or older child), who is reading aloud and thereby implicitly colluding with Monteiro Lobato, and the listener (usually a younger child). In the case of *Peter Pan*, for example, it is evident that a work which contains no apparent original political message becomes part of Monteiro Lobato's opposition to the Vargas dictatorship. The enormous popularity of Monteiro Lobato's children's works helped disseminate liberal, secular, and internationalist ideas to adults and children alike in a state that was authoritarian, Catholic, and nationalist. Dona Benta, the grandmother and educator always ready to open up the children's and dolls' horizons, proved an ideal front for Monteiro Lobato to disseminate his liberal, anti-Getúlio Vargas program. Except in the case of *Peter Pan*, it seems to have been an excellent resistant translation strategy and to have worked, for it is always more difficult for a dictatorship to object to statements in children's literature, especially with the displacement caused by the double framing of Dona Benta's retellings. As mentioned above, Monteiro Lobato's works were and indeed still are extremely popular in Brazil.

Monteiro Lobato: Persona Non Grata

Monteiro Lobato was despised by the Estado Novo nationalist government of Getúlio Vargas for his internationalism, his negative comparisons of Brazil to the United States and the United Kingdom, his atheism, and his continual meddling in politics. Some of his comments seem clearly socialist as well: "o sonho duma ordem social nova em que a felicidade coubesso ao maior número" (the dream of a new social order where the greatest number can be happy; 1948:148)) and "Querem que o país todo se torne um sítio de Dona Benta, o abençoado refúgio onde não há nem opressão nem cárceres—lá não se prende nem um passarinho na gaiola. Todos são comunistas à sua moda, e estão realizando a República de Platão, com um rei-filósofo na pessoa de uma mulher" (They want the whole country to become the farm of Dona Benta, the blessed refuge where neither oppression nor prisons exist—there not even a bird is locked up in its cage. They are all communists in their own way, and they are building Plato's Republic, with a philosopher-king in the form of a woman; 1948:308–9). Monteiro Lobato was frequently suspected of being a communist and was invited to join the Brazilian Communist Party when it was legalized in 1945, but he could not accept its discipline and declined the invitation. These features of his political positioning serve as background to his political persecution. In March 1941 Monteiro Lobato was accused of sending an insulting letter to dictator Getúlio Vargas, the President of the Republic, and to General Gois Monteiro. He was imprisoned for six months on 20 March 1941, of which he served three, despite considerable protest from intellectuals against his imprisonment.

The subversive and resistant nature of Monteiro Lobato's rewritings and translations for children was not lost on the regime. *Peter Pan* was one of the texts that caused considerable political trouble for him. In June 1941 a São Paulo public prosecutor, Clóvis Kruel de Morais, recommended to the Tribunal de Segurança Nacional (the National Security Tribunal) that the distribution of *Peter Pan* be prohibited because it would give children the wrong opinion of the government of Brazil, molding "o espírito da criança à mentalidade demolidora do nacionalismo" (the spirit of children into a mentality that would destroy nationalism; qtd. in Azevedo 1997:307) and giving an impression that Brazil was an inferior country compared to Britain.

As an instance in which Monteiro Lobato betrays Brazil, one passage cited by the prosecutor occurs when Emília asks whether English children play with a "boi de xuxu," a sort of toy animal made by sticking pieces of wood into a vegetable, a chayote, a common practice in rural areas of Brazil where children had to improvise toys out of odds and ends. Dona Benta replies that English children are very spoiled and given all the toys they want, and that toys are not incredibly expensive as they are in Brazil. High-quality German toys made in Nuremberg are also praised, but she says that in Brazil the toy industry is only just beginning. Here Monteiro

Lobato is inserting his opinions of the economic protectionism of Getúlio Vargas's Estado Novo government.

Another report to the Tribunal de Segurança Nacional by Tupy Caldas accused Monteiro Lobato's works of being excessively materialistic and lacking any kind of spiritualism; he argued that they should be banned because they were dangerous to the national educational program, failing to contribute to the formation of a "juventude patriótica, continuadora da tradição cristã, unificadora da Pátria" (patriotic youth, continuing the Christian tradition, and unifying the Nation; qtd. in Carneiro 1997:76). As a result of instructions given by the Tribunal de Segurança Nacional, the São Paulo Department of Social and Political Order (DEOPS) apprehended and confiscated all the copies of Monteiro Lobato's *Peter Pan* that it could find in the state of São Paulo.

Aware of the subversive role that books could play in fostering resistance, Vargas himself underlined this very danger:

> Todo e qualquer escrito capaz de desvirtuar esse programa é perigoso para o futuro da nacionalidade. O nosso mal até aqui foi justamente dar liberdade excessiva aos escritores, quando é o livro o mais forte veículo de educação. (Qtd. in Carneiro 1997:76)

> All written matter capable of perverting this program is dangerous for the future of the nation. Our problem thus far has been that we have given excessive freedom to our writers, even though books are the most powerful means of education.

Predictably, Monteiro Lobato's anticlericalism was unpopular with the right wing of the Catholic Church.[8] The combination of Monteiro Lobato's resistant publishing, writing, translation, and public statements made his imprisonment inevitable.[9]

Resistance, Activism, and Translation

Throughout Monteiro Lobato's career as a writer and translator, certain themes repeat themselves: the need to modernize, industrialize, and "Americanize" Brazil; to make it more efficient and competitive; to improve the health and well-being of its people; to extend education through the growth of reading books; and to give more freedom to women. The old, slow, rustic, and backward Brazil was dominated by the large estate owners, the latifundiários, the Catholic Church, and the nationalist policies of the Getúlio

Vargas government. Despite their avowed nationalism, all these interests acted in collusion with international trusts, particularly Standard Oil, and failed to develop a Brazilian policy for prospecting for oil and developing the vast mineral resources of the country. These opinions are found throughout his pamphlets, his stories for children, and his translations and rewritings. He frequently selected works to translate, such as Henry Ford's *My Life and Work* and *Today and Tomorrow*, that directly fit in with his political and economic beliefs. He also shaped his translations and rewritings of children's books by changing the place of enunciation and framing the stories as retellings by Dona Benta interspersed with pertinent and critical comments by the children and dolls from the Sítio do Picapau Amarelo. Publishing was Monteiro Lobato's life, and during the repressive Vargas regime, particularly after the proclamation of the Estado Novo in 1937, publishing translations and rewritings was one of the few possible forms of resistance to the stiff censorship and the stifling nationalism that dominated economic, political, and cultural policies.

This analysis of the resistant translations of Monteiro Lobato illustrates that resistance in translation can be very different from the notion of resistance described in the work of authors such as Antoine Berman, Lawrence Venuti, and Tejaswini Niranjana, who see resistance primarily encoded in the formal elements and strategies of the translated work. For Berman a resistant translation must be open to the foreign: "l'essence de la traduction est d'être ouverture, dialogue, métissage, décentrement. Elle est mise en rapport, ou elle n'est rien" (1984:6; cf. Berman 1992:4, "the essence of translation is to be an opening, a dialogue, a cross-breeding, a decentering. Translation is 'a putting in touch with,' or it is nothing"). Berman suggests that translation, particularly the translation of novels in France up to the period of his analysis, has been domesticated to French classical norms; it has been *ethnocentrique*—all texts have had to be adapted to the French way of thinking; *hypertextuelle*—the resulting translation has been another text, a pastiche, or a variation rather than the original; and *platonicienne*—it has been more concerned with ideas than form. Opposing these standards, Berman argues that a translation should be *éthique*—it should respect the original; *poétique*—it should attempt to keep the style of the original; and *pensante*—it should think about the original as a whole (1985:47ff.).

Lawrence Venuti's (1992, 1995, 1998a, 1998b) ideas about resistant translation are well known. He argues in favor of the kind of translation that according to Philip Lewis (1985), contains "abusive fidelity," where the translator should cultivate "polysemy, neologism, fragmented syntax, discursive heterogeneity" and what he later calls "the remainder," using Jean-Jacques Lecercle's term (Venuti 1992:12). Such translations will be "strange and estranging" and "mark the limits of dominant values in the target language culture and hinder those values from enacting an imperialistic domestication of a cultural other" (Venuti 1992:13).

In *Siting Translation* (1992) Tejaswini Niranjana draws heavily on Benjamin and Derrida to support her ideas on postcolonial translation. Following Benjamin, she gives examples of translations of a twelfth-century Indian *vacana* that fail to "understand the special significance inherent in the original which manifests itself in its translatability" (Niranjana 1992:180). These translations assimilate Śaivite poetry to a Christian neocolonialist discourse, using terms generally associated with Christianity. Niranjana retranslates the passage leaving untranslated the proper names and certain key words, such as the name of the god Guhēśvara and *linga*. She believes her translation resists dominant "homogenizing and continuous narratives," arguing that the postcolonial translator should attempt to find the richer complexity of "our notions of the 'self', a more densely textured understanding of who 'we' are" through interventions that avoid the idea of purity and that demonstrate that origins are never monolithic (Niranjana 1992:185–86).

Berman, Venuti, and Niranjana all focus on the importance of resistant language in translations. The use of fluent, easy-to-read language in the target text is seen as reflecting an inability to accept the foreign or extend one's horizons beyond one's immediate culture. Such a view is criticized by, among others, Douglas Robinson, who takes issue with the elitism apparent in Venuti's view of resistant language and the "holding back from communication" in Niranjana, which will hamper rather than help the social effect of a translation (1997a:93; 1997b:158). Indeed, foreignizing translations have clear disadvantages for encouraging direct action, as their awkwardness may be associated with the authoritarian discourse of textbooks or legalese (Robinson 1997b:162).

The analysis of Monteiro Lobato's work developed here locates resistance in translation in quite different elements. Monteiro Lobato's resistant translations are part of his overall publishing project through which he attempted to defy the Getúlio Vargas regime. The resistance of Monteiro Lobato's translations is seen particularly in the frames with which he surrounds and manipulates his rewritings of classic stories for children.

The language he chooses is straightforward and simple, contrasting with the more formal Portuguese of previous works written for children. The works he selects to translate and have translated, mostly from English, challenge the French dominance of literature imported into Brazil. Dona Benta's retellings emphasize Monteiro Lobato's secular liberalism, his hatred of the traditional dominant oligarchies, and his belief in the need for greater economic freedom and planned use of natural resources. These points are reinforced by the paratextual commentaries of the children and dolls, who are unafraid of questioning the status quo, who are avid to learn, and who represent the enterprising citizens of the future Brazil.

Moreover, Monteiro Lobato's work illustrates an important way in which developing nations such as Brazil can use original works from the First World. Monteiro Lobato translates the original stories, localizing them and changing the original emphasis. In *D. Quixote das crianças*, for example, he "translates" the original difficult stylistics of the Portuguese translation of Cervantes into much simpler and more readable language, the language of Brazil in his day. He writes, "usamos a linguagem a mais simplificada possível, como a de Machado de Assis, que é o nosso grande mestre" (we use the most simplified language possible, like that of Machado de Assis, our great master), where Portuguese classical writers, by contrast, used a much richer language and more complex constructions (Monteiro Lobato 1957:190–91). Similarly he injects Brazilian reality into his translations, as in his version of *Peter Pan* when he compares North American Indians ("redskins") to Brazilian Indians and the *caboclos* (half-Indians) (1971:26). Both Berman and Venuti write from the point of view of members of a dominant culture, and they are speakers of a dominant language; they believe that their languages have always resisted the foreign. By contrast Monteiro Lobato was struggling to give value to his own language, the Portuguese of Brazil, dominated at the time by the norms of Portugal. Thus his strategy was not to emphasize the linguistically foreign, but rather to attempt develop the particularly Brazilian characteristics of Portuguese. This leads us to conclude that the contrast between domestication and foreignization in resistant translations is not quite so simple and may well depend on the place of enunciation and reception. Viewed from Brazil, Monteiro Lobato's translations can be seen as liberating colloquial Brazilian Portuguese from the shackles of Luso Portuguese. But if we move our perspective to Portugal, his language can be seen as foreignizing standard Portuguese with a Brazilian flavor.

In 1928 Oswald de Andrade published his *Manifesto antropofágico* (*Anthropophagic Manifesto* or *Cannibalistic Manifesto*), in which he presented the image of the Brazilian cannibal, who would "devour" the enemy, so he could take over the enemy's soul. Though never mentioning translation, Andrade says that the Brazilian writer, like the cannibal, should not take in the foreign influence in a passive way, but rather should transform it actively into something new. The original work should be actively swallowed and reproduced in a different form. Although Monteiro Lobato was not a member of the modernist group of 1922 who introduced the idea of anthropophagy in art, Adriana Vieira sees an anthropophagic component of Monteiro Lobato's writing in his use of the original text in a "cannibalistic" way, adapting the original and putting his own characteristic Brazilian mark on it, as do the later writers and translators Haroldo and Augusto de Campos (Vieira 2001:153). Although Monteiro Lobato is adapting popular literature within a commercial setting and the de Campos brothers are translating much more erudite non-commercial and high-art literature, Vieira believes that they can be compared because Monteiro Lobato, like the de Campos brothers, uses the original text in an anthropophagic way, adapting the original and putting his own characteristic Brazilian mark on it. As we have seen, the foreign becomes domesticated, but it is a resistant domestication that contains marked Brazilian characteristics and is used for specific Brazilian ideological purposes that involve dissent and subversion.

Notes

1. *Urupês* went into five editions, and the first edition of *Narizinho* sold 50,500 copies, 30,000 of which were distributed to schools in the state of São Paulo.

2. Monteiro Lobato was also a major public figure in Brazil from 1918 to 1927 because, in addition to the success of his books and his work as a publisher, he wrote a regular column for the influential newspaper *O Estado de São Paulo* and became publisher of the middlebrow journal *Revista do Brasil*, after purchasing it in 1918.

3. All translations in this essay are my own, unless otherwise indicated.

4. The Estado Novo refers to the Brazilian regime after the internal coup staged by Getúlio Vargas and a number of hardline generals in order to reduce opposition and to maintain Vargas in power as dictator. The presidential elections of 1938 were postponed; the Communist Party was banned; and censorship was strengthened.

5. This facet of Monteiro Lobato's thinking is also reflected in his 1926 novel *O presidente negro ou o choque das raças: Romance americano do ano 2228* (The Black President or the Clash of Races: An American Novel of 2228), set in the futuristic United States in 2228 when the whites are divided and Jim Roy becaomes the first black president. The whites reunite and initiate a campaign to sterilize the blacks, with

the sterilization drug disguised as a hair-straightening treatment. Monteiro Lobato tried to publish an English translation of the book in the U.S., but it was considered too racially provocative by a number of publishers, and he never attempted to publish again in an English-speaking country. The Brazilian text was reissued as *O presidente negro* in 2009 by Editora Globo after having been out of print for many years.

6. Tomé de Sousa (1503–79) was Governor General of Brazil from 1549 to 1553.

7. Pedrinho mentions he has already read the legends of Charlemagne, and Dona Benta suggests they read *Orlando Furioso* together (Monteiro Lobato 1957:18).

8. For an example of these views see Brasil, *A literatura infantil de Monteiro Lobato, ou Comunismo para crianças* (The Children's Literature of Monteiro Lobato or Communism for Children; 1957), in which he accuses Monteiro Lobato of encouraging a communist revolution, bad manners within the family, atheism, and rebellion against the right to own private property.

9. On 30 December 1940 Monteiro Lobato gave an interview to the BBC in which he emphasized the indebtedness of Brazil to England and stressed the fact that Brazil had lost touch with the traditional English values of civil liberties, *habeas corpus*, calm when facing danger, solidarity, and resistance.

ELSE R. P. VIEIRA

Growing Agency: The Labors of Political Translation

"WHAT if Bernardo is born in prison? And what if he is snatched from me at childbirth like all those *desaparecidos* in Argentina? The world knows about all those innocent babies who were taken away from their mothers. Who will feed him? Who will give him affection? Who will bring him up? Who will see to his future? What will his future be like?" These thoughts haunted me as the due date of the birth of my first child and the deadline to submit a political translation were both fast approaching.

It all started when I was in the fifth month of my pregnancy in early October 1980. A representative of Vozes, which is a most reliable, well-established, and professional publishing house in Brazil, comparable to Routledge in the English-speaking world, based in Petrópolis, near Rio de Janeiro, flew to Belo Horizonte, the capital of the central state of Minas Gerais, Brazil, where I lived. He had a proposal for me: to translate from English into Portuguese a recently accepted doctoral dissertation written by René Dreifuss for the program in Political Science of the University of Glasgow. The thesis was on the history of Brazil.[1]

I need to clarify that my role was to be more than just translating. I would only translate part of the manuscript, but what was further expected of me was organizing a team of translators, typists, and everything I would need to produce a quality translation of a 1,200-page text in limited time. The task also involved stylistic adjustments to make the text flow better for non-academic readers. The moment seemed to be opportune for the publishers to bring Brazilian history to a broader spectrum of the public. Or perhaps it was the other way round: the country was ready to learn more. Adjustments included, for example, toning down the dense thesis style to make it more reader friendly. We would have less than five months to produce camera-ready hard copy for the publishing house. They needed the pages in early February so that the book could be printed by 31 March 1981, the seventeenth anniversary of the coup d'état that established the dictatorship in Brazil. The publishers were going to speed up the printing process, but we as translators would have to speed up the translation process as well.

But speeding up meant in no way lessening the quality of the translation. It would have to meet the standards of the publisher, myself, and the author as well. The professionalism of the publishing house is important to stress. They were aware that the pressures were great and told me that I should propose what I would need to accomplish the task. No limits were set on the resources, including the number of co-translators and extra costs for full-time typists. This is of course very unusual. At the same time the publishing house was adamant and unyielding about the time limits. They would not negotiate about the deadline and they made it clear that no extensions would be given for submission of the camera-ready hard copies.

There were challenges in the proposal and it's good to work when you have a sense that there are challenges ahead of you. The offer was irrefutable.

Bonding the Publishing House, the Author, and the Translator

Vozes is one of the five largest publishing houses in Brazil. Its social-political agenda dates back to its beginning in the nineteenth century, when the two Franciscan monks who founded the firm used to print books for the free school São José. The books printed in the early days had a fundamental role in the resistance to the growth and spread of positivism in the nineteenth century. Together with the dissemination of religious culture, Vozes has stood for fostering Catholic intellectual movements. This trend in some ways anticipates the groundbreaking historical leap that the Catholic Church made in Latin America in the 1960s, which came to be known as Liberation Theology. In the 1970s during the institutionalized political repression, Vozes was brave enough to publish books such as *Tortura nunca mais* (Torture Never More) and *A voz dos vencidos* (The Voice of the Defeated), as well as books with themes leading to reflection in areas of the humanities (philosophy, theology, psychology) that were frowned upon by the dictatorship. Major anthropologist Darcy Ribeiro, leading liberation theologians Gustavo Gutiérrez and Leonardo Boff, and philosopher Michel Foucault are some of its renowned authors.

When the representative of the publishing house came to me, the author, René Dreifuss, came also. This was very important in establishing rapport among the author, translator, and publisher, and it was important in my decision to accept the job. It was not only that René was the author; he would join the team as the expert on political science providing terminological support for the translators. The manuscript was dense with the specific terminology of political theory. Normally a translator is given time to study the subject matter of a project and to become familiar with the terms and the theory involved. But this was not going to be possible for us because of the time constraints we were working under.

There was another important point related to his visit: empathy among the team. The author was a young man about my age, the father of a toddler. There was an immediate sense of affinity which became ever more evident in the course of the negotiations. The prospect of working with him was very positive as well. He looked and sounded extremely intelligent and knowledgeable. He was a polyglot. He spoke German at home (his German-Jewish parents managed to escape from the concentration camps in Germany); Spanish is the language of Uruguay, where his parents fled and where he was born and grew up. He spoke English with an American accent because he took his senior year in high school in the United States. He also had Yiddish arising from his university education in Haifa. His Portuguese was heavily mixed with Spanish, but his English was strong.

As we discussed the possible translation, we began talking in Portuguese, but because of the disturbing interference of Spanish in his Portuguese, we decided to use English as the means of communication. We soon realized that my American accent in English was very similar to his, and we had a good laugh finding out that I had also been a senior in a high school in the United States about the same time that he was there. At that time my own accent was markedly American, as I had not yet done much work in Britain. We didn't talk much about these affinities at the time, but they led to our immediate bonding.

There was another factor at work related to the effects of censorship in a dictatorship. There is no freedom of speech under dictatorships, so we learn to detect and read other signs, such as expression, tone of voice, gestures, subtexts, and dates. Intelligence sparkled from the author's eyes. Professionalism was underlying every word of the publisher's representative. The fact that the launch for the book was to be 31 March was very important to everyone involved. Even though it was not verbalized as such, it put history and politics on the agenda. For the first time in my life as a translator, I accepted the terms of a translation contract without seeing the book. But I trusted the publishing house which in turn trusted this young scholar who came to my house. To the implicit bonding shared with the other translators I shall return.

Translation and Life-bearing

To me what in other circumstances would have been perceived as a daunting deadline was not a major concern even though word-processors were unavailable at the time. The fact is that I was going to have to clear my desk for the baby's birth anyway. The immensity of the task is something that I recognized but at the time it did not strike me as a reason to hold back either. This was fine with me.

I cannot downplay the fact that I was half way through my pregnancy. There is something extraordinary about a pregnant woman and her relationship to life-giving; it is something visceral. At that time I did not feel that it was a reason to hold back either. The role of pregnancy was also important in other ways. At that time in Brazil we had an intuition that something was about to happen in the country. When it would happen we did not know, but we knew that it would happen. Like the birth of a baby: we don't know exactly when the baby will come, but we know an immense event is before us. At the time I could not have put words to it, but from my current perspective I can: the feeling that I was giving birth to a new life merged with the feeling that my country would also have a new beginning; it was just a matter of time. It may also be the case that I projected the birth of my child onto my wish that Brazil would break free from the crystallized reactionary state we had been plunged into.

It must be said that even though we did not know how much we could trust the dictatorship at the time, things were changing. In part because of international pressures, in part because of growing dissatisfaction within because of rampant inflation, the gradual re-democratization of the country was announced at the end of General Ernesto Geisel's term as president (1974–79). His successor, General João Baptista Figueiredo (1979–85), gave amnesty to the political exiles (August 1979) who were then beginning to return to the country. The return of political exiles is a very interesting phenomenon. Even though we could not feel secure about how much we could talk about history and politics, the exiles were living history who acted as a testimony to facts that were suppressed. They also brought to the country ideas from outside that were suppressed inside Brazil by the repressive regime. Could we talk about history and politics? No, but we felt them.

I agreed to start the translation as soon as the volume arrived, which would be in a few days. It was the unspoken that was important, a shared feeling among the three of us in the negotiation that something very big, momentous, was ahead of us. Was this the projection of our wishful thinking or were there signs of change in the air? We didn't know, but we went for it. It was a shared conviction.

Even seconds had to be counted. Once I agreed to the contract, I immediately contacted three other translators. They accepted the challenge and they had great enthusiasm when I described the project. They did not ask anything beyond what I could say and they started organizing their lives to begin what would be a very demanding task in a few days.

The Pandora Box

The manuscript arrived. It was a big box full of Xeroxed pages. The cover bore an impressive and technical title: "State, Class, and the Organic Elite: The Formation of the Entrepreneurial Order in Brazil (1961–1965)." The first thing I had to do was to apportion the 1,200 pages to the four translators involved, including myself. So I started reading the book. Time pressure and the implicit trust in the publishers had been reasons enough for me not to examine the material beforehand, but when it arrived I read the manuscript through in fascination and despair. The thesis style could be heavy at times but the manuscript gripped me in ways I could not understand fully. I had one of the most meaningful experiences that a translator can have: to find an author who was saying the things I would like to say. René was saying all the things that I felt but could not utter. Some of them we had intuitions about, but, as I said, under a dictatorship history is suppressed or distorted and freedom of speech is banned. We had lived for 16 years without the permission to say anything. Even though we had strong intuitions about where history was falsified, we were not given access to the facts. Here in the manuscript the author had the data to prove our suspicions, and he provided all the information and facts for a new view of the history of the dictatorship, whereas we, Brazilians, had only sharp suspicions. This was an important experience: the author complementing what we would like to say. We were nearly there.

But the more the thesis gripped me, the more it scared me. The translation process had started without previous examination of the book and in a sense the act of translating was already a fait accompli. I had agreed to the translation and everything else that followed, but the question was how to go about it. There were moments that I wished I had not signed the contract and had not involved others in the process by commissioning the other translators. Yet there was no going back. I could not and never intended to claim innocence, and in fact I would feel ashamed to try to do so: it was very clear from the beginning that there was a strong political dimension to the history of Brazil that was about to be translated. Of course I was aware from the start that there was something political about it. First, the thesis was produced at the University of Glasgow; Scotland is political and Glasgow is particularly political. Second, the thesis was produced by a political scientist. Finally, the date envisaged for the launch, the anniversary of the coup d'état, also made the political dimension of the project obvious and inescapable.

Vozes, the publishing house, was entering the market very close to the publication of Fernando Gabeira's *O que é isso companheiro?* (1979), literally "What's this, comrade?", whose later film version was titled in English *Four Days in September* (1998). Gabeira was one of the young people who had been involved in the kidnapping of the American Ambassador Charles Burke Elbrick on 4 September 1969 in exchange for the liberation of 15 political prisoners. The strategy of kidnapping is in many cases a weapon of the powerless; in this specific case it was devised as a response to the Ato Institucional 5 (Institutional Act number 5), issued by the Brazilian government on 13 December 1968, which intensified repression under the dictatorship. As a result of the act, Congress was closed, those who opposed the regime were barred from political life for ten years; the right to *habeas corpus* was suspended; freedom under vigilance became the norm. Opposition and dissident voices had no outlet. Human rights were enormously violated. The kidnapping was a way of exerting pressure on the government in the face of the abolished constitutional guarantees of personal freedoms. The violation of constitutional rights escalated when a military junta, by means of Institutional Act 12, prevented Vice-President Antônio Aleixo from taking over during the period when President General Costa e Silva had surgical treatment in the United States.

Gabeira and other young people had radicalized the situation in Brazil by using the kidnapping and the subsequent international attention focused on Brazil to exert pressure on the government. The strategy worked. The Brazilian government promptly negotiated with the kidnappers and the American ambassador was safely released. But Gabeira and the rest of the group in turn became political prisoners. By virtue of the strategy of kidnapping as a form of liberation that they had inaugurated, however, they were later released abroad as political exiles through the subsequent kidnapping of the German ambassador to Brazil.

As mentioned, in 1979 the army had given amnesty to political exiles, who gradually began returning to Brazil and were seeking channels to publish their memoirs. Gabeira's book triggered a very important moment in Brazilian literature, which gave currency to the term *Memorialismo*, referring to the vigorous genre associated with the narratives of those exiled by the recent dictatorship (1964–85). Vozes had in fact mentioned to me that the launch date somehow related to this more autobiographical genre because the publishing house wanted to introduce another slant to the timid but growing field of the suppressed historiography of the dictatorship. For the first time we began to have the voice of history that was silenced. We didn't know what had happened to the exiles, but they were speaking the voice of the past.

We had this first story from Gabeira, but we asked to what extent was this just an individual story? It reflected the history of the country, but just as seen through the eyes of one person. By contrast our translation was a thorough and dense analysis of the historical events that transcended a single individual: it signaled the shift from story to history. Even though I could not claim innocence, because the signs were clear to me, I could not have foreseen the extent of what the thesis exposed. The scale of the events became known to the world at large in 1999 with the Pinochet case when, again because of international pressure, the CIA opened to the public the archives related to the involvement of the United States in the political affairs of Latin America. In fact between 1976 and 1980, René had done extensive research in the archives in Brazil and the United States, including those of the CIA.

The thesis exposed, among other things, the shams and shames of Brazilian official history. As we translated, what was meant to be factual evidence for a thesis produced abroad turned out in Brazil to be open denunciation of those still in power in a repressive dictatorship. All the names were there, what they had contributed to the coup, how the army had been involved. All the tactics and strategies they had used to get hold of power were laid bare.

Worst of all, it was clear that the dictatorship lacked credibility and trustworthiness. It was not certain to what extent it was responding to international pressure in fact or in appearance only, giving the impression that it was becoming more flexible. Was the apparent change merely a front restricted to a small area of life? The lack of the government's credibility was patent even in the name and date of the coup d'état. It was labeled a democratic revolution, but in fact it was a coup that used repression and torture to achieve its aims. The contradiction is blatant in the very date of the coup d'état; it actually occurred on the first of April but, in a stroke reminiscent of Gabriel García Márquez, the military government had pre-dated it to the last day of March. They bypassed its obvious connection with April Fool's Day.

To return to the period of negotiations about the translation, at the time it was stated that the regime was beginning to be flexible and the return of the exiles seemed to confirm these statements. But could we trust these pronouncements? There was so much uncertainty. Looking back now, we can see that it was a period of transition of regimes, from the late 1970s to 1985, but we could not know that at the time. And we could not trust the leaders and the government. We could only experience life as it was lived, we could not theorize it. A period of transition is a period of great uncertainty because the rules of the game are not clear. And there is a pervasive sense of pressure for change. What has been crystallized for a long time begins to change very very quickly: there is a sense of urgency in the air. We had to make agonizing choices, usually in a hurry, as was the case with me, but without knowing for sure what the rules of the game were.

In fact the decision to translate Dreifuss's book was not agonizing at the moment I decided: it was a matter of conviction. But it became agonizing after I laid my hands on the material. One question we always ask ourselves in such situations is whether we should add to the crystallized situation or whether we should commit ourselves to the possibility of change rather than to a certainty of where we are going.

We went on. Our situation reminds me of that of Fernando Meirelles, the director of *City of God*, with whom I worked closely in 2004. He told me about the process of making the film.[2] Contrary to what he had envisaged, at each stage of the film, he failed to receive the expected financing. So every week he would scrape up whatever amount he had in investments until he finally realized that he would finance the film himself until the very end. But he went straight on. He used a very interesting image, that of one of the arcanes of the tarot cards, who looks aloft while walking toward a cliff. Enthusiasm is a heavy drug, and this is a conclusion that I share with him in relation to the translation I produced of the history of the dictatorship in Brazil.

We shared the unspoken conviction that a country has the right to know its own history. So we walked toward the precipice.

Hatching the Translation Team: Uncle Sam's Nephews and Nieces

The three other translators also acted on implicit trust and unspoken conviction. There was an unspoken decision to go for it. Like me they were also fascinated by the revelations of this twentieth-century Tiresias. Each sentence we translated was a renewed challenge to the official history we had been swallowing for 16 years. What I had experienced when I first approached the book to apportion the task I saw happening to the team as well, namely fascination with what the book revealed. We felt enthusiastic about the continual challenge to official history that we saw on every page. It was a revelation to see who the actors in history actually were.

One interesting coincidence about the team of translators is that the four of us had all spent our senior year of high school in the United States. The team of translators consisted of Ayeska Branca de Oliveira Farias, my sister Ceres Ribeiro Pires de Freitas, Glória Maria de Mello Caravalho, and myself. Two of us, Ayeska and Ceres, had been to the United States in 1967, and Gloria and I were there in 1968. This, of course, also coincidentally applies to the author. Coincidentally? Not really. It was so good to find in the book that we were translating yet another explanation for the shared experience binding author and translators together. In one of the interesting parts we translated, the author René coined a very apposite term to describe a certain category of people to whom we belonged: Uncle Sam's nephews. He describes how the think-tanks and strategists of multinational interests allied with the Brazilian oligarchy and formed a political military complex to act against the nationalist President João Goulart and the social forces aligned with him, namely students, clergy, union leaders, rural workers, intellectuals, and artists.

In chapter 7 of the book we were translating, we learned about an intellectual campaign of which we had all been potential targets. An all-pervasive ideological campaign emerged consisting of the bourgeoisie in alliance with multinational think-tanks to infiltrate those mobilized groups. In order to get to the mobilized youth in Brazil, they would approach the best students who were 17 or 18 years old and offer them scholarships to schools in the United States. Thus, many teenagers were sent out of the country to the United States, subsidized by programs intended to captivate their hearts and minds, for the tactical upbringing of the future "nephews of Uncle Sam." These "nephews" (and nieces) would in future "extirpate the Marxist cancer," "exorcize the Cuban heresy" from Brazil, and become future leaders for the political, economic, military, and cultural transnationalization of Brazil.

The five of us were then, theoretically, among Uncle Sam's nephews and nieces. We recognized ourselves as being part of this program, yet with a difference. All of us were given scholarships to spend a year in the United States as part of the country's policy of captivating the hearts and minds of the young. Yet paradoxically, lived history—the history we actually experienced in the United States—was one of contestation and had a liberating effect on us, even as the dictatorship in Brazil was intensifying its repressive mechanisms, particularly as a consequence of the landmark Institutional Act 5 mentioned above.

Certainly in my specific case and I believe in Gloria's, the captivation of hearts and minds backfired. It was an instance of *o tiro saiu pela culatra* or "the bullet shot through the butt," as the Portuguese saying goes. The American way of life did not quite captivate my heart, but individuals and the experience of lived history in that landmark year in the United States did. The cultural ferment in 1968 left an indelible imprint on my life and worldview. The intended program was turned upside down. I lived a groundbreaking moment in the contestation of history: the demonstrations around the assassination of Martin Luther King, the protests against the Vietnam War, and the emerging feminist movement. I suspect this experience psychologically prepared me—and the other translators in the team as well—for our decision to translate the book. In different ways all of us were affected by historical contestation. Part of our enthusiasm about the project was the recovery of the belief in the mutability of history. So all of us went on: perhaps toward a precipice but with our heads aloft.

Thoughts on Teamwork

In our project the bonding between translators and author was too evident to be left unreflected upon. In my thoughts about this phenomenon of strong empathy between author and translator, two theorists are illuminating. The first is Antoine Berman, who in *The Experience of the Foreign* (1992) discusses the German Romantics' momentous undertaking of translations as part of the attempt to better understand their own culture. The desire for the foreign is for Berman part of the wish to transform a national culture through a confrontation with the non-native. Gayatri Spivak's words are also quite eloquent in this context. She sees translation as "an act of intimacy": in the effort to communicate with others across space, the translator "surrenders to the other," but this surrender also allows for fraying (1993:184). The more I translated, the more I worked with the team, the more I saw that all of us— albeit in agonizing fear—"surrendered to the other," to this brilliant stranger who in 1,200 pages said all that Brazilians needed and wanted to hear. He was an other, but at the same time he was a mirror of ourselves. He verbalized what Brazil seemed to be waiting for, but Brazil also seemed to be waiting for us as translators to cast into words of our own idiom what all of us perceived but did not have the courage or the facts to express. We wanted what the other had to say, collectively and individually.

In our case the act of intimacy was multilayered. As mentioned, we recognized our own personal stories embedded in the nation's history that we were translating; we partook in the writer's sense of history as well because he shared so much with us. But our translation of René also enacted a "contained alterity," in which the translator tries to keep the fraying down to a minimum (Spivak 1993:180–81). The fascination of putting into our language what was latent in us and what the author had verbalized in another idiom could not obscure other difficulties. The spell of the enthusiasm did not make me blind to the fact that teamwork breeds problems. All of the translators were competent ones and I was sure the results would be good. But all four of us had different rhythms and demands on us, as well as different ways of absorbing this immense task on top of our previous commitments. There were also unexpected events. Just one example: we were all of childbearing age and one of the children of a translator had chicken pox. We were working within a very tight deadline and except, of course, in the case of the chicken pox, I could not be flexible about unsteady production. At stake was also the fact that I had to do a considerable amount of editing to make the styles of the four translators consistent.

A major difficulty was the author's Babelic language. René's writing was in English, but the latent structure of his writing was German, the language he spoke at home. His sentences were extremely long and the word order was unfamiliar and resonated of German. Not all of us had a background in German to enable us to address this problem in his writing. The publishing house had asked us to make the style more reader friendly, but the author did not always like it when we broke long sentences in two, for example, or when we changed the word order. Another problem was that he could not avoid the temptation to change the text as we went along; he always wanted to add more and more evidence to prove his thesis. This meant that we were often translating a text in the making and also translating more than we had committed ourselves to. And all this under the pressure of time . . .

Another problem was that the text had errors in its details. The author was a genius in terms of politics, but he was writing about a country whose geography, history, and government he had not studied as much as had the translators, all Brazilians. The errors were in the small details, but they were there. For example, he referred to the state of Espírito Santo as being in the northeast, an error any Brazilian could spot. Moreover, he added a nonexistent rung in the hierarchy of the air force in Brazil. He would not accept our corrections and he insisted on putting the same mistakes into the translated text. Well, the public would interpret this as an unforgivable mistake of the translators. But he was adamant, even after we showed him the state on the map. Of course, in my view, such errors would cause his outstanding contribution—in fact a paradigm shift in the historiography of Brazil and Latin America—to lose credibility. He could fall into the same lack of credibility as the dictatorship he was unmasking. The only way out I found was to negotiate: he would accept relocating the state of Espírito above Rio (to the center east), and we would close our eyes to the nonexistent rung in the air force, as we could no longer waste so much time on such details. In fact, we counted on Vozes's proofreader to detect the problem, but as it happened, because of time pressure, this stage was eventually wiped out.

The Baby

All of this was happening while Bernardo was growing and growing and growing in me. The ultrasound scans showed that the baby was a big, big boy. Father and mother started to choose a name, as parents do. Gustavo? Bernardo? We chose Bernardo and we used to talk to Bernardo every day. He inhabited our daily lives and conversation even before he was born. And this baby was growing so fast and I am very short. It was becoming ever so difficult for me to reach the 1,200 pages on my desk—more than 1,200 pages in fact because a translation from English into Portuguese is always longer than the original.

I was growing so big and Bernardo was giving every sign that he would soon show his face. We have an expression in Portuguese, *mostrar a cara*, literally 'to show his face': it is used politically as well as to designate the moment a baby appears at birth. By that time I was in agonizing fear of any harm being done to my child about to be born. So I added a statement to my preface to the translation saying that all the content expressed in the book was the author's responsibility. I had no conviction about what I was saying: I was thinking about the baby. The translation process that I have described was one of great empathy. All of us as translators wanted to make the author's words our own. The manuscript also seemed to be waiting for us as persons and as translators. Anyone doing research on this translation would recognize the disingenuousness of the preface. René, in fact, later shifted this remark to his own foreword, thus disengaging all involved in the process from responsibility for its content.

The Final Moments

The deadline came to submit the translation to the publisher. We had made it. With ups and downs, with a sense of revelation that was the author's but that had become ours as translators also, we handed the book to Vozes, the publisher. The book would be published with the less technical title *1964: A conquista do Estado; Ação política, poder e golpe de classe* (1964: The Conquest of the State: Political Action, Power, and a Class Coup). It would list the names of the translators. It would be launched on 31 March, the anniversary of the coup d'état. We were in utter dread and agonizing fear as well. The censors could be reading it soon, with our names on it.

I had some time to organize my life for the birth, to clear my desk and my space at the university. As soon as the translation was handed in, I turned to decorating the baby's room. One day, the twelfth of February, I woke up feeling a bit different. I had been feeling very, very tired ever since I had handed the book in. We were driven while we were working: it's only when you finish that you realize how tired you are. And I was very heavy by that time as well. But that day was my husband's birthday. So I plucked up some energy to prepare for the friends and relatives who would be coming by later in the day for the celebration. It was then that the contractions started. Bernardo seemed to want to come a few days early to give himself as a birthday present to his father.

In no time I had to apologize to the guests. I looked down: the waters had broken. I rushed with the final preparations to go to maternity. And the joy: I had not quite finished everything, but most was ready for Bernardo.

Yet the thought in the back of my mind was whether the censors would spoil that beauty. There was a threat looming in the air: had the censors already examined the translated book? Had the police been following my movements? Will they come? Will I ever see my baby? On the way to maternity, joy was mixed with a most memorable plea: spare me censors, I'll burn the translation. I cry in joy and despair every time I think of that trip to the hospital.

Fortunately I come from a culture that celebrates life. When I got to maternity, the friends and relatives were already there to celebrate the father's birthday and the son's birth. What a relief. I had an army of relatives and friends to protect me from the wrath of political censorship.

But labor did not progress. The doctor showed me with ultrasounds that Bernardo was a big, big boy. It would have to be a Cesarean section. That was the hardest moment, when I realized I would be totally vulnerable and immobilized. The doctor said I was very tense and they would have to give me something to relax. I had no choice at that point any more.

I woke up with a touch on my hand. It was the pediatrician showing me Bernardo, this hungry, hungry boy who needed his mother. The censors and the police had not come. I had one of the most beautiful moments of my life, looking at a gorgeous baby opening his eyes to life while my country was also starting a new moment.

The Visibility of Translation as Midwifery

I could not attend the launch, but it was a big event. The book became a bestseller for some three years. It produced controversies. It produced debates. It was very beautiful to see a culture of silence opening itself to dialogue.

A funny detail. The first review of the book, by a prominent weekly, *Veja*, paid a major compliment to the translation. One of the reviewer's first remarks was how good the translation was: the book read as if it had been written in Portuguese. There is some value attached to transparency. Or to put it differently: I do not measure the translator's (in)visibility by the criterion that the translated text reads as if it were written in the language of the translation or not. I take readability and fluency to be basic quality requirements of any published material, whether original or translation. But then the reviewer spotted an error: the translator seems to have recreated the hierarchy of the Brazilian air force. I was too happy to tell the story behind that new rung to *Veja*; I just let it go. Otherwise, justifying the error in terms of the writer's obstinacy, I would also be exposing his ignorance of this detail and diverting attention from his major accomplishment. This mistake, like a drop in an ocean, would stand out even more if justified. I opted to protect the writer's credibility. One problem in a translation of 1,200 pages is inevitable anyway.

This experience afforded me a much higher level of visibility than I had ever had before in my life: enabling my country's right to know its own history. Meditating on this experience of political translation as agency during the preparation of this essay has been important for me. All the decisions of the actual experience were made so quickly and so intensely. In such situations it often takes time to truly understand what one has lived.

The parallel between the gestation and the translation is something I like very much. It reminds me of a Greek word *maieutics*, which means literally 'the work of a midwife'. The word has been used by great philosophers, particularly Plato, to refer to how we deliver to people knowledge that they actually already possess, but that they possess unconsciously. It may be that in Brazil the knowledge delivered by our team of author and translators was not really unconscious but repressed, because we Brazilians had to live every day with the unspeakable fear of members of our families being victimized.

Ironically as a mother about to give birth to a child, I could not give the final push to Bernardo to bring him into the world. But I helped give the final push to a new understanding of the history of my country.

Notes

1. Because of censorship, repression, and the distortion of history under dictatorships, the displacement of the narrative of history is a phenomenon commonly associated with such regimes. As a result the narrative of history must often be produced outside the country in question. Under Pinochet, for example, Chilean exiles produced the most valuable films and documentaries contesting the distorted official history of the country, using footage that they had somehow smuggled abroad.

2. This statement is found in the chapter he wrote for publication in my book *City of God in Several Voices: Brazilian Social Cinema as Action* (2005). See Meirelles (2005).

MARIA TYMOCZKO

The Space and Time of Activist Translation

> [I have] faith in the capacity of human beings to change what human
> beings have created. Resistance and change are not only possible but
> continuously happening. But the effectiveness of resistance and the real-
> ization of change depend on people developing a critical consciousness
> of domination and its modalities, rather than just experiencing them.
>
> NORMAN FAIRCLOUGH, *Language and Power*

R ELATED to calls for action that have been sounded in translation studies, the essays in this volume document some of the many forms
that activist translation has taken historically and that it can take at present. The ethical and ideological import of the studies is central, demon-
strating that translators have been and can be agents of significant social
change. The essays also show that discourses about activism in translation
have evolved considerably since the topic was first raised in translation
studies.

Translation, Resistance, Activism

The specificity of activist translation strategies, the wide range of objectives
of resistance in translation, and the many motivations for activism among
translators are evident in this collection. Here the targets of activist translation include European colonialism and imperialism, the focus of the Hispanic revolutionary movement and its translators discussed by Georges L.
Bastin, Álvaro Echeverri, and Ángela Campo. Motivated by earlier revolutionary movements in the United States and France, the translators promoting revolution in Hispanic America were often themselves militants or
networked with those plotting armed rebellion. In turn Puaʻalaʻokalani D.
Aiu discusses the second-generation imperialism of the United States and
its appropriation of the Hawaiian Islands—the act that arguably initiated
U.S. pretensions as an imperial power, antedating the imperialist moves of

the United States after 1898 in the Caribbean and the Philippines, and U.S. neoimperialism since the beginning of the twentieth century. Aiu focuses on the use of both translation and the refusal to translate as tools in Hawaiian political and cultural movements since the 1970s. From the mid-nineteenth century, U.S. imperialism has depended on translating Hawaiians into English, a goal that almost completely succeeded but that has met activist opposition for the last half century. Still another descendant of European imperialism in the form of a coalition of nationalist, capitalist, and religious interests is discussed in Antonia Carcelen-Estrada's study of the "pacification" of the Huaorani in the Ecuadorian Amazon undertaken in the middle of the twentieth century and still continuing. Here the government of Ecuador—in an almost classic iteration of earlier Spanish conquests in the Americas and a reproduction of patterns of the Spanish colonial government—allied itself with the translation programs of Protestant missionaries in order to gain access to the oil-rich resources of Huaorani lands. Carcelen-Estrada explores not only efforts to translate the identities of Huaorani communities associated with translation protocols for the Bible into Huao Terero but also the resistance to translation implicit in the identity performances of the Huaorani themselves.

A less overtly political field of action, one more restricted to cultural issues per se, is represented in Denise Merkle's study of the secret publishing networks in England in the second half of the nineteenth century; she shows that translators and publishers—many of them prominent and well-known figures—made activist interventions to shift sexual mores in Britain by publishing translations that put sexually explicit and homoerotic texts in circulation, thus contesting dominant norms in England. Similarly, as Nitsa Ben-Ari demonstrates, through translations the erotic found expression in modern Hebrew language and culture and in the young state of Israel, despite the dominant puritanical nationalist ethos; surprisingly the translations in question involved vastly different text types, ranging across pornography, twentieth-century erotic classics, and medical manuals. Likewise, in the study by Brian James Baer, the translation of Western classics is shown to have been used in the Soviet Union to oppose a broad field of rigid socialist cultural norms. In another context all three of these case studies might be analyzed primarily as the relationship between translation and literary systems. Setting these translators in the context of resistance, engagement, and activism, however, indicates the ideological force of the movements and the breadth of the targets of activist translation, including linguistic and textual norms, sexual and spiritual values, right-wing and left-wing ideologies.

Still other goals of resistance and activism in translation are revealed in the essays of Paul Bandia, John Milton, and Else Vieira. They deal with resistance to the oppression of twentieth-century dictatorships, the hier-archies of the modern postcolonial nations of Africa, and, by extension, many regimes of the contemporary world. These essays confirm that op-position to a wide field of social constructs—class structures, material in-equities, social hierarchies, specific governmental policies, and the narra-tion of approved histories—can all be actively engaged by translators and translations. In turn Mona Baker demonstrates how narrative theory can be useful in evaluating activist projects, and she details how electronic and media networking has made it possible for contemporary translators to join in networks linking activists around the world, allowing translators to participate in and engage with international questions of every sort.

The studies in this volume attest that for more than two centuries translation has been involved in a broad range of actions, including revo-lution, nation building, and resistance to military oppression and physical force. Translational activism has supported the development of language movements, shifts in cultural values (involving both indigenous values and foreign importations), gender liberation, avant-garde art movements, and more. Similarly, the range of power structures that translation has opposed is impressive, including colonial regimes and dictatorships, with translators defying imprisonment and death; government and military interests; laws, official policies, and state values; religious institutions; official histories; lit-erary establishments; constraints on discourse; multinational corporations; and the diffuse structures of neocolonialism and globalization. This wide range of opponents and institutions targeted by translators must be factored into general discussions of translation, resistance, and activism.

In pursuing their varied struggles, mobilized translators adopt a wide variety of linguistic and textual strategies to achieve their goals, and they engage in many types of action as well. As the essays here illustrate, sometimes the fact of translation itself—whatever the textual strategy—is the primary activist achievement. This was the case when documents as-sociated with the U.S. and French revolutions were translated into Spanish at the end of the eighteenth century and two centuries later when Else Vieira led a team of translators who prepared for publication a history re-vealing the details of the rise of the ruling Brazilian dictatorship. Textual production per se is currently operative when groups of translators work together to disseminate news that is suppressed, ignored, or distorted by mainline information networks. At other times the refusal to translate is the most effective activist posture. The case of translational silence in the Hawaiian cultural revival and the endurance of the Huaorani people in the Amazon stand as examples in this volume, but zero translation has been well documented as an effective strategy in many political and ideological contexts. As is clear, activist translation does not merely take the form of communication; it can also involve blocking communication and refusing to transmit cultural information.

Sometimes activist translation strategies depend on the choice, manipulation, or even displacement of text types and genres. Old and canonical texts can be revived for these purposes or new texts introduced. Examples of the manipulation of genre include the development of erotic materials in modern Hebrew via the rather unexpected text type of medical manuals; similarly the reframing of children's books in Brazil as an activist translation method was used by Monteiro Lobato to promote political discourses during a period of dictatorship. At times activist translators amplify translated texts, providing elaborate commentaries and paratextual materials that serve as a guide for political or ideological readings; the methods of Richard Burton in his voluminous commentary on *The Arabian Nights* stand as an example. At other times engaged translators simplify translated texts in order to serve specific engaged purposes. Sometimes activist translation strategies turn on the insertion of the foreign into a culture and at other times they turn on the refusal of the foreign. There is no single textual or discursive strategy that can be identified paradigmatically with translational resistance, engagement, or activism. No single strategy has been historically privileged by successful activist translators—no such claim can be made for literal or free, acceptable or adequate, formal-equivalence or dynamic-equivalence, domesticating or foreignizing, or any other binary—and the essays above testify to this truth. Activist translation strategies are selected, invented, and improvised for their tactical values in specific situations, contexts, places, and times.

Although some of the activist translations and translation movements discussed in this book can be read as initiated by isolated individuals, as a whole the essays show that engaged translators are usually networked with other translators and other activists in common enterprises. One sees in the essays here that translators have cooperated with organizations and groups of many types, from armed militants to legal experts, from secret societies to mobilized artistic movements and dissident publishers, from NGOs to protest movements of many types. Above all activist translators tend to be networked with each other, illustrated in an intimate way by the very personal account of Else Vieira. It is striking that mobilized translators often become founders of discursivity, not merely by importing new cultural discourses in their translations but also by initiating discourses through the representations in their translations and constructions deriving implicitly and explicitly from their translation choices.

Another important conclusion that follows from the studies in this volume is that there are limits to translational resistance associated with the very values that translators are engaged in changing. Put another way, paradoxically many of the translations exhibit collusion with dominant thinking even as they attempt to shift their target culture and target readers in directions that diverge from the dominant. One sees an example in the suppression by García de Sena of anything that might challenge the hierarchy of the Catholic church in Hispanic America, thus leading to the muting of ideas pertaining to separation of church and state in his 1807 Spanish translations of the writings of Thomas Paine and other revolutionary documents from the United States, as discussed in the essay by Bastin, Echeverri, and Campo. Similarly, as Merkle indicates, even as Richard Burton attempted to open up late Victorian society to greater freedom in sexual mores, he perpetuated many of the imperialist, racist, and patriarchal presuppositions of British culture in his orientalist and misogynist representations. We have seen that resistance and activism of all types are always metonymic activities and that not everything problematic in a society can be opposed or shifted at one and the same time, a factor that is particularly apparent during cultural crises and times of rapid social change. Nonetheless it can be dislocating to see this fissuring materialized in translations and to realize that arguably progressive translators collude with values currently considered objectionable.

The wide variation in the targets of resistance, the goals of engaged translators, the strategies of translation, the affiliations of translators, and even the collusive aspects of their work results from the extreme cultural specificity of activist translations. All translations are located in their own time and space, but the situated quality of activist translations stands in high relief. The cultural specificity of such translations is connected with the subject positions of the translators and the programmatics of the activist interventions undertaken. Contextually driven motivations are paramount in the strategies chosen by activist translators because the stakes of their choices are high, particularly in agonistic and polarized power struggles. Careful attunement of translation strategy to context is driven by the political sensitivities of the target populations and the translators' investment in influencing their audiences. Because struggles and contestations are inherently in flux and often undergo rapid change, activist strategies cannot be static; they must be precisely adjusted to the historical, political, and cultural requirements of the time. In a sense activist translations constitute a limiting case of speech acts governed by stringent felicity conditions, determined both by significant presuppositions and by socially determined signals of implicature, all of which are extremely context sensitive and context dependent.[1] In a highly charged or polarized ideological context, any utterance or language act including translation will be scrutinized for its implications and its conformity to particularized communicative expectations and presuppositions. Insofar as conditions are volatile or in flux, these conditions can change suddenly and rapidly, necessitating strategical agility in translation as in other forms of activist interventions.

Another way to look at this issue is to see the challenges facing activist translators and the readers of activist translations in terms of relevance theory.[2] For activist translations context is *relevant* in the strongest sense of the word. Relevance theory is useful for teasing apart and exploring the complexities of activist translation because an engaged translation product or practice can only be understood in terms of the precise context of its performance and delivery. Moreover, in translating, rather than communicate or perform a political or ideological position directly in their own voices and persons, translators elect to speak or act indirectly via their translations. To put it another way, a translation is a text about a text or a form of contextually situated metastatement; this is the case even if the metastatement is seemingly only a form of reported speech or quotation uttered in a new context (cf. Jakobson 1959:233; Holmes 1994:23–33; Lefevere 1985, 1992). Thus a translation strategy must be carefully chosen to suit the target context even as the context itself is highly relevant to the significance of the strategy deployed. Obviously any scholarly assessment of translation strategies must be equally nuanced.

A translation's ideology is determined only partially by the content of the source text—the subject and the representation of the subject—even when the content itself is overtly political and enormously complicated as a speech act, with locutionary, illocutionary, and perlocutionary aspects of the source text all contributing to the ideological effect in the source context. The ideological value of the source text is in turn complemented by the fact that translation is a metastatement, a statement about the source text and its content that constitutes an interpretation of the source text; in quoting a source text, a translator creates a text that is a representation with its own proper locutionary, illocutionary, and perlocutionary forces determined by factors in the receptor context. Thus, even in a simplified model, the ideology of a translation will be an amalgam of (1) the subject and content of the source text and their representation in the source text; (2) the various speech acts instantiated in the source text related to the source context; (3) the translator's representation of the source content and the source text; (4) the relevance of the target context of the translation; (5) the various speech acts of the translation itself addressing the receptor context; and (6) any resonances and discrepancies that exist between the two "utterances" of source text and translation. A translator can also address the target audience directly in paratextual materials.[3] An activist translator makes strategic choices at all these textual levels, choosing strategies for their power and effect in the context of the specific audience addressed. In addition to the ideological parameters that operate at the level of the translated text, there are of course external factors that relate to a translation's ideological significance: the identity and affiliations of the author, the identity and affiliations of the translator, the connections of the translator with various social and political movements, the reception context (such as reviews, censorship, legal action) of the translation, and so forth.

At the level of both the text and the metatext, the receptor context frames the meaning of a translation: in this sense, among others, Gideon Toury (1985:19, cf. 1980:28) is accurate in his dictum that translations are "facts" of the receiving cultures. Metatextual implicatures are assumed or constructed by translators and in turn metatextual inferences are made by the audiences or readers of translations, situating a translator's work and the source text with respect to the immediate receiving context. A translator's position can be judged by inferences resulting from the choice of text, from choices at the microlevels of the text (such as word choice or phrasing), from form, from omissions and silences, from additions and explicitations, and so forth, not all of which are consciously perceived by a reader. In assessing the political or ideological significance of an activist translation, therefore, a reader's inferences take into account much more than the message of the source text and the message of the author or speaker of that source text. The shift of context entailed in the place of enunciation of the translator introduces a new field of considerations relevant to the interpretation of the message, requiring inferences about metatextual issues as well as textual ones. All of these considerations have been instantiated and addressed in the essays in this collection.

As we have noted, at times translators guide readers' responses by making direct comments in their own voices to accompany the translations, most notably in paratextual commentary including notes, introductions, and critical essays, thus framing a translation and explaining how it should be read, what inferences should be drawn, and what ideological import the translation has in the receptor context. The extensive commentaries on U.S. revolutionary documents by the Spanish translators discussed by Bastin, Echeverri, and Campo stand as good examples, promoting new revolutionary models directly through persuasive argument, as well as through the ostensive value of the translated texts themselves. Similarly the commentaries of Richard Burton discussed by Merkle have this character, and indeed the commentaries are often as long as or longer than the translations themselves. The metacommentaries within Monteiro Lobato's children's literature described by Milton also operate in this way, which explains why his *Peter Pan* was censored in 1941 during the Getúlio Vargas period.

No activist translation strategy can ever have a fixed or absolute meaning divorced from context, whether that strategy depends on domestication (including radical domestication such as womanhandling or cannibalization), foreignization, or even silence. It is relevance within a context that establishes meaning. Similar surface structures in translational acts can diverge at the level of deep structure, and divergent translation strategies may function in similar ways despite surface differences. Even the communicative function of translation can be open to question or negation, as we have seen; this is one reason that silence or refusal to translate can be such a powerful ideological tool of resistance or engagement. As Aiu observes at the end of her essay about the Hawaiian cultural revival, "The irony is that in this situation both translation and non-translation work to empower Hawaiians."

What follows from the extreme cultural specificity of engaged translations is that any particular activist translation strategy will be time limited. That is, if translation as an activist intervention is highly culturally structured, temporally specific, and context sensitive, it follows that a translation strategy will generally be extremely situated in its temporal, cultural, and ideological moment. Not only is it illusory to attempt to prescribe or promote a single textual strategy for translational resistance or activism in general, such a theoretical posture would actual impede translational activism. Any given strategy geared to a specific time, place, or political context will normally be durable only for a restricted period of time. Because strategies of resistance and activism in translation are so context sensitive, they are liable to rapid alteration, as tactics of activism in general are: a resistant or engaged translation strategy will be characteristic of a particular time, place, movement, group of people, audience, or even a single translator—or some intersection of these factors. Thus in order to understand an activist strategy, it may be necessary to minutely situate the translation in its cultural context: a scholar must understand the relevance of the year, the place, the particular political situation, the specifics of a struggle at a specific time, the actors involved, the translator's identity and role in the partisan engagement, and so forth. Things that are possible in one year, may not be possible in another year. Some opportunities close down and others open up. It is a truism to say that translations grow old but it may be the case that resistant and activist translations are among those that age the fastest.

Contextual Shifts and Activist Translation Strategies in Ireland, 1880–1980

Paradoxically the wide array of targets, goals, and strategies of activist translations apparent in a heterogeneous collection of studies such as those above has its counterpart in the variations of activist translation strategies that characterize any specific ideological struggle employing translation as an operational component over an extended period of time. The theoretical conclusions that emerge from a survey of a range of activist situations can be confirmed by examining the variation in and shifts of goals, strategies, and tactics in activist translation movements of long duration, that is, in specific histories of translational activism across time. Indeed, if the place of activism is held constant, the variation through time of activist translational methods can be seen more clearly, with the time-limited quality of translation strategies and goals becoming particularly evident.

Consideration of Irish cultural nationalism, one such extended cultural struggle using translation, illustrates both the temporal and contextual specificity of activist strategies and also the wide variation in translation strategies deployed effectively over a long span of time and even at a single point of time, depending on the characteristics of competing discourses and the nature of the political contestation. The wide array of translation types across time and the specificity of strategies in relation to context that have been associated with cultural nationalism in Ireland since 1880 are illuminated by political events of the times, the political positioning of individual translators and their translations, and the position of the branch of nationalism that individual translators were engaged with. These positions are staked out with respect to England and the world, of course, but they are equally marked with respect to internal Irish political and ideological debates. Obviously within the framework of this short essay, the evidence from such a long period can only be illustrated in summary fashion; nonetheless, a few key cases of the translation of early Irish literature into English in relation to their political contexts serve to indicate the main points of the argument. Even in an abbreviated treatment, the highly variable nature of the activist translations of early Irish literature is manifest, and it is evident that shifts in strategy correlate with political and historical developments.[4] The brief survey below demonstrates not only that no single strategy of activist translation has been privileged in Ireland but also that the strategies actually documented are quite divergent, responding to the immediate needs of the historical and cultural moment, and determined by the microcontexts of competing discourses at a particular point in time. Moreover, it is evident that the individual strategies found in Ireland's translational history did not sustain themselves over an extended span of time, in part because no given strategy could meet the changing ideological needs of the nation for long. These variations are especially striking in view of the fact that Ireland is a small culture which has had a relatively homogeneous population until recently; moreover, cultural nationalism in Ireland was a fairly unified movement for decades after 1880.[5]

Although such questions can be traced in the translation history of early Irish literature into English from the late eighteenth century onwards, the starting point for this survey is Standish O'Grady's *History of Ireland: The Heroic Period*, the two volumes of which appeared respectively in 1878 and 1880. The work was radical in its day because O'Grady offered English readers a popularized history of Ireland and an introduction to the traditional native heroes. As is well known, O'Grady took up this task when he found an English-language treatment of Irish history in the library of a country house that he was visiting; the book radicalized him because he realized that despite his Irish university education, he had never been exposed to the pre-English history of his own country. O'Grady set out to introduce Anglophone Irish readers to their cultural heritage, and his writing became a transformative experience for many people, earning him the sobriquet "Father of the Irish Revival." A modern scholar looking at O'Grady's work is surprised and even at times appalled, therefore, by the extreme domestication of the Irish source texts, O'Grady's activist agenda notwithstanding. Almost everything in the two volumes is assimilated to the standards of English language and literature: genre, plot, episode, character type, material culture, cultural concepts, and even names. Nonetheless the popularity of O'Grady's *History* and the fact that he initiated discourses of cultural nationalism with his work suggest that his assimilative translation strategy was artistically and ideologically successful.

This paradox is explained by O'Grady's political and historical context. A Unionist, he wrote at a time when the question of Home Rule dominated Irish and English political debate and when achieving Home Rule seemed eminently possible. An assimilationist posture toward Ireland's native heritage might therefore have seemed judicious: it was consonant with the drive for a form of sovereignty that parliamentary means could achieve within the structure of the United Kingdom. O'Grady's translations repudiated stereotypes about the Irish that had become generalized in England for more than two centuries, portraying the Irish as other, barbarian, wild, unable to govern themselves, and so forth, all of which had been used to justify English colonial rule and later the incorporation of Ireland into the United Kingdom.[6] O'Grady's translation strategies have the strengths of their weaknesses: his collusion with English norms is inextricable from his strategic promotion of the Irish as heroic, noble, civilized, and just as capable of self-government (and Home Rule) as the English. They reflect the social and ideological fissures of his rapidly changing era (cf. Laclau and Mouffe 1985).[7]

Scarcely a decade later such an assimilationist strategy was no longer viable. After the fall of Charles Stewart Parnell in 1891, hopes of Home Rule were largely abandoned as no longer possible in the changed political circumstances. Far from trying to assimilate to English standards, which may have seemed appropriate when Home Rule appeared likely, cultural autonomy and disambiguation from England became dominant nationalist goals of the period. Irish cultural nationalism had also matured in the decade since O'Grady had published his seminal work. The Gaelic Athletic Association had been founded in 1884, promoting the replacement of English sports with native Irish ones. In 1893 the Gaelic League was established and almost immediately ignited enthusiasm for an Irish language revival. By the 1890s many more people had also become conversant with the main lines of Irish patriotic history, the principal stories of native Irish tradition, and the repertory of native Irish heroes, in part because of the success of O'Grady's writings and other popularized treatments. The development of children's books in English presenting summaries of medieval Irish tales and historical narratives as a prelude to the conventional political history of Ireland also dates from the period after O'Grady's translations, and some of those publications had been incorporated into school curricula. These materials had educated the rising generation of Irish citizens on a shared cultural heritage featuring icons from a literature and history that owed no debt to English master narratives. Although no single political platform unified the population, increasingly the concept of an Irish Ireland—an Ireland that rooted its identity in its native language, history, and cultural traditions—had caught the popular imagination. After 1891, therefore, it became important to dissimilate Irish culture from English culture: cultural difference was stressed and even constructed. Rather than shifting Irish texts to dominant English standards, for more than a quarter century after Parnell's fall engaged translators employed strategies that furthered goals of an Irish Ireland. O'Grady's translation strategies based on domestication to English norms were no longer culturally or ideologically ascendant or appropriate.

Beginning in 1898, the centenary commemoration of the iconic but failed Rising of 1798, there was a turn toward more overt activism including the publication of nationalist and republican newspapers, demonstrations for and against various political causes, disruptions of recruitments for the British army, actions supporting the Boers against the English in the Boer War (1899–1902), and the like. It is no accident that the translations of Irish literature between this period and the establishment of the Irish state in 1922 are all considerably less domesticated to English standards than O'Grady's work and that they are much more politically and ideologically explicit and marked. Although the translations accede to (or collude with) standards of decorum common to Victorian English proprieties and Irish Catholic morality and although they tend to elide many of the distinct formal aspects of Irish narrative in favor of genres and styles that were already established in the European literary repertory, nonetheless all the translations of the period offer more assertive representations of the Irishness of Irish stories, heroes, culture, and values than O'Grady had done.[8]

Translation from Irish into English was an explicit political act from the 1890s to 1922, when the Irish state was established. Translators appropriated Irish-language materials for Ireland's immediate purposes of cultural independence and its long-term goals of political autonomy, selecting strategies that were compatible with discourses current in Irish cultural nationalism. Translations from Irish literature developed models of heroism and fostered a spirit of armed resistance, even as they fortified the Irish with images that repudiated centuries of English prejudice and stereotyping. As a group the translators constructed discourses that focused on heroic biography and a sacrificial ethos, emphasizing the tragic inevitability of internecine war in the source texts. These interpretations of Ireland's old heroic tales did not merely fit the values of the time: they were prophetic, setting a trajectory leading to the revolutionary military action of the Rising of 1916, the Irish war of independence, and Ireland's civil war.

The activist translations of the time were interwoven with other projects and programs of the Irish political and cultural landscape contesting British dominion, including the language movement, the athletic program, handcraft movements, publication of nationalist newspapers, a retooling of the educational system, the development of a national literature in both English and Irish, and the establishment of an Irish dramatic movement that staged formal theatrical productions, as well as rousing skits, amateur theatricals, and *tableaux vivants* reinforcing many of the same messages as the translations of the early literature. Cultural actions in turn had counterparts in the projects of other groups promoting social change including agrarian reform and labor organization, with paramilitary training an important component of the activism. In most cases translators were affiliated with at least one branch of the nationalist movement and in many cases they played multiple roles. The Irish translators epitomize the way that engaged translators historically have had collective affiliations with larger activist movements and political programs, including various forms of progressive cultural activities.

Despite the commonality of cultural assertion that unifies the translations from this period of Irish history, there are striking differences in the actual translation strategies employed. Three examples illustrate the divergences and differing stances in the political field of Irish cultural nationalism. The relationship to and implications of the strategies are apparent if one asks about the ways that context provides a structure of relevance for reading the texts and about the inferences it is possible to draw from the representations and the formal characteristics of the divergent translation strategies.

We can begin with Eleanor Hull's compendium of translations and refractions from the Ulster Cycle, published as *The Cuchullin Saga* (1898). By calling the stories *sagas*, Hull evoked comparison with Icelandic literature, suggesting an affinity between the tradition of Irish heroism and Germanic—specifically Viking—heroic tradition. The representation of early Irish literature in terms of the Icelandic sagas invokes ideological (counter)discourses about nobility, heroism, and the valorization of preindustrial ideals and ways of life that were already well established in England and Europe.[9] In fact Hull's title suggests a parallel to many of the most famous Icelandic texts, including *Njal's Saga* and *Egil's Saga*. By implicitly appropriating discourses in circulation about the Vikings for Irish heroes, Hull casts a very different light on the native Irish from the common derogatory English stereotypes or even the romantic representations of Matthew Arnold in "On the Study of Celtic Literature" (1867), who had celebrated the Celts for their emotional sensitivity, their attunement to natural magic, their melancholy, and the like. Hull's image was pertinent to the times, particular the centenary of the Rising of 1798, when cultural nationalists in Ireland were celebrating the patriotic history and fallen military heroes of the nation.

By contrast in *Cuchulain of Muirthemne* (1902), Augusta Gregory translated a selection of the ancient aristocratic heroic tales from the Ulster Cycle in the guise of short prose narratives recounted in the rural Kiltartan dialect. Here the heroic tales are presented as folk narratives, with Gregory's choice of form and the Hiberno-English dialect underscoring this association.[10] What relevance did her context have for Gregory's choices and what political and ideological inferences could her readers draw from her translation choices? This translation strategy would have suggested discourses associating Ireland's glorious and heroic past with the contemporary peasantry as its legitimate heirs, thus valorizing rural Ireland as the touchstone for an emerging nationalist ethos. In doing so Gregory evoked romantic ideas about the folk that had served as the foundation for nationalist movements across Europe throughout the nineteenth century. This ideological stance came naturally to Gregory, who was herself a gifted collector of folk literature.

Quite a different strategy is manifest in Mary A. Hutton's *The Táin: An Irish Epic Told in English Verse* (1907). Hutton constructs a more militaristic heroic version of Irish culture, recasting the medieval Irish prose narratives with their poetic inserts as verse epic. Hutton assimilated the Irish form to dominant European standards for epic, namely long-line narrative poetry, rendering the Irish texts as blank verse. Because she divided her translation into "books" and included formulaic phrases (not always found in the source text), the translation has a Homeric ring. The blank verse and the high register of the language suggest the poetry of Shakespeare and Milton as well. In this representation the Irish hero Cú Chulainn is implicitly compared with the Greek Achilles, a comparison that had been made explicit earlier by Alfred Nutt in *Cuchulainn, the Irish Achilles* (1900). In her translation Hutton reinforced yet another popular nationalist discourse about the Irish: that their culture could claim an antiquity, dignity, and military tradition equal to those of Greece, appropriating the prestige of Greek culture for the Irish cultural revival. Hutton was an active member of the Gaelic League in Belfast, and her work perhaps reflects the ethos of that organization, elevating the status of Irish culture and Irish language texts as a way of bypassing English dominance. This translation was favored by the Gaelic League, and it is telling that Hutton's version was also used by Patrick Henry Pearse (an important member of the Gaelic League and later one of the martyrs of the Rising of 1916) in educating the boys at St. Enda's, his school for young nationalists. The boys were encouraged to model themselves after Cú Chulainn, whose words the school rendered as the motto over the main door: "I care not though I were to live but one day and one night provided my fame and my deeds live after me." It would seem that readers were encouraged to make revolutionary inferences as well as cultural ones from Hutton's translation strategy.

What should be noted here is that during the decade 1898–1907 there were a number of divergent translation strategies being deployed for activist ideological and political purposes, all valid and useful for Irish nationalism in general, but each related to specific discourses and ideological positions of the time. This set of Irish examples indicates how activist translators are generally engaged with larger political movements; indeed each of these three translators was affiliated with one or more specific groups in the nationalist field, often multiply connected with the movement in different roles including teacher, poet, playwright, folklorist, publisher, scholar, and the like. The proliferation of translation strategies, each effective in its own way, reminds us that it is rash and shortsighted to imagine that any specific translation strategy can be prescribed as the privileged vehicle of translational resistance or activism even in a very specific context. In one sense the translation strategies of Hull, Gregory, and Hutton were competing, as were the discourses and political postures they implied, yet the evidence can also be interpreted in another way. In the case at hand, a relatively small and homogeneous culture at a particular moment in history, during a period when the Irish nationalist movement was also relatively unified, a variety of divergent translation strategies were all effective for activist purposes. Those purposes—though nuanced and distinct in their implications and differing in the inferences that readers could draw—were compatible in the main and tended in the same direction. In fact one can argue that there was added value accruing from the deployment of multiple distinct translation strategies: the nation as a whole could simultaneously conceive the Irish heroes as being ancient, dignified, noble, and militarily adept as the Greeks; heroic and valiant as the Vikings;[11] and standing for the ancestors of the simple, moral, dignified, and upstanding Irish peasants, the bedrock of the nation.[12]

A new stage of the Irish translation record is apparent after 1922 and the founding of the Irish state. Prima facie it would seem that there should have been an increase in the number of translations of early Irish literature and other Irish cultural materials into English after independence, with increased possibilities for representing and celebrating the distinctive features of Irish culture and Irish literature in the new nation. The actual historical record is therefore counterintuitive, because in fact translation of the early literature into English virtually ceased in Ireland for almost half a century. Paradoxically once Ireland began the process of nation building, discourses about and representations of Irish culture became even more circumscribed than they had been under English rule.

This phase of zero translation can be interpreted in several ways. It could be (and was) justified by the official promotion of Irish as the first language of the nation. The justification is hard to sustain with respect to medieval texts in Old and Middle Irish, however, because those states of the language must be translated even for native speakers of Modern Irish. Such translations could hardly have compromised the viability of Modern Irish as a living language. It is also possible to correlate the lack of translations with censorship in the new state. Particularly after the Censorship of Publications Act of 1929, when clerical standards were formalized in official regulations, it would have been virtually impossible to translate much of the early literature in full. Because the early tales include sexual and scatological elements, close translations would have violated common values and even laws pertaining to sexuality and decency in general. Many, perhaps most, of the early stories have episodes involving nakedness, sexual assignations, sexual offers and provocations, fornication, infidelity, adultery, and so forth, all of which violated standards inherited from both Victorian norms and Catholic mores. Cultural restrictions became even more severe in Ireland after the adoption of the de Valera constitution in 1937, which wrote into law and codified many features of the dominant ethos pertaining to sexuality, chastity, and gender roles.

Again, however, there is another way to regard the absence of translations of early Irish materials after 1922. It can be looked on as a form of committed silence: an active engagement with Irish cultural nationalism and a commitment to maintain the (now petrified) identity constructions and representations of Irish culture that had been developed between 1890 and 1922, during the Irish revival and the Irish struggle for independence. Such a commitment could only be enacted by silence and zero translation. Retranslation of the early texts with more frank representations of the actual characteristics of Irish literature, culture, and history would have exposed the manipulations of the earlier phases of cultural nationalism and the constructivist representations of earlier translations. It would also have displayed characteristics of early Irish culture that could have drawn Anglophile censure or mockery during the founding years of the infant state, a period when, like any postcolonial nation, Ireland was particularly vulnerable. Indeed for decades after the independence of the Irish state, Ireland continued to regard itself as embattled: the partition of the island after 1921 and the continued inclusion of Northern Ireland in the United Kingdom made this sense of contingency more than cultural paranoia.

After 1922 Irish nationalists were faced with a double bind: early Irish literature and the literature of the Irish revival were both important to preserve, promote, and celebrate as important elements of Ireland's distinct national culture. It would have been damaging to the new nation-state to have updated translations reveal that many of the founding cultural documents—upon which Ireland had implicitly based its claim to sovereignty—were immoral according to the standards of the new state:

indecorous because of humor, "low" language, incidents of drunkenness and erratic behavior, free sexual behavior, gross actions, and so forth. Similarly new close translations would have revealed the manipulations of the preexisting work of the cultural revival, thus doubly undermining the state's moral legitimacy and its claim to sovereignty. In consequence, even before the promulgation of official censorship, the period after independence is marked by the production of rewritings and sanitized retellings of the early literature rather than close translations. Continuing the earlier translation project of the Irish revival, these refractions became part of the educational program of Irish schools, incorporated into the teaching of language, literature, and history.[13] In a sense an official version of the early mythos was created that diverged from the actual medieval texts; this received body of narrative became part of cultural literacy in the Irish state, and it spawned a vast number of cleaned-up (i.e., censored and self-censored) versions of early Irish literature that have continued to the present day in the form of children's books, popular histories, narratives at visitors centers, and so forth.

At the same time the old texts were available without abridgment in the early language itself—Old, Middle, and early Modern Irish—even though the material was not translated in full into English in Ireland.[14] The early texts were known to scholars and freely studied and translated by students, provided they could manage the early language. Thus scholars constituted a sort of secret society, to which entrance requirements were fairly stringent.[15] This paradoxical program of both silence and openness was institutionalized in the Mediaeval and Modern Irish Series, an instructional series for language students published without translations; the series began to be issued in 1931 and continues to be part of the publication repertory of the School for Celtic Studies, a branch of the Dublin Institute for Advanced Studies, and it includes a number of the "problematic" early tales.

In several of the studies in this volume, we have seen that silence and the refusal to translate can be an active weapon in a cultural or political struggle. Under this last interpretation of the absence of translations of medieval texts in Ireland after 1922, there was an open conspiracy of silence about the actual nature of much early Irish literature, culture, and history. Rather than being a form of resistance against the dominant English norms supporting colonial oppression, the translational silence after 1922 can be interpreted as active support for the dominant brand of nationalism and a form of collusion with the dominant norms of the emerging state. The translational silence in Ireland after 1922 illustrates that similar translation strategies can have different meanings depending on sociocultural and geopolitical context, involving both different presuppositions and different inferences. By letting the old translations stand, translators after 1922 tacitly assented to the earlier textual representations and implicitly subscribed to the established nationalist view of the past, but with very different motivations. It is ironic that the social norms of the emerging state had been partially constructed by the literary, dramatic, and translation movements before 1922 but that in many ways those national norms later became oppressive and regressive constraints not only on individual lives but also on the production of literature and other arts in the new republic.

As we have seen, scholars and writers who chose translational silence after 1922 were not engaged with any specific activist movement nor did they support any particular microposition in the political spectrum; rather they participated in the dominant nationalist project of the new state. To understand their position, therefore, it is necessary to contextualize them within the larger geopolitical context of Ireland's position in the world as an emerging postcolonial nation. We should note, moreover, that this national project was not without its opponents, including translators. One type of resistance to the dominant ethos of the republic took the form of translations and refractions with significant erotic elements, such as "Phallomeda" and "The Healing of Mis" by Austin Clarke (1976), some of which circulated privately when publication was not possible.

These dominant representations of early Irish literature and culture did not get systematically challenged in translation until the publication of *The Táin* (1969) by Thomas Kinsella, almost a half century after the establishment of the Irish state.[16] In his translations Kinsella represented the distinctive form of early Irish heroic literature (a mixture of poetic and prose forms of various types) by mirroring the formal variation with modern English analogues. He also highlighted distinctive features of Irish culture, including the cattle-based economy, the laws permitting concubinage and polygamy, and some of the native religious beliefs, in part by importing relevant Irish words for some of these cultural concepts into his texts or by creating English words and phrases that would foreground culturally distinct elements.[17] In these respects Kinsella constructed translations that were resistant linguistically, conceptually, and culturally (cf. Sommer 1992).

At the same time Kinsella challenged dominant nationalist values by transposing passages of the texts that had been suppressed in earlier English translations, including sections that undermined the notion of the sexual "purity" of early Irish culture.[18] He represented the sexual and scatological elements of the texts graphically in his translations, even heightening these elements in some cases.[19] By translating the humor of the stories, Kinsella undermined the solemn veneration of the early texts and Ireland's received patriotic history that orthodox nationalism insisted on. Most significant for Kinsella's activist strategies, he interrogated Irish heroism itself by presenting the heroes and their deeds in ways that challenged the representations of his predecessors. Reproducing the self-reflexivity of the ethos of many of the early tales, as well as the humorous light cast on the heroic figures, Kinsella included the moral foibles and failings of the heroes and stressed the heroes' hyperbolic and grotesque nature, even as he translated in full the extreme heroic deeds found in the medieval texts. Thus, Kinsella represented the complex stance toward heroic culture characteristic of many medieval Irish stories, a stance that self-reflexively questions the dominant premises of its own inherited warrior tradition. By extension within the context of the established identification between the medieval heroes and the heroes of 1916, Kinsella's translations of the early texts also examine the inherited nationalistic heroic ethos of his own time in a complex translational version of *mise en abîme*.[20] Implicitly his work invites reconsideration of the heroic pieties of the dominant Irish national narratives and patriotic history that had been in the making for more than a century, reflecting simultaneously on the traditional medieval heroes and the historical figures of the modern period, particularly those like Pearse who had avowedly modeled themselves on their medieval predecessors.

Kinsella's translations transgressed traditional English values and textual standards far more than did those of his predecessors in terms of propriety, mores, text types, narrative genres, assumptions about culture, and so forth. At the same time, in representing both the heroic deeds and the self-reflexive tone with which heroism is presented in medieval Irish literature, his translations depart significantly from the work of earlier translators; Kinsella interrogated and challenged the values of Irish cultural nationalism, inviting reconsideration of the nationalist representations of medieval Irish heroism and by extension the patriotic narrative of nation in Ireland itself. These challenges to both English and Irish culture are embodied specifically in his representations of the principal hero of the Ulster Cycle, Cú Chulainn. In both the early texts and Kinsella's translations, Cú Chulainn is larger than life in heroic deeds, but he is also louse ridden, he leaves his post for a sexual assignation, he lies, and he engages in unheroic acts. The hyperbolic yet flawed nature of Kinsella's hero—fully transposed from the source texts—resonates with the hyperbolic veneration of modern Irish heroes in the Irish Republic who were themselves flawed, as human beings inevitably are.[21] Kinsella interrogated Irish heroism but did not repudiate it: in doing so he gave contemporary Irish nationals a way to have their medieval and modern heroic traditions and to be simultaneously liberated from many of their oppressive constraints.

Kinsella's work was an immediate success and inspired many popular spin-offs, perhaps the most well known of which is the album *The Táin* composed and recorded by Horslips in 1973. The modern resonance of Kinsella's work—including the humor, the hyperbole, and the questioning of received values—fit with the ambience of the times. The ascendancy of the United States geopolitically and culturally allowed Ireland to shift its focus away from an obsessive fixation on England, moving beyond that polarized opposition to affiliation with the more open mores and self-reflexive humor characteristic of the U.S. The fact that the United States had received so many Irish immigrants aided in this shift. Nationalist movements opposing colonialism and civil rights movements worldwide reinforced and valorized Kinsella's insistence on cultural autonomy and resistance against dominant oppressive cultural standards. Moreover, cultural shifts in the 1960s—from the rock music of the Beatles and acerbic comic television series to the sexual liberation sweeping Western culture—all made Kinsella's translation strategies timely.

In the series of translations being tracked here, it is possible to discern the three stages of writing often discussed in postcolonial theory.[22] O'Grady's versions of early Irish tales—highly adapted and domesticated to English standards both formally and culturally—embody the tendency in postcolonial cultures to introject the colonizers' values and standards, even as they construct resistant representations asserting Irish cultural difference. A second stage is marked by the tendency to define the colonized culture's identity and values in terms of polar opposites to those of the colonizers. This is the place of enunciation of most of the translations between 1890 and 1922: they are less domesticated than O'Grady's work, but nonetheless tied to English standards by the very insistence on negating those standards or by the tendency to define Irishness in opposition to Englishness. The third stage of postcolonial writing emerges in Kinsella's work, namely an active attempt to define an autonomous cultural stance separate and distinct from that of the colonizers, irrespective of the colonizing power's approbation or condemnation.[23]

Clearly the successful engaged translation strategies in Kinsella's work are radically different from those used before 1922. In light of the cultural specificity of activist translation strategies, it is interesting to note that there was a relatively small window of time in which Kinsella's translation strategies in *The Táin* were optimal. It is doubtful whether his representations of Irish heroism in particular would have been nearly so palatable either to himself or to readers had *The Táin* been launched a mere three years later. After the resurgence of British oppression in Northern Ireland—manifest in the determination to suppress the civil rights movement and epitomized in the killings of Bloody Sunday on 30 January 1972—issues related to Irish nationalism, attitudes toward England, and views of heroism changed considerably throughout Ireland, north and south. Moreover, once the cruelty of governmental forces and Protestant paramilitary groups in Northern Ireland had accelerated and in turn revitalized the IRA, Kinsella's own politics might have restrained his humor and his interrogations of Irish heroism as a whole.[24] It is fortunate that Kinsella published his translations in 1969 when Ireland was receptive to the humor and self-reflexivity of his engaged translation strategies, or the nation and the world might have missed a great masterpiece of translation and twentieth-century writing.

A sign of the narrow window of opportunity for Kinsella's translation strategy mixing heroism, humor, and the deconstruction of heroism is the translational posture of Seamus Heaney.[25] Heaney began to translate the Middle Irish text *Buile Suibhne* shortly after Bloody Sunday when he moved to the Republic of Ireland in 1972. Published more than a decade later, the translation is an indirect one, with Heaney relying on the edition and translation of J. G. O'Keeffe (1913). In part the exercise was biographical: Heaney was drawn to the character Sweeney as a sort of alter ego, attracted by the rhyming of their two names, by the fact that Sweeney like himself was from the north of Ireland, and by Sweeney's flight in the tale southwards away from war. Driven mad by war, Sweeney spends the rest of his life living in the wilderness in sympathy with the natural world, a fate Heaney perhaps imagined for himself at the time. The choice of Sweeney also reflects the repudiation of the heroic character Cú Chulainn, similarly a northern figure, and, by extension, repudiation of the entire tradition of Irish heroism. Early in the escalation of hostilities in Northern Ireland, Cú Chulainn had been appropriated and revalorized as a symbol of heroism and violent confrontation by both sides of the conflict, figured, for example, in wall murals in Catholic and Protestant areas alike. The partisan use of Cú Chulainn complicated the position of writers from Northern Ireland who wished to indicate their Irishness and their northern affiliation by utilizing early Irish literature in their writing, yet who also wished to distance themselves from violence, as Heaney did. As I remember from conversations at the time with poets from Northern Ireland, one result was to disparage Cú Chulainn and reject him as a useful symbol, because he was seen as too violent and too "masculine," in favor of more "feminine" models such as various strong female figures of Irish literature or, in fact, Sweeney. There are traces of these discourses in Heaney's poetry and essays, and they motivate his choice of text, his translation strategy, his representations, and his construction of discourses in *Sweeney Astray*, which was finally published in 1983, almost exactly a century after O'Grady's landmark refractions. The translation presents ironies on many levels, not least that Heaney privileges a seemingly antiheroic and pacifist *Irish* tale for translation in the 1970s but later—after becoming a Nobel laureate—chooses to translate *Beowulf* (2000), the canonical text celebrating early *English* heroism.

The Time and Space of Activist Translation

This brief sketch of the diverse politicized translation strategies in Ireland over the course of a century and the radical shifts driven by contextual change within an extended history of activist translation confirms the findings of the essays in this volume as a whole. The Irish evidence also documents the varied goals that activist translators pursue and the engaged affiliations that they maintain even within a single small culture. The Irish case illustrates that activist translation strategies are highly variable and that they are sensitive to context, minutely located in time and space. The situated nature of engaged strategies and the impact of cultural, political, historical, and temporal factors become particularly evident when one holds the spatial and national context constant. In a longitudinal study of this sort it is also in some ways easier to trace how activist translation strategies respond to the specific ideological demands of the moment.

The Irish data demonstrate that many translation strategies are extremely time limited. Here the radical shift in translation norms in the period after the appearance of O'Grady's assimilationist texts illustrates how an approach that was socially transformative in one decade becomes useless and perhaps unacceptable a short time later. An even shorter window of time available for a specific engaged translation strategy is apparent in the case of *The Táin* by Thomas Kinsella, for within three years the political events in Northern Ireland put Kinsella's translation strategy into question in some quarters. Finally, despite the same temporal, historical, and political context, with translators sharing most of what Gideon Toury (1995:56–58) has called "initial" norms, the Irish data demonstrate that different translators choose different strategies in order to position their translations in relation to specific partisan debates so as to create particularized representations with ideological implications. Here one can cite the translations that appeared in the same decade by Eleanor Hull, Augusta Gregory, and Mary Hutton, all of whom agreed on the desideratum of producing translations that would support Irish cultural nationalism and dispel English stereotypes of the Irish. Nonetheless the implementation strategies in their translations of how to constitute representations of Irish culture are radically different albeit in ways complementary. These examples indicate how futile it is to attempt to promote or prescribe a single strategy for activist translation as the correct or privileged approach in one place and time, not to mention across time and space in general.

The essays in this book converge on the same basic conclusions. To understand resistance in translation, we must ask "resistance to what?" To address engagement in translation, we must explore the causes a translator is committed to and engaged with. In an investigation of any activist translation or translation movement, the motivations and purposes of activism must be determined. The problem of defining the object of resistance, engagement, and activism returns us again to the choices translators make and to the metonymic nature of both translation and activism. Translators decide to privilege specific aspects of a source text in their transmissions, their silences, their constructions, and their representations, especially in activist situations. Those choices are not random but are driven by the immediate ideological, political, and cultural contexts the translator is working in and translating for. They are also driven by the translator's affiliations and place of enunciation in those contexts. All these factors are minutely specific in time and space, and that specificity is never more operative than in instances of engaged translation, because a successful activist translation must fit the felicity conditions of its time.

No writer or translator can engage all struggles. This is one reason that an activist translation strategy is often extraordinarily time limited: it can change from year to year and sometimes even from month to month. A corollary is that not all resistant or activist translation goals will be viewed as positive by all readers or critics: because societies are heterogeneous and because they also change through time, one person's liberation is another's agitation, cooptation, or even imprisonment. As Baer indicates in his essay above, it can even be difficult to perceive translational activism in another context. Moreover, to say that a translation is resistant, engaged, or activist does not suffice to conclude that it is ethical or responsible. The process of choice that is intrinsic to translation makes translations inherently controversial, none more so than activist translations. In turn the controversial potential in any translation—but especially activist ones—will have ethical dimensions involving contestations about responsibility and affiliation. The heterogeneity in social views about values has a direct correlation with regimes of translation and hence with debates about how translations should be undertaken, debates that often take a prescriptive turn.

Thus, to say that a translation is activist does not suffice to conclude that it is responsible, that it is effective, or that it has followed a certain procedure, employed a specific strategy, or created specific representations. We have seen that activist translation movements typically have collusive aspects. Because the methods chosen for realizing a translator's goals are those that seem most likely to succeed at a particular moment in a particular context and a particular ideological framework, engaged translation strategies are inevitably pragmatic, hybrid, adventitious, and improvised so as to be most effective as determined by the judgment of the translator at the time. No activist strategy can simply be prescribed for all times and all places, nor can a totalizing critical analysis of resistant or engaged translation practices be effective. The wide range of activist translation goals and strategies and the cultural specificity of those goals and strategies in relation to the time and space of translation are confirmed not only by examining a wide range of case studies but also by following the changes over time in extended histories of translational activism.

As the studies in this collection indicate, whatever the data used, it is clear that activist translations are not merely communicative transactions. Nor are activist translations effective primarily because of their form, style, or textual strategies. Rather activist translations are performatives— they are acts within broader fields of specific political and ideological programs of action and their effectiveness is a function of their performative nature. The flexibility and pragmatism of activist translators enable translations to participate in many different types of political movements and to serve those movements in very diverse ways. Challenging hostile cultural frameworks, introducing newness into the world, changing societies, and confronting oppression and physical coercion are not easy processes, yet as a mode of activism, translation has vitality, adaptability, and robustness that give it a protean participatory power.

Notes

1. The notions of felicity conditions and implicature are associated with the work of Austin (1975), Searle (1969), and Grice (1975, 1981). See also the general discussion in Lyons (1977:2.592–613, 725–45).

2. See Sperber and Wilson (1995) on relevance theory.

3. Cf. Tymoczko (2003a, 2007:254–55).

4. More detailed discussions of the translations considered below are found in Tymoczko (1999).

5. On the extent of historical and current diversity in Ireland, see Cronin and Ó Cuilleanáin (2003).

6. The stereotyping of the Irish is discussed in Curtis (1968, 1971).

7. O'Grady's project can be compared to those of the translators discussed above by Baker, Bastin et al., and Vieira, where translation of the texts per se is paramount, whatever the textual strategy.

8. The use of European formal analogues is significant. The Irish had been oriented to the Continent for almost 2000 years; after the seventeenth-century English conquest, Ireland used its European affiliations in various ways to maintain its culture and to leverage some independence from English colonial rule.

9. See Helgason (1999).

10. Many of the tales about Cú Chulainn and the Ulster Cycle heroes had in fact persisted in Irish oral tradition to the twentieth century, so Gregory's representation was not altogether fanciful. See Ó Súilleabháin (1970:597–99).

11. This was a representation that itself challenged Anglo-Saxonist discourses of the time. Cf. Curtis (1968, 1971).

12. There were still other translation strategies of the period that constructed alternate representations of the early Irish, among the most interesting of which is A. H. Leahy's *Heroic Romances of Ireland* (1905–06). Leahy appropriated the prestige of medieval romance (including Arthurian romance) for the Irish; this was a genre that had high standing in English culture, particularly among the Pre-Raphaelites, and Leahy's formal archaizing style is reminiscent of translations associated with that movement. Hence Leahy offered another set of images that were useful for Irish cultural nationalism. The representations in scholarly translations were useful in still other ways; see Tymoczko (1999:73–74, 122–41).

13. This development was prefigured by the use of sanitized versions of early Irish literature, particularly stories about Cú Chulainn, at St. Enda's under the direction of Pearse. Cf. Tymoczko (1999:74, 80).

14. Some scholarly translations (at times expurgated) of the early texts appeared in England (for example in the Irish Texts Society's publications), others in Scotland, and still others in the United States and Germany, but almost none of the secular vernacular literature that might be considered morally controversial was translated in Ireland itself.

15. The parallels with Merkle's study above are obvious.

16. I have written extensively on Kinsella's translation strategies elsewhere (Tymoczko 1999), so here I will summarize his work briefly, concentrating on its significance for the question of activism and translation.

17. We can compare here the insistence on the use of Hawaiian words for distinct conceptual and metaphorical thinking discussed by Aiu above.

18. Here we can compare the projects of the activist translators discussed above by Merkle and Ben-Ari.

19. At the end of *Táin Bó Cúailnge*, for example, Kinsella deviates from the main manuscript he is translating to import erotic or scatological passages from another manuscript, thus amplifying these features in his translation (cf. his endnotes, 1970/1969:280–83).

20. The identification of the heroes of the war of independence with the medieval heroes was part of mainstream Irish discourse: a statue of the dying Cú Chulainn by Oliver Sheppard in the General Post Office in Dublin serves as the memorial to the heroes of the Rising of 1916.

21. Not accidentally, Joyce also represents his protagonist Stephen Dedalus as louse ridden, ironically identifying his hero with Cú Chulainn here and elsewhere; see the arguments in Tymoczko (1994:88–89; cf. 2004:46–47). The hyperbole of the early texts is also mirrored in modernist Irish writing, notably James Joyce's *Ulysses* and *Finnegans Wake* and Flann O'Brien's *At Swim-Two-Birds*. As author and translator Kinsella follows a path already trodden by Ireland's great modernist writers.

22. Cf. Tymoczko (1999:178–80) and sources cited.

23. It is noteworthy that Kinsella's text was published initially by Dolmen Press, one of the few independent presses in Ireland at the time, an artistic and ideological choice for Kinsella. In view of his strong assertion of Ireland's autonomous cultural heritage, it is interesting to note that Kinsella's *Táin* was published for mass-market

distribution by Oxford University Press in 1970 and has remained in print since. Obviously things were changing in England as well as in Ireland.

24. The escalating bitterness of the political climate in Northern Ireland and changes in the Irish political context associated with the Troubles in Northern Ireland may have contributed to Kinsella's decision not to finish a second volume of translations from the Ulster Cycle, a project he was actively working on when I first met him in the mid 1970s.

25. See Tymoczko (2000c) for a more extensive analysis of this case.

Works Cited

Abramovich, Fanny. 1982. "Lobato de Todos Nós," in Paulo Dantas (ed.), *Vozes do tempo de Lobato*. São Paulo: Traço. 145–57.

Achebi, Chinua. 1994/1959. *Things Fall Apart*. New York: Anchor.

Adejunmobi, Moradewun. 1998. "Translation and Postcolonial Identity: African Writing and European Languages," in Lawrence Venuti (ed.), *Translation and Minority*. *The Translator* 4.2.163–81, special issue.

Aiu, Pua'ala'okalani D., 1997. "This Land Is Our Land: The Struggle to Define Place in Hawai'i: An Analysis of the 1991 Kaho'olawe Island Conveyance Commission Hearings." Dissertation, University of Massachusetts Amherst.

Akhmatova, Anna. 1967–68. *Sochineniia*. 2 vols. Munich: Inter-Language Literary Associates.

Allison, Ann. 2000/1996. *Permitted and Prohibited Desires: Mothers, Comics, and Censorship in Japan*. Berkeley: University of California Press.

Almog, Oz. 1997. *Ha'tzabar: dyokan* [The Sabra: A Profile]. Tel Aviv: Am Oved.

Álvarez, Román, and M. Carmen-África Vidal (eds.). 1996. *Translation, Power, Subversion*. Clevedon: Multilingual Matters.

Anderson, Benedict. 2006. *Imagined Communities*. Rev. ed. London: Verso.

Andrade, Oswald de. 1928. "Manifesto antropófago." *Revista de Antropofagia* 1:1.

Andrews, Lorrin. 2003. *A Dictionary of the Hawaiian Language*. Honolulu: Island Heritage.

Anonymous, trans. 1883. *The Kama Sutra of Vatsyayana Translated from the Sanskrit; In Seven Parts with Preface, Introduction and Concluding Remarks*. 3 vols. Part 1, London; parts 2–7, Benares: Hindoo Kama Shastra Society.

Anonymous, trans. 1886. *The Perfumed Garden of the Cheikh Nefzaoui: A Manual of Arabian Erotology (XVI. Century)*. Cosmopoli: Kama Shastra Society of London and Benares.

Arakaki v. Cayetano, 324 F.3d 1078 (9th Cir. 2003).

Arakaki v. Lingle, 423 F.3d 954 (9th Cir. 2005), rev'd, 547 U.S. 1189 (2006).

Armas Ayala, Alfonso. 1970. *Influencia del pensamiento Venezolano en la revolución de independencia de Hispanoamerica*. Caracas: Instituto Panamericano de Geografía e Historia.

Austin, J. L. 1975. *How to Do Things with Words*. 2nd ed. Ed. J. O. Urmson and Marina Sbisà. Cambridge: Harvard University Press.

Azevedo, Carmen Lucia de, Marcia Camargos, and Vladimir Sachetta. 1997. *Monteiro Lobato: Furacão na Botocúndia*. São Paulo: SENAC.

Baer, Brian James. 2005. "Translating the Transition: The Translator-Detective in Post-Soviet Fiction," in Dirk Delabastita and Ranier Grutman (eds.), *Fictionalizing Language Contact: Translation and Multilingualism. Linguistica Antverpiensia* 4:243–54, special issue.

Baker, Mona. 2006. *Translation and Conflict: A Narrative Account*. London: Routledge.

———. 2009. "Resisting State Terror: Theorizing Communities of Activist Translators and Interpreters," in Esperanza Bielsa and Christopher W. Hughes (eds.), *Globalization, Political Violence, and Translation*. London: Palgrave Macmillan. 222–42.

Bakhtin, Mikhail. 1981. *The Dialogic Imagination: Four Essays*. Ed. Michael Holquist. Trans. Caryl Emerson and Michael Holquist. Austin: University of Texas Press.

———. 1984. *Rabelais and His World*. Trans. Helene Iswolsky. Bloomington: Indiana University Press.

Bandia, Paul. 1993. "Translation as Cultural Transfer: Evidence from African Creative Writing." *TTR* 6:2.55–78.

———. 1996. "Code-Switching and Code-Mixing in African Creative Writing: Some Insights for Translation Studies." *TTR* 9:1.139–54.

———. 2006. "African Europhone Literature and Writing as Translation: Some Ethical Issues," in Theo Hermans (ed.), *Translating Others*. 2 vols. Manchester: St. Jerome. 2.349–61.

Barsky, Robert. 1996. "The Interpreter as Intercultural Agent in Convention Refugee Hearings." *The Translator* 2:1.45–63.

Bassnett, Susan. 1998. "When Is a Translation not a Translation?" in Susan Bassnett and André Lefevere (eds.), *Constructing Cultures: Essays on Literary Translation*. Clevedon: Multilingual Matters. 25–40.

———. 2002. *Translation Studies*. 3rd ed. London: Routledge.

Bassnett, Susan, and Harish Trivedi, eds. 1999. *Post-Colonial Translation, Theory and Practice*. London: Routledge.

Bastin, Georges L. 2004. "Traducción y emancipación: El caso de la Carmañola." *Boletín de la Academia Nacional de Historia de Venezuela* 345:199–209.

Bastin, Georges L., Ángela Campo, and Álvaro Echeverri. 2004. "La traducción en América Latina: Una forma de traducir propia y apropiada," in Andrea Pagni (ed.), *Espacios de traducción en América Latina. Estudio: Revista de Investigaciones Literarias y Culturales* 26, special issue.

Bastin, Georges L., and Elvia Rosa Castrillón. 2004. "La carta dirigida a los Españoles Americanos: Una carta que recorrió muchos caminos." *Hermeneus* 6:273–90.

Bastin, Georges L., and Adriana Díaz. 2004. "Las tribulaciones de la Carmañola (y la Marsellesa) en América Latina." *TRANS* 8:29–39.

Batllori, Miguel. 1953. *El Abate Viscardo: Historia y mito de la intervención de los Jesuitas en la independencia de Hispanoamérica.* Caracas: Instituto Panamericano de Geografía e Historia.

Ben-Ari, Nitsa. 1997. *Roman im he'avar: ha'roman ha'histori ha'yehudi-germani min ha'mea ha-19 u'tzmichata shel sifrut leumit hadasha* [Romance with the Past: The Nineteenth-Century German-Jewish Historical Novel and the Emergence of a National Literature]. Tel Aviv: Dvir; Jerusalem: Leo Baeck.

———. 2000. "Ideological Manipulation of Translated Texts." *Translation Quarterly* 16/17:40–52.

———. 2002. "The Double Conversion of Ben-Hur: A Case of Manipulative Translation." *Target* 14:2.263–302.

———. 2006a. *Dikuy ha'erotiqa: cenzura ve'cenzura-azmit ba'sifrut ha'ivrit 1930–1980.*[Suppression of the Erotic: Censorship and Self-Censorship in Hebrew Literature 1930–1980] Tel Aviv: Tel Aviv University Press.

———. 2006b. *Romanze mit der Vergangenheit.* Trans. Dafna Mach. Tübingen: Niemeyer Verlag.

———. 2006c. *Suppression of the Erotic in Modern Hebrew Literature.* Ottawa: Ottawa University Press.

Bennett, W. Lance, and Murray Edelman. 1985. "Toward a New Political Narrative." *Journal of Communication* 35:4.156–71.

Ben-Yehuda, Netiva. 1981. *Bein ha'sphirot: 1948* [Between Calendars: 1948]. Jerusalem: Keter.

Berman, Antoine. 1984. *L'Épreuve de l'étranger.* Paris: Gallimard.

———. 1985. *Les Tours de Babel: Essais sur la traduction.* Mauvezin: Trans-Europ-Repress.

———. 1992. *The Experience of the Foreign: Culture and Translation in Romantic Germany.* 1984. Trans. S. Heyvaert. Albany: State University of New York Press.

————. 2000. "Translation and the Trials of the Foreign." 1985. Trans. Lawrence Venuti, in Lawrence Venuti (ed.), *The Translation Studies Reader*. London: Routledge. 284–97.

Beti, Mongo. 1971. *The Poor Christ of Bomba*. Trans. Gerald Moore. London: Heinemann.

————. 1984. *Main basse sur le Cameroun: Autopsie d'une décolonisation*. Rouen: Éditions Peuples Noirs.

————. 1985. *Lament for an African Pol*. Trans. Richard Bjornson. Washington: Three Continents Press.

————. 1987. *Remember Reuben*. Trans. Gerald Moore. London: Heinemann.

————. 1993. *La France contre l'Afrique: Retour au Cameroun*. Paris: La Découverte.

————. 1994. *Histoire du fou*. Paris: Juillard.

————. 1999. *Trop de soleil tue l'amour*. Paris: Julliard.

————. 2003. "The Publication of *Trop de soleil tue l'amour*: Interview with Mongo Beti." By Boniface Mongo-Mboussa. www.africultures.com/anglais/articles_anglais/intbeti.htm.

Bey, Essad. 1935. *A luta pelo petróleo*. Trans. Charlie W. Frankie. São Paulo: Companhia Editora Nacional.

Bhabha, Homi K. 1994. *The Location of Culture*. London: Routledge.

————. 2004/1994. *The Location of Culture*. London: Routledge.

Biale, David. 1997/1992. *Eros and the Jews: From Biblical Israel to Contemporary America*. Trans. Carmit Guy. Berkeley: University of California Press.

Boéri, Julie. 2008. "A Narrative Account of the Babels vs. Naumann Controversy." *The Translator* 14:1.21–50.

————. In progress. "Babels, the Social Forum and the Conference Interpreting Community: Overlapping and Competing Narratives on Activism and Interpreting in the Era of Globalisation." Dissertation, University of Manchester.

Boéri, Julie, and Stuart Hodkinson. 2005. "Babels and the Politics of Language at the Hearth of Social Forum." *Euromovements*. www.euromovements .info/newsletter/babel.htm. 1 April 2005.

Borges, Jorge Luis. 2000. "The Translators of the Thousand and One Nights," trans. Esther Allan, in Lawrence Venuti (ed.), *The Translation Studies Reader*. London: Routledge. 34–48.

Bourdieu, Pierre. 1980. *Le Sens pratique*. Paris: Éditions de Minuit.

————. 1982. *Ce que parler veut dire*. Paris: Librairie Arthème Fayard.

————. 1990. *The Logic of Practice*. Stanford: Stanford University Press.

Brasil, Sales. 1957. *A literatura infantil de Monteiro Lobato, ou Comunismo para crianças*. Bahia: Aguiar and Souza.

Brisset, Annie. 1990. *Sociocritique de la traduction: Théâtre et altérité au Québec (1968-1988)*. Longueuil, Québec: Le Préambule.

———. 1996. *A Sociocritique of Translation: Theatre and Alterity in Quebec, 1968–1988.* 1990. Trans. Rosalind Gill and Roger Gannon. Toronto: University of Toronto Press.

Brodhead, Richard. 1993. *Cultures of Letters: Scenes of Reading and Writing in Nineteenth-Century America.* Chicago: University of Chicago Press.

Brodsky, Joseph. 1992. "Poetry as a Form of Resistance to Reality." *PMLA* 107:2.220–25.

Bruner, Jerome. 1991. "The Narrative Construction of Reality," *Critical Inquiry* 18:1.1–21.

Buckley, Sandra. 1997. *Broken Silence: Voices of Japanese Feminism.* Berkeley: University of California Press.

Budberg, Moura. 1971. "On Translating from Russian," in *The World of Translation: Papers Delivered at the Conference on Literary Translation Held in New York City in May 1970 under the Auspices of P.E.N. American Center.* New York: P.E.N. American Center. 145–51.

Burke, William. 1808/1976. *Additional Reasons for our Emancipating Spanish America: Deduced, from the New and Extraordinary Circumstances, of the Present Crisis: And Containing Valuable Information, Respecting the Late Important Events, both at Buenos Ayres, and in the Caraccas, as well as with Respect to the Present Disposition and Views of the Spanish Americans: Being Intended as a Supplement to the "South American Independence."* New York: AMS Press.

Burton, Isabel, and Justin Huntly McCarthy, eds. 1886–88. *Lady Burton's Edition of her Husband's "Arabian Nights": Translated Literally from the Arabic.* 6 vols. London: Waterlow and Sons.

Burton, Richard F., trans. 1885–86. *A Plain and Literal Translation of the Arabian Nights' Entertainments, now Entituled [sic] The Book of the Thousand Nights and a Night, with Introduction, Explanatory Notes on the Manners and Customs of Moslem Men and a Terminal Essay upon the History of The Nights.* 10 vols. Benares: Kamashastra Society.

———, trans. 1886–88. *Supplemental Nights to the Book of the Thousand Nights and a Night, with Notes Anthropological and Explanatory.* 7 vols. N.p.: Printed by the Burton Club for Private Subscribers only. [Verso of title page reads: Illustrated Benares Edition.]

[Burton, Richard F., and Forester Fitzgerald Arbuthnot, trans.] 1885. *Ananga-ranga (Stage of the Bodiless One), or, The Hindu Art of Love, (Ars amoris indica). Translated from the Sanskrit, and annotated by A.F.F. & B.F.R.* Cosmopoli: Kama Shastra Society of London and Benares.

Burton, Richard F., and Leonard C. Smithers, trans. 1890. *Priapeia or the Sportive Epigrams of Divers Poets on Priapus: The Latin Text now for the First Time Englished in Verse and Prose (the Metrical Version by "Outidanos") [Good for Nothing] with Introduction, Notes Explanatory and Illustrative,* and *Excursus, by "Neaniskos" [A Young Man].* Cosmopoli: Printed by the translators.

———, trans. 1894. *The Carmina of Caius Valerius Catullus, Now First Completely Englished into Verse and Prose; the Metrical Part by Capt. Sir Richard F. Burton, R.C.M.G., F.R.G.S., etc., etc., etc., and the Prose Portion, Introduction, and Notes Explanatory and Illustrative by Leonard C. Smithers.* London: The Translators.

Carneiro, Maria Luiza Tucci. 1997. *Livros proibidos, idéias malditas: O deops e as minorias silenciadas.* São Paulo: Estação Liberdade.

Catford, J. C. 1965. *A Linguistic Theory of Translation: An Essay in Applied Linguistics.* London: Oxford University Press.

Cheung, Martha. Forthcoming. "From Partial Modernization to Total Transformation: Translation and Activism in Late-Qing China," in Julie Boéri and Carol Maier (eds.), *Compromiso social y traducción/interpretación; Translation/Interpreting and Social Activism.* ECOS: Granada.

Cheyfitz, Eric. 1997. *The Poetics of Imperialism: Translation and Colonization from "The Tempest" to "Tarzan."* Expanded ed. Philadelphia: University of Pennsylvania Press.

Clarke, Austin. 1976. *Selected Poems.* Portlaoise: Dolmen Press.

Clay, John. 1964. *Chadar ha'mitot shel Fanny Hill* [Fanny Hill's Bedroom]. Trans. Avner Carmon. Tel Aviv: Olympia.

Clealand, John. 1964. *Bita ha'tzeira shel Fanny Hill* [Fanny Hill's Youngest Daughter]. Trans. A. Rodan. Tel Aviv: Olympia.

Cleary, David. 1990. *Anatomy of the Amazon Gold Rush.* Iowa City: University of Iowa Press.

Cleland, John. 1964. *Zichronoteha shel eshet taanugot: Fanny Hill* [*Memoirs of A Woman of Pleasure: Fanny Hill*]. Trans. G. Kasim. N.p.: Great Art and A.I.

Cohen, Haim. 1973. *Al sepharim asurim* [On Forbidden Books]. Tel Aviv: Am Oved.

Colligan, Colette. 2002. "Obscenity and Empire: England's Obscene Print Culture in the Nineteenth Century." Dissertation, Queen's University at Kingston, Canada.

Cooper, George, and Gavin Dawes, 1985. *Land and Power in Hawai'i.* Honolulu: Benchmark Books.

Cronin, Michael, and Cormac Ó Cuilleanáin, eds. 2003. *The Languages of Ireland.* Dublin: Four Courts.

Curtis, L. Perry, Jr. 1968. *Anglo-Saxons and Celts: A Study of Anti-Irish Prejudice in Victorian England.* Bridgeport, CT: University of Bridgeport.

———. 1971. *Apes and Angels: The Irishman in Victorian Caricature.* Washington: Smithsonian Institution Press.

Dawes, Gavin. 1968. *Shoal of Time: A History of the Hawaiian Islands.* Toronto: Macmillan.

DeChaine, D. Robert. 2002. "Humanitarian Space and the Social Imaginary: Médecins Sans Frontières/Doctors Without Borders and the Rhetoric of Global Community." *Journal of Communication Inquiry* 26:4.354–69.

Decker, Clarence E. 1952. *The Victorian Conscience.* New York: Twayne.

De Man, Paul. 1978. "The Epistemology of Metaphor," in Sheldon Sacks (ed.), *On Metaphor.* Chicago: University of Chicago Press. 11–28.

De St Jorre, John. 1994. *The Good Ship Venus: The Erotic Voyage of the Olympia Press.* London: Hutchinson.

Diener, Peter. 1984. "Shakespeare en Russie et les ambiguités de son interprétation politique," in Jean-Paul Debax and Yves Peyré (eds.), *Coriolan: Théâtre et politique.* Toulouse: Université de Toulouse–Le Mirail, Service des Publications. 207–16.

Dingwaney, Anuradha, and Carol Maier, eds. 1995. *Between Languages and Cultures: Translation and Cross-cultural Texts.* Pittsburgh: University of Pittsburgh Press.

Doe v. Kamehameha Schools/Bernice Pauahi Bishop Estate, 416 F.3d 1025 (9th Cir. 2005), rev'd in part, 470 F.3d 827 (9th Cir.) 2006) (en banc).

Dreifuss, René Armand. 1980. "State, Class, and the Organic Elite: The Formation of the Entrepreneurial Order in Brazil (1961–1965)." Dissertation, University of Glasgow.

———. 1981. *1964: A conquista do Estado; Ação política, poder e golpe de classe.* Trans. Ayeska Branca de Oliveira Farias, Ceres Ribeiro Pires de Freitas, Else Ribeiro Pires Vieira (supervisor), and Glória Maria de Mello Carvalho. Petrópolis: Editora Vozes.

Dworkin, Andrea. 1981/1979. *Pornography: Men Possessing Women.* London: Women's Press.

Elliot, Elisabeth. 1958. *Through Gates of Splendor.* New York: Harper and Row.

Ellis, Havelock. 1890. *The New Spirit.* London: Walter Scott.

Ellis, Roger, and Liz Oakley-Brown, eds. 2001. *Translation and Nation: Towards a Cultural Politics of Englishness.* Clevedon: Multilingual Matters.

Ermolaev, Herman. 1963. *Soviet Literary Theories, 1917–1934: The Genesis of Socialist Realism.* Berkeley: University of California Press.

———. 1985. "Socialist Realism," in Victor Terras (ed.), *Handbook of Russian Literature.* New Haven: Yale Univerity Press. 429–31.

Escobar, Arturo. 2008. *Territories of Difference: Place, Movements, Life, Redes.* Durham: Duke University Press.

Eshed, Eli. 2000. *Mi'Tarzan ve'ad zbeng: ha'sipur al ha'sifrut ha'popularit ha'ivrit* [From Tarzan to Zbeng: The Story of Israeli Pop Fiction]. Tel Aviv: Babel.

E-Shen Lu, Flora. 1999. "Changes in Subsistence Patterns and Resource Use of the Huaorani Indians in the Ecuadorian Amazon." Dissertation, University of North Carolina at Chapel Hill.

Etkind, Efim. 1963. *Poeziia i perevod*. Moscow-Leningrad: Sovetskii Pisatel'.

———. 1968. *Mastera russkogo stikhotvornogo perevoda*. 2 vols. Leningrad: Sovetskii Pisatel'.

———. 1978. *Notes of a Non-Conspirator*. Trans. Peter France. Oxford: Oxford University Press.

———. 1997. *Mastera poeticheskogo perevoda*. Moscow: Akademicheskii Proekt.

Even-Zohar, Itamar. 1990. *Polysystem Studies. Poetics Today* 11 no. 1, special issue.

———. 2005. "Culture Planning and Culture Resistance in the Making and Maintaining of Entities." *Papers in Culture Research* at www.tau.ac.il/~itamarez/ez_vita/EZ-TOCS-Books.html.

Ewick, Patricia, and Susan S. Silbey. 1995. "Subversive Stories and Hegemonic Tales: Toward a Sociology of Narrative." *Law and Society Review* 29:2.197–226.

Fairclough, Norman. 1989. *Language and Power*. New York: Longman.

Fanon, Frantz. 1966. *The Wretched of the Earth*. 1961. Trans. Constance Farrington. New York: Grove Press.

———. 1967. *Black Skin, White Masks*. 1952. Trans. Charles Lam Markmann. New York: Grove Press.

Fedorov, Andrei. 1958. *Vvedenie v teoriiu perevoda: Lingvisticheskie problemy*. 2nd ed. Moscow: Literatyry na Inostrannykh Iazykakh.

Feiner, Shmuel. 1998. "Ha'isha ha'yedhudia ha'modernit: mikre-mivchan be'yachasei ha'haskala ve'hamoderna" [The Modern Jewish Woman: A Test Case in the Relationship between Haskalah and Modernity], in Israel Bartal and Isaiah Gafni (eds.), *Eros, erusin ve'isurim* [Sexuality and the Family in History]. Jerusalem: Zalman Shazar Center for Jewish History. 253–304.

Fessenden, Tracy, Nicholas F. Radel, and Magdalena J. Zaborowska, eds. 2001. *The Puritan Origins of American Sex: Religion, Sexuality, and National Identity in American Literature*. New York: Routledge.

Fisher, Walter. 1984. "Narration as a Human Communication Paradigm: The Case of Public Moral Agreement." *Communication Monographs* 51:1–22.

———. 1985. "The Narrative Paradigm: In the Beginning." *Journal of Communication* 35:4.74–89.

———. 1987/1989. *Human Communication as Narration: Toward a Philosophy of Reason, Value, and Action*. Columbia, S.C.: University of South Carolina Press.

———. 1997. "Narration, Reason, and Community," in Lewis P. Hinchman and Sandra K. Hinchman (eds.), *Memory, Identity, Community: The Idea of Narrative in the Human Sciences*. Albany: State University of New York Press. 307–27.

Fitzpatrick, Elizabeth B. 2000. "Balai Pustaka in the Dutch East Indies: Colonizing a Literature," in Sherry Simon and Paul St-Pierre (eds.), *Changing the Terms: Translating in the Postcolonial Era.* Ottawa: University of Ottawa Press. 113–26.

Fleishman, Lazar. 1990. *Boris Pasternak: The Poet and His Politics.* Cambridge: Harvard University Press.

Flotow, Luise von. 1997. *Translation and Gender: Translating in the "Era of Feminism."* Manchester: St. Jerome.

Flower, Desmond, and Henry Maas, eds. 1967. *The Letters of Ernest Dowson.* London: Cassell.

Fone, Byrne R. S. 1995. *A Road to Stonewall.* New York: Twayne.

Forel, Auguste. 1931. *Ha-sheela ha'minit* [*The Sexual Question*]. 3 vols. Tel Aviv: Mitzpah.

Foucault, Michel. 1976. *Histoire de la sexualité.* 3 vols. Paris: Gallimard.

Fox, Renée C. 1995. "Medical Humanitarianism and Human Rights: Reflections on Doctors Without Borders and Doctors of the World." *Social Science and Medicine* 41:12.1607–17.

France, Anna Kay. 1978. *Boris Pasternak's Translations of Shakespeare.* Berkeley: University of California Press.

Freidberg, Maurice. 1962. *Russian Classics in Soviet Jackets.* New York: Columbia University Press.

———. 1997. *Literary Translation in Russia: A Cultural History.* University Park, Pa.: Pennsylvania State University Press.

Fryer, Peter. 1966. *Private Case—Public Scandal.* London: Secker and Warburg.

Fuentes, Bertha C. 1997. *Huaomoni-Huaorani-Cowudi: Una aproximación a los Huaorani en la práctica política multi-étnica ecuatoriana.* Quito: Abya-Yala.

García Canclini, Nestor. 1989. *Culturas híbridas: Estrategias para entrar y salir de la modernidad.* Mexico City: Grijalbo.

García de Sena, Manuel, trans. 1811/1949. *La independencia de la Costa Firme justificado por Thomas Paine treinte años há.* Caracas: Instituto Panamericano de Geografía e Historia.

Gay, Peter. 1998. *Pleasure Wars.* New York: W. W. Norton.

Gentzler, Edwin. 1996. "Translation, Counter-Culture, and *The Fifties* in the USA," in Román Álvarez and M. Carmen-África Vidal (eds.), *Translation, Power, Subversion.* Clevedon: Multilingual Matters. 116–37.

———. 2001. *Contemporary Translation Theories.* 2nd ed. London: Routledge.

———. 2002. "Translation, Poststructuralism, and Power," in Maria Tymoczko and Edwin Gentzler (eds.), *Translation and Power.* Amherst: University of Massachusetts Press. 195–218.

———. 2008. *Translation and Identity in the Americas: New Directions in Translation Theory.* London: Routledge.

Gessen, Masha. 1997. *Dead Again: The Russian Intelligentsia after Communism.* London: Verso.

Gilman, Sander. 1993. *Freud, Race, and Gender.* Princeton: Princeton University Press.

Ginsburg, Mirra. 1971. "Translation in Russia: The Politics of Translation," in *The World of Translation: Papers Delivered at the Conference on Literary Translation Held in New York City in May 1970 under the Auspices of P.E.N. American Center.* New York: P.E.N. American Center. 351–60.

Glazov-Corrigan, Elena. 1994. "A Reappraisal of Shakespeare's *Hamlet*: In Defence of Pasternak's *Doctor Zhivago.*" *Forum for Modern Language Studies* 30:3.219–38.

Gluska, Mordechai. 1979. *Ha'hagbalot al chofesh ha'bituy mi'taamei musar* [Moral Limitation of the Freedom of Expression]. Tel Aviv: n.p.

Grases, Pedro. 1981a. *Preindependencia y emancipación: Protagonistas y testimonios.* Caracas: Editorial Seix Barral.

———. 1981b. *Instituciones y nombres del siglo XIX.* Caracas: Editorial Seix Barral.

———. 1997. *La conspiración de Gual y España y el ideario de la independencia.* 3rd ed. Caracas: Biblioteca de la Academia Nacional de la Historia.

Grases, Pedro, and Alberto Harkness. 1953. *Manuel García de Sena y la independencia de Hispanoamérica.* Caracas: Publicaciones de la Secretaría General de la Décima Conferencia Interamericana.

Greenawalt, Kent. 1995. *Fighting Words: Individuals, Communities, and Liberties of Speech.* Princeton: Princeton University Press.

Greenblatt, Stephen. 1992. *Marvelous Possessions: The Marvels of the New World.* Oxford: Clarendon Press.

Gregory, Augusta, trans. 1902. *Cuchulain of Muirthemne.* New York: Oxford University Press, 1973.

Grice, H. P. 1975. "Logic and Conversation," in P. Cole and J. L. Morgan (eds.), *Syntax and Semantics, 3: Speech Acts.* New York: Academic Press. 41–58.

———. 1981. "Presupposition and Conversational Implicature," in P. Cole (ed.), *Radical Pragmatics.* New York: Academic Press.

Gudkov, Lev. 1995. "The Intelligentsia and the Intellectuals," in Germann Diligenskii (ed.), *Russia on the Threshold of an Uncertain Future.* Commack, N.Y.: Nova Science Publishers. 169–93.

Haddawy, Husain, trans. 1990. *The Arabian Nights.* New York: W. W. Norton.

Hallewell, Lawrence. 1985. *O livro no Brasil.* São Paulo: Queiroz.

Halverson, Sandra. 1999. "Image Schemas, Metaphoric Processes, and the 'Translate' Concept." *Metaphor and Symbol* 14:3.199–219.

Hatim, Basil. 1999. "Implications of Research into Translator Invisibility." *Target* 11:2.201–22.

Hauerwas, Stanley, and David Burrell. 1989. "From System to Story: An Alternative Pattern for Rationality in Ethics," in Stanley Hauerwas and L. Gregory Jones (eds.), *Why Narrative? Readings in Narrative Theology.* Grand Rapids, Mich.: William B. Eerdmans. 158–90.

Heaney, Seamus, trans. 1984/1983. *Sweeney Astray: A Version from the Irish.* New York: Farrar, Straus, Giroux.

———, trans. 2000. *Beowulf: A New Verse Translation.* New York: Farrar, Straus, and Giroux.

Helgason, Jón Karl. 1999. *The Rewriting of Njáls Saga: Translation, Politics, and Icelandic Sagas.* Clevedon: Multilingual Matters.

Hermans, Theo, ed. 1985. *The Manipulation of Literature: Studies in Literary Translation.* London: Croom Helm.

———. 1999. *Translation in Systems: Descriptive and System-oriented Approaches Explained.* Manchester: St. Jerome.

———, ed. 2006. *Translating Others.* 2 vols. Manchester: St. Jerome.

Hinchman, Lewis P., and Sandra K. Hinchman, eds. 1997. *Memory, Identity, Community: The Idea of Narrative in the Human Sciences.* Albany: State University of New York Press.

"History of SIL." www.sil.org/sil/history.htm Accessed 17 July 2007.

Hodkinson, Stuart, and Julie Boéri. 2005. "Social Forums after London: The Politics of Language." *Red Pepper.* www.redpepper.ord.uk/Jan2005/x-Jan2005-ESF.html. 1 April 2005.

Holland, Peter. 1999. "'More Russian Than a Dane': The Usefulness of *Hamlet* in Russia," in Shirley Chew and Alistair Stead (eds.), *Translating Life: Essays in Transpositional Aesthetics.* Liverpool: Liverpool University Press. 315–38.

Holmes, James S. 1994. *Translated! Papers on Literary Translation and Translation Studies.* 2nd ed. Amsterdam: Rodopi.

Hull, Eleanor, ed. 1898. *The Cuchullin Saga in Irish Literature: Being a Collection of Stories Relating to the Hero Cuchullin. Translated from the Irish by Various Scholars: Compiled and Edited with Introduction and Notes by Eleanor Hull.* London: David Nutt.

Hung, Eva, and Judy Wakabayashi, eds. 2005. *Asian Translation Traditions.* Manchester: St. Jerome.

Hunnicutt, Alex. 2004. "Burton, Sir Richard F." in glbtq: An Encyclopedia of Gay, Lesbian, Bisexual, Transgender, and Queer Culture. Chicago: glbtq, inc. www.glbtq.com/social-sciences/burton_rf,2.html. Accessed 15 December 2008.

Huntington, Samuel. 1993. "The Clash of Civilizations." *Foreign Affairs* 72:3.22–49.

———. 1996. *The Clash of Civilizations and the Remaking of World Order.* New York: Touchstone.

———. 2004. *Who Are We? The Challenges to America's National Identity.* New York: Simon and Schuster.

Hutton, Mary A., trans. 1907. *The Táin: An Irish Epic Told in English Verse.* Dublin: Maunsel.

Jakobson, Roman. 1959. "On Linguistic Aspects of Translation," in Reuben A. Brower (ed.), *On Translation.* Cambridge: Harvard University Press. 232–39.

James, C. Vaughan. 1973. *Soviet Socialist Realism: Origins and Theory.* New York: St. Martin's.

Jerez, Jesús de Manuel, Juan López Cortés, and María Brander de la Iglesia. 2004. "Translation and Interpreting: Volunteer Work and Social Commitment." piit.beplaced.com/ECOSarticle.htm. 1 April 2005.

Joyce, James. 1939. *Finnegans Wake.* New York: Viking.

———. 1996/1916. *Dubliners: Text, Criticism, and Notes.* Ed. Robert Scholes and A. Walton Litz. New York: Penguin.

Kabbani, Rana. 1986. *Europe's Myths of Orient.* London: Macmillan.

Kahn, Fritz. 1962. *Chayenu ha'miniyim: madrich ve'yoetz le'chol ish ve'isha [Our Sex Life: A Guide and Counselor for Everyone].* Trans. Baruch Karu. Jerusalem: Achiasaf.

Kahoʻolawe Island Conveyance Commission; Public Hearings. 1991. Maui, Hawaii: Kahoolawe Island Reserve Commission.

Kameʻeleihiwa, Lilikalā. 1992. *Native Land and Foreign Desires: Pehea La E Pono Ai?* Honolulu: Bishop Museum Press.

Kane, Joe. 1995. *Savages.* New York: Knopf.

Kapnist, Petr Ivanovich. 1901. *Socheneniia.* Vol. 2. Moscow.

Kattan, Victor. 2004. "It's Not Who You're Against; It's Who You're For." *Palestine Monitor.* www.palestinemonitor.org/new_web/palestine_center_stage_european_social.htm. 1 April 2005.

Kibbey, Ann. 1986. *The Interpretation of Material Shapes in Puritanism: A Study of Rhetoric, Prejudice, and Violence.* Cambridge: Cambridge University Press.

Kimerling, Judith. 1996. *El derecho del tambor: Derechos humanos y ambientales en los campos petroleros de la Amazonía Ecuatoriana.* Quito: Abya-Yala.

Kingsland, Rosemary. 1980. *A Saint among Savages.* London: Collins.

Kinsella, Thomas, trans. 1970/1969. *The Táin.* London: Oxford University Press.

Kirkwood, William G. 1992. "Narrative and the Rhetoric of Possibility." *Communication Monographs* 59:30–47.

Kom, Ambroise. 2000. "La langue française en Afrique noire postcoloniale," in *La malédiction francophone.* Hamburg: Lit Verlag. 97–105.

Komissarov, Vilen. 1998. "Russian Tradition," in Mona Baker (ed.), *Routledge Encyclopedia of Translation Studies.* London: Routledge. 541–49.

Kon, Igor S. 1995. *The Sexual Revolution in Russia: From the Age of the Czars to Today.* Trans. James Riordan. New York: The Free Press.

Koshiyama, Alice Mitika. 1982. *Monteiro Lobato: Intelectual, empresário, editor.* São Paulo: Queiroz.

Kourouma, Ahmadou. 1998. *En attendant le vote des bêtes sauvages.* Paris: Seuil.

Kristeva, Julia. 1969. *Sēmeiōtikē: Recherches pour une sémanalyse.* Paris: Seuil.

———. 1974. *La Révolution du langage poétique.* Paris: Seuil.

Labou Tansi, Sony. 1979. *La Vie et demie.* Paris: Seuil.

———. 1988. *Les Yeux du volcan.* Paris: Seuil.

Laclau, Ernesto, and Chantal Mouffe. 1985. *Hegemony and Socialist Strategy: Towards a Radical Democratic Politics.* London: Verso.

Lakoff, George, and Mark Johnson, 1980. *Metaphors We Live By.* Chicago: University of Chicago Press.

Landers, Vasda Bonafini. 1982. *De Jeca a Macunaíma: Monteiro Lobato e o Modernismo.* Rio de Janeiro: Civilização Brasileira.

Lane, Edward William, trans. 1839–41. *The Thousand and One Nights, Commonly Called, in England, The Arabian Nights' Entertainments: A New Translation from the Arabic, with Copious Notes.* 3 vols. London: Charles Knight.

Lane-Mercier, Gillian. 1997. "Translating the Untranslatable: The Translator's Aesthetic, Ideological, and Political Responsibility." *Target* 9:43–68.

Laor, Yitzhak. 1995. *Anu kotvim otach moledet* [We Write You, Motherland]. Tel Aviv: Ha'kibbutz Ha'meuchad.

Lavallé, Bernard. 1993. *L'Amérique espagnole de Colomb à Bolivar.* Paris: Éditions Belin.

———. 2002. "Americanidad exaltada/Hispanidad exacerbada: Contradicciones y ambigüedades en el discurso criollo del siglo XVII peruano," in Catherine Poupeney Hart and Albino Chacón Gutiérrez (eds.), *El discurso colonial: Construcción de una diferencia americana.* Heredia, Costa Rica: EUNA (Editorial Universidad Nacional). 17–36.

Lawrence, D. H. 1961/1929. *A Propos of Lady Chatterley's Lover and Other Essays.* Harmondsworth: Penguin.

Leahy, A. H., trans. 1905–6. *Heroic Romances of Ireland: Translated into English Prose and Verse, with Preface, Special Introductions, and Notes.* 2 vols. London: David Nutt.

Lefevere, André. 1982. "Mother Courage's Cucumbers: Text, System, and Refraction in a Theory of Literature." *Modern Language Studies* 12:3–20.

———. 1985. "Why Waste Our Time on Rewrites? The Trouble with Interpretation and the Role of Rewriting in an Alternative Paradigm," in Theo Hermans (ed.), *The Manipulation of Literature: Studies in Literary Translation.* London: Croom Helm. 215–43.

———. 1992. *Translation, Rewriting, and the Manipulation of Literary Fame.* London: Routledge.

Lefevere, André, and Kenneth David Jackson, eds. 1982. *The Art and Science of Translation. Dispositio* 7, special issue.

Lefkowitz Horowitz, Helen. 2002. *Rereading Sex: Battles over Sexual Knowledge and Suppression in Nineteenth-Century America.* New York: Vintage.

Le Guin, Ursula K. 1969. *The Left Hand of Darkness.* New York: Ace Books.

Leighton, Lauren. 1991. *Two Worlds, One Art: Literary Translation in Russia and America.* Dekalb: Northern Illinois University Press.

Levý, Jiří. 1967. "Translation as a Decision Process." *To Honor Roman Jakobson: Essays on the Occasion of His Seventieth Birthday, 11 October 1966.* 3 vols. The Hague: Mouton. 2.1071–82.

Lewis, Philip E. 1985. "The Measure of Translation Effects," in Joseph F. Graham (ed.), *Difference in Translation.* Ithaca: Cornell University Press. 31–62.

Liefeld, Olive Fleming. 1990. *Unfolding Destinies: The Untold Story of Peter Fleming and the Auca Mission.* Grand Rapids: Zondervan.

López, Casto Fulgencio. 1997. *Juan Picornell y la conspiración de Gual y España.* 2nd ed. Caracas: Biblioteca Nacional de la Historia.

Loseff, Lev. 1984. *On the Beneficence of Censorship: Aesopian Language in Modern Russian Literature.* Trans. Jane Bobko. Munich: Sagner.

Loth, David. 1961. *The Erotic in Literature.* London: Secker and Warburg.

Lyons, John. 1977. *Semantics.* 2 vols. Cambridge: Cambridge University Press.

MacIntyre, Alasdair. 1981. *After Virtue.* London: Duckworth.

Malena, Anne. 2002. "La Louisiane: Une trahison américaine telle qu'illustrée dans la traduction de *Vue de la colonie espagnole du Mississippi* de Berquin-Duvallon," in Denise Merkle (ed.), *Censure et traduction dans le monde occidental, Censorship and Translation in the Western World. TTR* 15:2.63–96, special issue.

Māmaka Kaiao. 1998. Ed. Komike Hua ʻŌlelo. Hilo: ʻAha Pūnana Leo.

Manton, Richard. 1984. *The Victorian Imagination.* New York: Grove.

Marcus, Steven. 1966. *The Other Victorians: A Study of Sexuality and Pornography in Mid-Nineteenth-Century England.* New York: Basic Books.

Marcuse, Herbert. 1955. *Eros and Civilization: A Philosophical Inquiry into Freud.* New York: Vintage.

Marshak, Samuil. 1990. *Sobranie sochinenii v chetyrekh tomakh.* 4 vols. Moscow: Pravda.

Mbembe, Achille. 2001. *On the Postcolony.* Berkeley: University of California Press.

McGee, Michael Calvin, and John S. Nelson. 1985. "Narrative Reason in Public Argument." *Journal of Communication* 35:4.139–55.

McGregor, Davianna P. 1990. "Ku Paʻa I ka ʻĀina." Dissertation, University of Hawaiʻi at Manoa.

M'Culloch, John. 1812. *Historia concisa de los Estados Unidos: Desde el descubrimiento hasta el año de 1807.* Trans. Manuel García de Sena. Philadelphia: T. and J. Palmer.

Mehrez, Samia. 1992. "Translation and the Postcolonial Experience: The Fran-cophone North African Text," in Lawrence Venuti (ed.), *Rethinking Translation*. London: Routledge. 120–38.

Meirelles, Fernando. 2005. "Writing the Script, Finding and Preparing the Cast," in Else R. P. Vieira (ed.), *City of God in Several Voices: Brazilian Social Cinema as Action*. Nottingham: CCC Press. 13–25.

Menchú, Rigoberta. 2005/1985. *Me llamo Rigoberta Menchú y así me nació la conciencia*. Ed. Elizabeth Burgos. Mexico City: Siglo XXI Editores.

Merkle, Denise. 1994. "Émile Zola devant la censure victorienne." *TTR* 7:1.77–91.

———, ed. 2002. *Censure et traduction dans le monde occidental, Censorship and Translation in the Western World. TTR* 15 no. 2, special issue.

———. 2003. "The Lutetian Society." *TTR* 16:2.73–101.

———. 2009. "Vizetelly & Company as (Ex)change Agent: Towards the Mod-ernization of the British Publishing Industry," in John Milton and Paul Bandia (eds.), *Agents of Translation*. Amsterdam: John Benjamins. 86–106.

Middleton, Tim. 2003. "From Mimicry to Menace: Conrad and Late-Victorian Masculinity," in Philip Holden and Richard J. Ruppel (eds.), *Imperial Desire: Dissident Sexualities and Colonial Literature*. Minneapolis: University of Minnesota Press. 135–51.

Milosz, Czeslaw. 1977. "On Pasternak Soberly," in *Emperor of the Earth: Modes of Eccentric Vision*. Berkeley: University of California Press. 62–78.

Min, Anchee. 2002. *Wild Ginger*. Boston: Houghton Mifflin.

Miron, Dan. 1993. "Hirhurim be'idan shel prosa" [Reflection in a Prose Era], in Zissi Stavi (ed.), *30 shana, 30 sipurim: mivhar ha'sipur ha'ivri ha'katzar mishnot ha'shishim ad shnot ha'tishim* [Thirty Years, Thirty Stories: An Anthology of Hebrew Stories from the 1960s to the 1990s]. Tel Aviv: Ye-diot Ahronot. 397–427.

Mishler, Elliot G. 1995. "Models of Narrative Analysis: A Typology." *Journal of Narrative and Life History* 5:2.87–123.

Mohica-Cummings v. Kamehameha. 2003. U.S. Dist. LEXIS 26804 (settled out of court).

Monteiro Lobato, José Bento. 1926. *How Henry Ford Is Regarded in Brazil*. Rio de Janeiro.

———, trans. 1926. Henry Ford, *Minha vida e obra*. São Paulo: Companhia Editora Nacional.

———, trans. 1927. Henry Ford, *Hoje e amanhã*. São Paulo: Companhia Editora Nacional.

———. 1944. *A barca de gleyre: Quarenta anos de correspondência entre Monteiro Lobato e Godofredo Rangel*. São Paulo: Companhia Editora Nacional.

———. 1947. *O escândalo do petróleo e ferro*. São Paulo: Brasiliense.

————. 1947. *Mr. Slang e o Brasil e o problema vital.* São Paulo: Brasiliense.

————. 1947. *O poço do Visconde.* São Paulo: Brasiliense.

————. 1947. *Reinações de narizinho.*São Paulo: Brasiliense.

————. 1948. *Prefácios e entrevistas.* São Paulo: Brasiliense.

————. 1951. "Traduções," in *Mundo da lua e miscelânea.* 5th ed. São Paulo: Brasiliense. 125–30.

————. 1954. *Aventuras de Hans Staden.* 9th ed. São Paulo: Brasiliense.

————. 1957. *D. Quixote das crianças.* 10th ed. São Paulo: Brasiliense.

————, trans. 1958. Lewis Carroll, *Alice no país do espelho.* 2nd ed. São Paulo: Brasiliense.

————. 1964. *O presidente negro ou o choque das raças: Romance americano do ano 2228.* 12th ed. São Paulo: Brasiliense.

————. 1968. *Historias de tia Nastácia.* 13th ed. São Paulo: Brasiliense.

————, trans. 1969. La Fontaine, *Fábulas.* 21st ed. São Paulo: Brasiliense.

————, trans. 1971. J. M. Barrie, *Peter Pan.* 16th ed. São Paulo: Brasiliense.

————, trans. 1973. Lewis Carroll, *Alice no país das maravilhas.* 11th ed. São Paulo: Brasiliense.

————, trans. 1992. Daniel Defoe, *Robinson Crusoé.* 12th ed. São Paulo: Brasiliense.

————. 2009. *O presidente negro.* Rio de Janeiro: Editora Globo.

Morgan, Edmund S. 1966. *The Puritan Family.* New York: Harper and Row,

Mosse, George L. 1985. *Nationalism and Sexuality: Middle-Class Morality and Sexual Norms in Modern Europe.* Madison: University of Wisconsin Press.

Nariño, Antonio, trans. 1794. "Declaración de los derechos del hombre y del ciudadano." Bogotá.

Nattrass, Mark S. 1993. "Delvin, Hart, and the Proper Limits of Legal Coercion." *Utilitas* 5:1.91–107.

Navarrete Orta, Luis. 1994. "Viscardo y Bolívar: Dos momentos del proyecto emancipador latinoamericano," in Beatriz Gonzáles Stephan, Javier Lasarte, Graciela Montaldo, and Maria Julia Daroqui (eds.), *Esplendores y miserias del siglo XIX: Cultura y sociedad en América latina.* Caracas: Monte Ávila Editores. 125–37.

Nelson, James G. 2000. *Publisher to the Decadents: Leonard Smithers in the Careers of Beardsley, Wilde, Dowson.* University Park: Pennsylvania State University Press.

Ní Chuilleanáin, Eiléan, Cormac Ó Cuilleanáin, and David Parris, eds. 2009. *Translation and Censorship: Patterns of Communication and Interference.* Dublin: Four Courts.

Nida, Eugene A. 1964. *Toward a Science of Translating: With Special Reference to Principles and Procedures Involved in Bible Translating.* Leiden: E. J. Brill.

Niranjana, Tejaswini. 1992. *Siting Translation: History, Post-structuralism, and the Colonial Context.* Berkeley: University of California Press.

Noumssi, Gérard Marie, and Michel Fosso. 2001. "Le Français en Afrique noire au début du troisième millénaire: Variation, problèmes socio-linguistiques, perspectives didactiques." *Présence Francophone* 56:73–91.

Novitz, David. 1997. "Art, Narrative, and Human Nature," in Lewis P. Hinchman and Sandra K. Hinchman (eds.), *Memory, Identity, Community: The Idea of Narrative in the Human Sciences.* Albany: State University of New York Press. 143–60.

Nutt, Alfred. 1900. *Cuchulainn, the Irish Achilles.* New York: AMS, 1972.

O'Brien, Flann. 1939. *At Swim-Two-Birds.* New York: Pantheon.

Ocampo López, Javier. 1999. *El proceso ideológico de la emancipación en Colombia.* Santafé de Bogotá: Planeta.

Ó Cuilleanáin, Cormac. 2004. "The Editor's Introduction," in Giovanni Boccaccio, *Decameron,* trans. Cormac Ó Cuilleanáin. Ware, Hertfordshire: Wordsworth. xi–lxxxi.

O'Grady, Standish. 1878–80. *History of Ireland: The Heroic Period.* 2 vols. London: Sampson Low, Searle, Marston, and Rivington.

O'Keeffe, J. G., ed. and trans. 1913. *Buile Suibhne (The Frenzy of Suibhne), being The Adventures of Suibhne Geilt: A Middle-Irish Romance.* London: Irish Texts Society.

Omer, Dan. 1966. *Ba'derech* [On the Way]. Jerusalem: Golgotha.

———, ed. and trans. 1967. *Nahama: shira bitniqit ameriqanit* [Howl: An Anthology of American Beat Poetry]. Jerusalem: Marcus.

Osborne, Hugh. 2001. "Hooked on Classics: Discourses of Allusion in the Mid-Victorian Novel," in Roger Ellis and Liz Oakley-Brown (eds.), *Translation and Nation: Towards a Cultural Politics of Englishness.* Clevedon: Multilingual Matters. 120–66.

Osorio, Jon K. K. 2002. *Dismembering Lāhui: A History of the Hawaiian Nation to 1887.* Honolulu: University of Hawai'i Press.

Ó Súilleabháin, Seán. 1970/1942. *A Handbook of Irish Folklore.* Detroit: Singing Tree.

Oxford English Dictionary. 1971. Compact Edition. Oxford: Oxford University Press.

Oz, Amos. 1982. *Menucha nechona* [A Perfect Peace]. Tel Aviv: Am Oved.

Pang, Gordon. 2006. "The Fight for Kaho'olawe." *Honolulu Advertiser.* 30 January:A1.

Pardo Tomás, José. 1991. *Ciencia y censura: La Inquisición española y los libros científicos en los siglos XVI y XVII.* Madrid: Consejo Superior de Investigaciones Científicas.

Parra-Pérez, Caracciolo. 1992. *Historia de la primera república de Venezuela.* Caracas: Biblioteca Ayacucho.

Pasternak, Boris. 1959. "Translating Shakespeare," trans. Manya Harari, in *I Remember: Sketch for an Autobiography,* trans. David Magarshack. New York: Pantheon. 123–52.

———. 1961. *Stikhi, 1936–1959. Stikhi dlia detei. Stikhi, 1912–1957, ne sobrannye v knigi avtora. Stati' i vystupleniia.* Ann Arbor: University of Michigan Press.

———. 1989–92. *Sobranie sochenenii v piati tomakh.* 5 vols. Moscow: Khudozhestvennaia Literatura.

Payne, John, trans. 1882–84. *The Book of the Thousand Nights and One Night: Now First Completely Done into English Prose and Verse, from the Original Arabic.* 9 vols. London: Printed for the Villon Society by Private Subscription and for Private Circulation Only.

Penzer, Norman M. 1967. *An Annotated Bibliography of Sir Richard Francis Burton, K.C.M.G.* London: Dawsons of Pall Mall.

Phillips, Richard. 1999. "Sexual Politics of Authorship: Rereading the Travels and Translations of Richard and Isabel Burton." *Gender, Place, and Culture* 6:3.241–58.

Picón-Salas, Mariano. 1994. *De la conquista a la independencia: Tres siglos de historia cultural hispanoamericana.* Mexico City: Fondo de Cultura Económica.

Picornell, Juan. 1797. *Derechos del hombre y del ciudadano, con varias máximas republicanas y un discurso preliminar dirigido a los americanos.* Madrid: Imprenta de la Verdad.

Plett, Heinrich F. 1991. "Intertextualities," in Heinrich F. Plett (ed.), *Intertextuality.* Berlin: De Gruyter. 3–29.

Portebois, Yannick. 2003. "A Publisher and His Books: The Catalogue of Vizetelly & Co., 1880–1890," in Marie Elena Korey et al., *Vizetelly & Compan(ies): A Complex Tale of Victorian Printing and Publishing.* Toronto: Governing Council, University of Toronto. 39–78.

Pukui, Mary K., and Samuel H. Elbert. 1986. *Hawaiian Dictionary.* Honolulu: University of Hawai'i Press.

Pym, Anthony. 1996. "Venuti's Visibility." *Target* 8:1.165–77.

———. 1998. *Method in Translation History.* Manchester: St. Jerome.

Quine, Willard V. O. 1959. "Meaning and Translation," in Reuben A. Brower (ed.), *On Translation.* Cambridge: Harvard University Press.

Rafael, Vicente. 1993. *Contracting Colonialism: Translation and Christian Conversion in Tagalog Society under Early Spanish Rule.* Rev. ed. Durham: Duke University Press.

Rattok, Lily. 2002. "Nashim be'milchemet ha'shichrur: mitos vezikaron" [Women in the War of Independence: Myth and Memory], in Hannah Naveh and Oded Menda-Levy (eds.), *Yom qrav ve'arbo ve'haboqer she'lemochorat*

[Battle Cry and the Morning After: Representations of the War of Independence in Israeli Literature]. Tel Aviv: Tel Aviv University. 287–303.

Reuben, David. 1970/1969. *Kol ma she'tamid ratzita ladaat al ha'min *aval lo heazta lisheol* [*Everything You Always Wanted to Know About Sex *But Never Dared to Ask*]. Trans. Eliezer Carmi. Tel Aviv: Bustan.

Rice v. Cayetano, 528 U.S. 495 (2000), rev'd 146 F.3d 1075 (9th Cir. 1998).

Rival, Laura. 2002. *Trekking through History: The Huaorani of Amazonian Ecuador.* New York: Columbia University Press.

Rivas Toledo, Alex, and Rommel Lara Ponce. 2001. *Conservación y petróleo en la Amazonía ecuatoriana: Un acercamiento Huaorani.* Quito: Abya-Yala.

Robinson, Douglas. 1997a. *Translation and Empire: Postcolonial Theories Explained.* Manchester: St. Jerome.

———. 1997b. "Tejaswini Niranjana, Retranslation, and the Problem of Foreignism." *TradTerm* 4:2.149–65.

Robinson, Paul. 1989/1976. *The Modernization of Sex: Havelock Ellis, Alfred Kinsey, William Masters, and Virginia Johnson.* Ithaca: Cornell University Press.

Rodríguez, Jaime. 1998. *La independencia de la América española.* Trans. Miguel Abelardo Camacho. Mexico City: Fondo de Cultura Económica.

Rodríguez Guerra, Cristóbal. 2002. "Plantas medicinales en peligro de extinción." *Revista de Aportes Andinos* 3 (August). www.uasb.edu.ec/padh/revista3/defensa/rodriguez.htm. Accessed 20 July 2007.

Rozencveig, Victor. 1993. "Three Masters of Russian Translation." *Meta* 38:4.643–57.

Roziner, Felix. 1991. *A Certain Finkelmeyer.* Trans. Michael Henry Heim. New York: W. W. Norton.

Rubinstein, Amnon. 1975. *Achifat musar be'chevra matiranit* [Moral Enforcement in a Liberal Society]. Jerusalem: Schocken.

Safir, Marilyn P. 1991. "Was the Kibbutz an Experiment in Social and Sex Equality?" in Barbara Swirski and Marilyn P. Safir (eds.), *Calling the Equality a Bluff: Women in Israel.* New York: Pergamon. 251–60.

Saglia, Diego. 2002. "Translation and Cultural Appropriation: Dante, Paolo, and Francesca in British Romanticism." *Quaderns* 7:95–109.

Sahlins, Marshall. 1981. *Historical Metaphors and Mythical Realities: Structure in the Early History of the Sandwich Island Kingdom.* Ann Arbor: University of Michigan Press.

Said, Edward, W. 1978. *Orientalism.* New York: Pantheon.

Sariola, Sakari. 1972. *Power and Resistance: The Colonial Heritage in Latin America.* Ithaca: Cornell University Press.

Sartre, Jean-Paul. 1988. *"What Is Literature?" and Other Essays.* Cambridge: Harvard University Press.

Schevill, Rudolph. 1936. "El Abate Marchena and French Thought of the Eighteenth Century." *Revue de Literature Comparée* 16:180–94.

Schwartz, Yigal. 1995. "Sifrut ivrit: ha'idan she'acharei" [Hebrew Literature: The Era After]. *Efes Shtayim* 3:7–15.

Searle, John R. 1969. *Speech Acts: An Essay in the Philosophy of Language.* Cambridge: Cambridge University Press.

Semenenko, Aleksei. 2007. *Hamlet the Sign: Russian Translations of "Hamlet" and Literary Canon Formation.* Stockholm: Stockholm University Press.

Sened, Yonat, and Alexander Sened. *Tandu.* 1973. Tel Aviv: Ha'kibbutz Ha'meuchad.

Shahar, David. 1982/1979. *Sochen hod malchuto* [*His Majesty's Agent*]. Jerusalem: Kana.

Shakespeare, William. 1957. *The London Shakespeare.* 6 vols. Ed. John Munro. New York: Simon and Schuster.

Shamma, Tarek. 2005. "The Exotic Dimension of Foreignizing Strategies: Burton's Translation of the *Arabian Nights.*" *The Translator* 11:1.51–67.

Shapira, Anita. 1997. *Yehudim chadashim, yehudim yeshanim* [New Jews, Old Jews]. Tel Aviv: Am Oved.

Shapiro, Treena. 2005. "Renaissance Waiting to Bloom." *Honolulu Advertiser,* 7 November:A1.

Shavit, Zohar. 1998. "The Status of Translated Literature in the Creation of Hebrew Literature in Pre-State Israel." *Meta* 43:1.46–53.

Shlapentokh, Vladimir. 1990. *Soviet Intellectuals and Political Power: The Post-Stalin Era.* Princeton: Princeton University Press.

"Sichot Maariv" [Maariv Conversations]. *Maarive.* images.maariv.co.il/cache/ART646685.html. Accessed 2 February 2004.

Simon, Sherry. 1996. *Gender in Translation: Cultural Identity and the Politics of Transmission.* London: Routledge.

Simon, Sherry, and Paul St-Pierre, eds. 2000. *Changing the Terms: Translating in the Postcolonial Era.* Ottawa: University of Ottawa Press.

Somers, Margaret. 1992. "Narrativity, Narrative Identity, and Social Action: Rethinking English Working-Class Formation." *Social Science History* 16:4.591–630.

———. 1997. "Deconstructing and Reconstructing Class Formation Theory: Narrativity, Relational Analysis, and Social Theory," in John R. Hall (ed.), *Reworking Class.* Ithaca: Cornell University Press. 73–105.

Somers, Margaret R., and Gloria D. Gibson. 1994. "Reclaiming the Epistemological 'Other': Narrative and the Social Constitution of Identity," in Craig Calhoun (ed.), *Social Theory and the Politics of Identity.* Oxford: Blackwell. 37–99.

Sommer, Doris. 1992. "Resistant Texts and Incompetent Readers." *Latin American Literary Review* 20:40.104–8.

Spechler, Dina R. 1982. *Permitted Dissent in the U.S.S.R.: Novy mir and the Soviet Regime.* New York: Praeger.

Speirs, Dorothy E. 2003. "Émile Zola's Novels," in Marie Elena Korey et al., *Vizetelly & Compan(ies): A Complex Tale of Victorian Printing and Publishing*. Toronto: Governing Council, University of Toronto. 79–105.

Sperber, Dan, and Deirdre Wilson. 1995. *Relevance: Communication and Cognition*. 2nd ed. Oxford: Blackwell.

Spiro, Melford E. 1965. *Children of the Kibbutz*. New York: Schocken.

Spivak, Gayatri Chakravorty. 1988. "Can the Subaltern Speak?" in Cary Nelson and Lawrence Grossberg (eds.), *Marxism and the Interpretation of Culture*. Urbana: University of Illinois Press. 271–313.

———. 1993. "The Politics of Translation," in Spivak, *Outside in the Teaching Machine*. London: Routledge. 179–201.

Stillman, Amy K. 1989a. "History Reinterpreted in Song: The Case of the Hawaiian Counterrevolution." *Hawaiian Journal of History* 23:1–30.

———. 1989b. "Traditionalists, Innovators, and Dance Competitions: Aspects of Preservation and Transformation in Hawaiian Dance." Unpublished paper presented at the Fourth Hong Kong International Dance Conference.

———. 1999. "'Aloha 'Āina': New Perspectives on 'Kaulana Na Pua'." *Hawaiian Journal of History* 33:83–99.

Stoll, David. 1985. *Pescadores de hombres o fundadores de imperio? El Instituto Lingüístico de Verano en América Latina*. Quito: Desco.

St-Pierre, Paul. 1993. "Translation as a Discourse of History." *TTR* 6:1.61–82.

Sturge, Kate. 2002. "Censorship of Translated Fiction in Nazi Germany," in Denise Merkle (ed.), *Censure et traduction dans le monde occidental, Censorship and Translation in the Western World. TTR* 15:2.153–70, special issue.

Talmon, A. B. 1938. *Chayey ha'min shel ha'adam* [Human Sexual Life]. Tel Aviv: Institute for Hygiene and Sexual Sciences.

Tarkovskii, Arsenii. 1982. *Izbrannoe: Stikhotvoreniia, poemy, perevody (1929–1979)*. Moscow: Khudozhestvennaia Literatura.

Thicke, Lori. 2003. "The Humanitarian Face of Translation." *Multilingual Computing and Technology* 13:4.n.p.

Tolstaia, Tatiana. 2002. "Perevodnye kartinki," in *Den': Lichnoe*. Moscow: Podkova. 245–75.

Toulabor, Comi. 1981. "Jeu de mots, jeux de vilain: Lexique de la dérision politique au Togo." *Politique africaine* 3:55–71.

Toury, Gideon. 1977. *Normot shel tirgum ve'hatirgum le'ivrit 1930–1945* [Norms of Translation and the Translation into Hebrew 1930–1945]. Tel Aviv: Porter Institute for Poetics and Semiotics.

———. 1980. *In Search of a Theory of Translation*. Tel Aviv: Porter Institute for Poetics.

———. 1985. "A Rationale for Descriptive Translation Studies," in Theo Hermans (ed.), *The Manipulation of Literature: Studies in Literary Translation*. London: Croom Helm. 16–41.

———. 1995. *Descriptive Translation Studies and Beyond*. Amsterdam: John Benjamins.

Turgenev, Ivan. 1972. *Hamlet and Don Quixote*. Trans. Robert Nichols. London: Folcroft Library Editions.

Tymoczko, Maria. 1994. *The Irish "Ulysses."* Los Angeles and Berkeley: University of California Press.

———. 1999. *Translation in a Postcolonial Context: Early Irish Literature in English Translation*. Manchester: St. Jerome.

———. 2000a. "Translation and Political Engagement: Activism, Social Change, and the Role of Translation in Geopolitical Shifts." *The Translator* 6:1.23–47.

———. 2000b. "Translations of Themselves: The Contours of Postcolonial Fiction," in Sherry Simon and Paul St-Pierre (eds.), *Changing the Terms: Translating in the Postcolonial Era*. Ottawa: University of Ottawa Press. 147–66.

———. 2000c. "Wintering Out with Irish Poetry: Affiliation and Autobiography in English Translation." *The Translator* 6:2.309–17.

———. 2003a. "Ideology and the Position of the Translator: In What Sense is a Translator 'In Between'?" in María Calzada Pérez (ed.), *Apropos of Ideology: Translation Studies on Ideology—Ideologies in Translation Studies*. Manchester: St. Jerome. 181–201.

———. 2003b. "Translation, Ideology, and Creativity." *Linguistica Antverpiensia*. New series. 2:27–45.

———. 2004. "Cú Chulainn, Finn, and the Mythic Strands in *Ulysses*." *ABEI Journal: The Brazilian Journal of Irish Studies* 6:41–58.

———. 2007. *Enlarging Translation, Empowering Translators*. Manchester: St. Jerome.

———. 2010. "Western Metaphorical Discourses Implicit in Translation Studies," in James St. André (ed.), *Thinking Through Translation with Metaphors*. Manchester: St. Jerome. 109–43.

Tymoczko, Maria, and Edwin Gentzler, eds. 2002. *Translation and Power*. Amherst: University of Massachusetts Press.

Uslar Pietri, Arturo. 1991. *La creación del nuevo mundo*. Madrid: Colecciones Mapfre.

Vargas Ugarte, Rubén. 1964. *La carta a los españoles americanos de don Juan Pablo Viscardo y Guzmán*. 2nd ed. Lima: Librería e Imprenta Gil.

Venuti, Lawrence, ed. 1992. *Rethinking Translation: Discourse, Subjectivity, Ideology*. London: Routledge.

———. 1995. *The Translator's Invisibility: A History of Translation*. London: Routledge.

———. 1998a. *The Scandals of Translation: Towards an Ethics of Difference*. London: Routledge.

———, ed. 1998b. *Translation and Minority*. *The Translator* 4 no. 2, special issue.

———. 2008. *The Translator's Invisibility: A History of Translation.* 2nd ed. London: Routledge.

Vieira, Adriana Silene. 2001. "Monteiro Lobato Translator." *CROP* 6:143–69.

Vieira, Else Ribeiro Pires. 1994. "A Postmodern Translation Aesthetics in Brazil," in Mary Snell-Hornby, Franz Pöchhacker, and Klaus Kaindl (eds.), *Translation Studies: An Interdiscipline.* Amsterdam: John Benjamins. 65–72.

———. 1999. "Liberating Calibans: Readings of *Antropofagia* and Haroldo de Campos' Poetics of Transcreation," in Susan Bassnett and Harish Trivedi (eds.), *Post-colonial Translation: Theory and Practice.* London: Routledge. 95–113.

Villanueva, Laureano. 1986/1883. *Biografía del Doctor José María Vargas.* Caracas: Ediciones del Rectorado de la Universidad Central de Venezuela.

Viscardo y Guzmán, Juan Pablo. 1799. *Lettre aux espagnols américains.* Philadelphia.

———. 1801. *Carta derijida a los Españoles Americanos.* Trans. Francisco de Miranda. London: Boyle.

———. 2002. *Letter to the Spanish Americans: A Facsimile of the Second English Edition (London, 1810).* Providence, R.I.: John Carter Brown Library.

Von Flotow, Luise. 1997. *Translation and Gender: Translating in the "Era of Feminism."* Manchester: St. Jerome.

Waisman, Sergio. 2003. "The Thousand and One Nights in Argentina: Translation, Narrative, and Politics in Borges, Puig, and Piglia." *Comparative Literature Studies* 40:4.351–71.

Wakabayashi, Judy. 2000. "Subversion, Sex, and the State: The Censorship of Translation in Modern Japan." *Translation Quarterly* 16/17:53–78.

Warnick, Barbara. 1987. "The Narrative Paradigm: Another Story." *Quarterly Journal of Speech* 73:172–82.

Webster, Nesta. 1936. *Secret Societies and Subversive Movements.* 5th ed. London: Boswell.

Weissbrod, Rachel. 1999. "Mock-epic as a Byproduct of the Norm of Elevated Language." *Target* 11:2.245–62.

Williams, Patricia. 1991. *The Alchemy of Race and Rights.* Cambridge: Harvard University Press.

Winter, Werner. 1964. "Translation as Political Action," in William Arrowsmith and Roger Shattuck (eds.), *The Craft and Context of Translation: A Critical Symposium.* Garden City, N.Y.: Anchor Books. 295–301.

Wolf, Michaela. 2002. "Censorship as Cultural Blockage: Banned Literature in the Late Habsburg Monarchy," in Denise Merkle (ed.), *Censure et traduction dans le monde occidental, Censorship and Translation in the Western World. TTR* 15:2.45–62, special issue.

Wright, Thomas. 1906/1968. *The Life of Sir Richard Burton.* 2 vols. New York: Burt Franklin.

Yizhar, S. 1998. *Malcolmia yefehfiya* [Lovely Malcolmia]. Tel Aviv: Zmora Bitan.

Zabus, Chantal. 1991. *The African Palimpsest: Indigenization of Language in the West African Europhone Novel*. Amsterdam: Rodopi.

Ziegler-Otero, Lawrence. 2004. *Resistance in an Amazonian Community: Huaorani Organizing against the Global Economy*. New York: Berghahn Books.

Ziolokowski, Margaret. 1998. *Literary Exorcisms of Stalinism: Russian Writers and the Soviet Past*. Columbia, S.C.: Camden House.

Zohar, Zvi, and Shmuel Golan. 1941. *Ha'chinuch ha'mini* [Sexual Education]. Tel Aviv: Sifriat Poalim.

Notes on Contributors

Puaʻalaʻokalani D. Aiu holds a Ph.D. in Communication Studies from the University of Massachusetts. She is the Administrator of the Hawaii State Historic Preservation Division and has also worked professionally in public relations. Dr. Aiu is an activist in the Hawaiian cultural revival, promoting the repatriation of Hawaiian territory and the revival of the Hawaiian language and Hawaiian culture.

Brian James Baer is Professor of Russian Translation at Kent State University. He is founding editor of the journal *Translation and Interpreting Studies* (*TIS*) and general editor of the Kent State Monograph Series in Translation Studies. His research focuses on Russian translation history, translation theory, and translation pedagogy. He is author of *Other Russias: Homosexuality and the Crisis of Post-Soviet Identity* (2009) and is presently completing an edited volume on translation in Eastern Europe and Russia.

Mona Baker is Professor of Translation Studies at the Centre for Translation and Intercultural Studies at the University of Manchester. She is author of *In Other Words: A Coursebook on Translation* (1992) and *Translation and Conflict: A Narrative Account* (2006). Editor of the *Routledge Encyclopedia of Translation Studies* (1998, 2001, 2009) and *Critical Concepts: Translation Studies* (4 vols., forthcoming), she is also founding editor of the journal *The Translator* and editorial director of St. Jerome Publishing. She is vice-president of IATIS (International Association of Translation and Intercultural Studies; www.iatis.org).

Paul F. Bandia is Professor of French at Concordia University in Montreal. His interdisciplinary research interests bring together postcolonial studies, sociolinguistics, cultural studies, and history. He has published widely in the fields of translation studies and postcolonial francophone literature and culture. Author of *Translation as Reparation: Writing and Translation in Postcolonial Africa* (2008), he is also co-editor of *Charting the Future of Translation History: Discourses and Methodology* (2006).

Georges L. Bastin holds a Ph.D. from the Université de Paris III and is Professeur agrégé in the Department of Linguistics and Translation at the Université de Montréal. He is author of *Traducir o adaptar?* (1998), co-editor of *Charting the Future of Translation History: Discourses and Methodology* (2006), and editor of two special issues of *Meta* (1999, 2000) on translation history. With research interests in the fields of translation pedagogy and translation history, he has published articles in the *Routledge Encyclopaedia of Translation Studies*, *Meta*, *TTR*, *The Translator*, *La Linguistique*, and other journals. He heads the Research Group on Translation History in Latin America (www.histal.umontreal.ca).

Nitsa Ben-Ari is head of Diploma Studies for Translation and Revision at Tel Aviv University. Her research areas are translation and ideology, including manipulation, subversion, and censorship. She is author of *Romance with the Past* (Hebrew 1997, German 2006), focusing on the role of nineteenth-century German-Jewish historical novels in the emergence of a new national Hebrew literature, and *Suppression of the Erotic in Modern Hebrew Literature* (English 2006, Hebrew 2006), discussing censorship and self-censorship in the formation of the "puritan Sabra" image in Hebrew literature. Dr. Ben-Ari has translated 26 books into Hebrew from English, French, German, and Italian, the latest being an annotated translation of Goethe's *Faust* (2006).

Ángela Campo is a doctoral student at the Université de Montréal. Currently doing research on terminology theory, she is a member of the Research Group on Translation History in Latin America.

Antonia Carcelen-Estrada is a doctoral student in Comparative Literature at the University of Massachusetts. She holds a degree in philosophy from the Universidad San Francisco in Quito and has worked as an activist in Ecuador. Her research focuses on the Huaorani community in the Amazon, as well as Kichwa communities in Ecuador and the United States. In her approaches to native populations in the Americas, she integrates translation studies, cultural studies, critical theory, and philosophy.

Álvaro Echeverri holds a Ph.D. from the Université de Montréal. His research interests include active methodologies for translator training, metacognitive aspects of translation and translation teaching, and the history of translation in Latin America. He is a member of the Research Group on Translation History in Latin America.

Denise Merkle teaches translation at the Université de Moncton and is a former president of the Canadian Association for Translation Studies. She is editor of *Censure et traduction dans le monde occidental/Censorship and Translation in the Western World* (a special issue of *TTR*, 2002), co-editor of *Des Cultures en contact* (2005), and co-editor of *Traduire depuis les marges/Translating from the Margins* (2008). She has published widely on Victorian translations and translators of French realist and naturalist writing and on translations produced by Québec and Acadian writers. Her studies center on the translator as an intercultural or transcultural agent, the sociology of translation, and the control of discourse.

John Milton is Associate Professor of English Literature and Translation Studies at the University of São Paulo. He has translated Brazilian poetry into English, notably the dramatic poem of João Cabral de Melo Neto, *Morte e Vida Severina* (2006), and his critical articles in translation studies have appeared widely. His current research interests focus on the interface of politics, economics, history, translation, and adaptation.

Maria Tymoczko is Professor of Comparative Literature at the University of Massachusetts; trained as a medievalist, she is also a specialist in Irish Studies. She is author of *Translation in a Postcolonial Context: Early Irish Literature in English Translation* (1999) and with Edwin Gentzler has edited *Translation and Power* (2002). Professor Tymoczko has published widely on translation theory and on translation as an engaged social practice. Her most recent critical study is *Enlarging Translation, Empowering Translators* (2007).

Else R. P. Vieira is Professor of Brazilian and Comparative Latin American Studies, Queen Mary College, University of London, where her specialties include Argentina, Chile, and Brazil. A former Professor in Comparative Literature at the Federal University of Minas Gerais, she has been visiting professor at the University of Oxford, held a Senior Research Fellowship at the University of Nottingham, and been associated with the Center for Latin American Studies at Harvard University and the University of California at Berkeley. She has published extensively on Brazilian translation and Brazilian film. She is editor of *City of God in Several Voices: Brazilian Social Cinema as Action* (2005).

Index

puritanism, 2, 17, 108–48, 228, 246
  New England puritanism, 131, 145,
    147–48
  resistance to, 108–48, 228
  sabra puritanism, 130, 133–34,
    136–37, 146–47
  Victorian puritanism, 108–28,
    130–32, 146
Pushkin, Alexander, 155
Pym, Anthony, 49–50

Quebec, 7, 61
  Révolution Tranquille, 61
Quemperi, 78
Quichua. *See* Kichwa
Quine, W.V.O., 20, 83, 87–88
Quito, 70
Qur'an, 6

Rabelais, François, 192
racism, 116–18, 124–26, 199, 209–10, 231
Radel, Nicholas F., 148
Radlova, Anna, 156
Rangel, Godofredo, 197
Raynal, Guillaume Thomas, 45
refusal to translate, 1, 78–86, 89–107,
    228, 230, 234, 242–45.
  See also silence; translation, non-
    translation; self-translation
relevance theory, 232–35, 240, 252
relexification, 168
Renaissance, 150
Reporters without Borders, 36
representation, 5, 9, 16–17, 62, 80–81,
    85–86, 130, 168, 170, 173, 177,
    185–86, 231–33, 237–48, 250–53
  deliberate misrepresentation, 175
  self-representation, 17, 67
Republic of Hawai'i, 91. *See also* Hawai'i
resistance
  as concept, 7–11, 15
Reuben, David, 141
Revista do Brasil, 209
revolution, 3, 42–64, 229, 235–42.
  See also France, United States
Ribeiro, Darcy, 213

Rio de Janeiro, 193–94, 196, 211
Ritte, Walter, 97
Rivet, Paul, 87
Roaring Twenties, 193
Robinson, Douglas, 207
Robinson, Paul, 147
Rodríguez, Jaime, 47
Roman Catholic Church, 45, 60, 205,
    212, 231, 238, 243
  Liberation Theology, 212
romanticism, 221, 240
Romashova, 162
Rome, 4, 157
  Roman literature, 5, 110–11, 122, 126.
    See also Latin
Rousseau, Jean-Jacques, 45, 47, 52
Routledge, 211
Royal Dutch Shell, 69, 74
Roziner, Felix, 153, 162–63
Russia, 13, 32–34, 149–67, 191
  literary translation as a form of
    political resistance in, 149–67
  Russian literature, 149–67.
  See also Soviet Union
Russian language, 2, 149–67

sabra, 130, 133–34, 144, 146–47
Saglia, Diego, 62
Saint Blas, 52
Saint Blas conspiracy, 52–53
St. Enda's school, 241, 253
Saint, Nate, 72–73
Saint, Rachel, 73, 87
samizdat, 161–62
Sandwich Islands. *See* Hawaiian Islands
San Francisco, 91
São José (free school), 212
São Paulo, 190, 198, 204, 209
  Department of Social and Political
    order (DEOPS), 205
Sartre, Jean-Paul, 11–12
  littérature engagée, 11–12
Scandinavia, 191
Schiller, Friedrich, 192
Schlegel, August Wilhelm, 14
Schleiermacher, Friedrich, 14